# Bridge to Literacy

## No Child — or Adult — Left Behind

© 2009 John Corcoran

Published by Kaplan Publishing, a division of Kaplan, Inc.
1 Liberty Plaza, 24th Floor
New York, NY 10006

Library of Congress Cataloging-in-Publication Data
Corcoran, John, 1937 Dec. 5-
   Bridge to literacy : no child--or adult--left behind / by John Corcoran.
      p.   cm.
   Includes bibliographical references.
   ISBN 978-1-4277-9829-9
   1. Literacy--United States.   I. Title.
   LC151.C63  2009
   302.2'244--dc22

                                                          2008027136

Printed in the United States of America

10 9 8 7 6 5 4 3 2 1

ISBN-13: 978-1-4277-9830-5

Kaplan Publishing books are available at special quantity discounts to use for sales promotions, employee premiums, or educational purposes. Please email our Special Sales Department to order or for more information at kaplanpublishing@kaplan.com, or write to Kaplan Publishing, 1 Liberty Plaza, 24th Floor, New York, NY 10006.

# *Endorsements*

Despite the noble efforts of many people at all levels of our society, the far-reaching problems of illiteracy in America have not been solved, or even contained. Illiteracy is an urgent matter that simply must be addressed. In this thoughtful and powerful book, *The Bridge to Literacy,* John Corcoran lays out the blueprint for what can and must be done. Everyone who really cares about our future and the need for a more literate America should walk the walk with John Corcoran through the pages of this book.

—Jim Duffy, former president of ABC-TV
and national spokesperson for Project Literacy U.S.

John Corcoran's newest book beckons each of us who recognizes literacy skills as a fundamental requirement for human growth and development to determine a way for those many adults and children who have not crossed the Bridge to Literacy to get in step. John offers for reflection what so many now know; he presents a courageous challenge to institutions of higher learning, while expressing his concern for the teachers who are not prepared to teach after receiving degrees.

—M. Therese (Terry) Kelly, BA, MLA, director and president of
New Heights Center and a practicing educational therapist

Until parents, teachers, and other professionals are taught to watch for the classic warning signs of dyslexia, children will continue to struggle and fall through the cracks in our education system—as John did. As John so clearly documents in this book, many professionals and organizations end up trying to help those with undiagnosed dyslexia—yet very few provide effective solutions.

—Susan Barton, founder of Bright Solutions for Dyslexia

This book is a "bridge" for all literacy advocates as we help one reader at a time who comes to our organizations or institutions with his/her hands reaching out for help to cross into the literate world. It is a "blueprint" for communities and schools to collaborate and work towards a common goal — how can we teach learners to read.

— Susan May, Reading Program Coordinator,
Marshall Community and Technical College

Most educators in the nation are trying to figure out how to close the achievement gap and stop the loss of 30 percent of our high school students. John Corcoran's book should be their road map. He not only exposes the problem as illiteracy but brilliantly outlines the solutions. Every educator and parent should read this book so that there will be no more excuses.

— Connie Messina, high school counselor

As a volunteer reading tutor, I have experienced firsthand the problems John Corcoran addresses capably in this book. The solutions he proposes are realistic, achievable — and necessary if our country is going to remain competitive in the world marketplace.

— Mike Hernacki, author and success coach

The saddest fact of American education today is despite all the data that show the way out of failure, especially with literacy, we persist in ignoring it. If heeded, this book could be very useful in leading the way.

— Ann Martin, language arts teacher for 30 years

# Bridge to Literacy

## No Child — or Adult — Left Behind

*by*

John Corcoran

KAPLAN PUBLISHING

To my wife,

Kathleen Marie Corcoran

# *Acknowledgments*

Most things in life are a team effort. As a builder, I know I was only as good as my subcontractors. Writing and publishing this book have been no different.

My researcher and writing assistant, Tricia Crisafulli, teamed up with me on this project for more than two years. As my teacher, she taught me about writing and the importance of research, interviews with experts, and endnotes. She also became a student, who learned the subject of literacy and embraced the nobility of the cause.

My agent, Doris S. Michaels, and her assistant, Delia Berrigan Fakis, of the DSM Literary Agency, believed in the project from the beginning and championed it to a successful conclusion.

My editor at Kaplan Publishing, Michael Sprague, enthusiastically embraced the importance of literacy and the longevity of this issue in America. Also a special thanks goes to the entire Kaplan team for their expertise, passion, and commitment to this project.

So many people played a part in the journey of this book, more than I can mention by name. Some who must be acknowledged individually include the following:

- Marianne Arling, the project director for The John Corcoran Foundation, who has the heart of a reading teacher, the curiosity and desire to learn all she can, and deep compassion for every learner

- Fran Thompson, a parent and an advocate, who critiqued the manuscript with knowledge and care

- Marion Zola, a screenwriter and a friend, who has loved this story for 20 years

- Vince Walter, a committed literacy advocate within Rotary International, who opened doors and embraced the vision

- Mike Vezo, a friend, for his expert advice and help and for his commitment to this cause

- The directors and supporters of the John Corcoran Foundation Inc.; the hundreds of tutors who have been trained by the Foundation and who have tutored more than 1,000 students in the past five years; our students' parents; and, of course, the most important ones, the students themselves, who spend many afterschool hours improving their reading skills.

To the many experts, including new readers, interviewed in this book and whose names are found throughout the chapters: thank you for graciously taking the time to share your knowledge, wisdom, and experience and to put your name on your beliefs. This book would not have the authority that it does without you.

Many family members, friends, colleagues, and associates who read the manuscript early on and offered help, encouragement, and advice. Your fingerprints are found throughout this book.

To my wife, Kathleen. We married January 30, 1965, "for better or for worse, richer or poorer, in sickness and in health." That says it all.

To my son, Johnny Corcoran; my daughter, Colleen Mertes; and her husband, Tod Mertes, who are always loving, positive, and encouraging about whatever I do and who know I feel the same about them.

To my grandchildren, Kayla, Stephanie, Bradley, Jace, and Sam — you make your grandparents proud.

I acknowledge with loving memory my parents, Jack and Agnes Corcoran. My father was the best man in my wedding; he was always, to me, the best man I have ever known. As for my mother, I always knew her love for me and my siblings. LOVE — the gift that keeps on giving. Thanks.

To all learners, children, youth, and adults and to all who teach them. I'll see you on the Bridge.

# Table of Contents

# *Foreword*

*by* Wilfrid J. Wilkinson
Rotary International President, 2007–08

For more than a century, Rotarians have established the reputation of helping others, one person at a time. Nowhere does this mission present itself more meaningfully than in the field of literacy, where millions of people need help worldwide. In recent years, there has been an increasing emphasis within Rotary on helping others by using all the tools that are available to us to improve literacy.

It is an established fact that to survive in today's society, we must be able to decode what we see and hear. In literacy, without decoding, a person cannot read and comprehend the written word. Without the critical skills required to read, it is nearly impossible to comprehend information and to learn.

While not everyone who reads this book will agree with all points that author John Corcoran makes, I think everyone will agree that we are facing a crisis in literacy. Interestingly enough, I'm told that the Chinese translation of the word *crisis* is "challenge plus opportunity." In *The Bridge to Literacy,* John clearly presents the challenge that we are facing today. At the same time, he gives many possible opportunities to meet and solve that challenge. In so doing, he has issued a clarion call for action — for all of us to join together to build the bridge to literacy.

In Rotary, we have a 4-Way Test of all things that Rotarians think, do, or say. Let's look at the issues surrounding literacy using the 4-Way Test.

## Is It the Truth?

In challenging us to build the bridge to literacy, John tells of his own personal experience of having "lived the lie" of not being able to read for so many years. He passionately describes the subculture of illiteracy in our society that is virtually invisible to the dominant literate culture. By denying the existence of the subculture of illiteracy and failing to offer the help that these children and adults need, we are forcing them not to tell the truth about their own inability to read, write, and spell.

## Is It Fair to All Concerned?

As the author shares from his personal experience, the reader hears the voice of the frightened little boy he once was, who tells us it's not fair that he didn't learn to read. We read of the troubled teenager he was later on, who knew it wasn't fair. And we hear from the businessperson he became, who met with troubled high school students struggling today with reading. As we picture them sitting with their arms crossed, we hear them saying, "It's not fair." While these images tug at our heartstrings, we realize that these children and young adults are being forced to live a lie about not being able to read — and it's not fair. It's especially unfair when we have the scientific knowledge and the means to deliver it as we build the bridge to reach them.

As the author notes in Chapter 3, "If we do not impart these skills to children, we are robbing them of a future." That certainly is not fair.

## Will It Build Goodwill and Better Friendships?

One of the values we stress in Rotary is helping others, one person at a time, empowering them to do what they can do best. As Peter Waite, executive director of ProLiteracy Worldwide, which advocates for adult learners, is quoted as saying in Chapter 4, "Learning how to read increases their self-confidence and sense of worth."

To be successful and stay the course, these adult learners need goodwill and supportive friendships. Adult students, who are often juggling home, job, children, and other responsibilities, need the support of family and friends to encourage them when they want to drop out.

The Computer-Assisted Literacy Solution (CALS), which is described in Chapter 9, stresses the importance of facilitators or encouragers, who are essential to the learning process. Although we use technology, and its power is very helpful in the delivery of literacy instruction to both adult learners and children, we continue to involve humans in the essential roles of friendship and support.

## Will It Be Beneficial to All Concerned?

John accurately points out the importance of helping even just one person. It could be said that when one person is helped, there is a huge multiplier effect — by 10, 20, or many more. When one person learns to read, it benefits the family, friends, and indeed everyone with whom this person comes in contact — even to the point of making a contribution to society as a whole, both economically and socially.

The cause of literacy easily meets the criteria of the 4-Way Test, while the status quo of illiteracy for so many is clearly a failure. Now we must address the challenge that lies in front of us. Many people, including those within our family of Rotary, have already contributed to helping build the bridge to literacy. Rotary has had many themes and projects over the years of helping other people.

Currently, with the CALS initiative for literacy, we are seeing the benefit of employing the power of technology both to reach people and also to remove some of the stigma of illiteracy. Learners who are using a computer can feel good about their ability to access technology tools like everyone else, while at the same time working on their literacy challenges at their own pace and with as much repetition as they need. This is a major plus. In this year of my leadership as Rotary International president, I have encouraged my fellow Rotarians to consider making CALS accessible along with the number of other literacy tools that we have within our organization.

I personally am committed to helping build the bridge to literacy. I hope that the readers of this book will consider what they each can do. Listen to the clarion call that the author has raised and join us in solving this crisis by meeting the challenge, using the opportunities that are available to us to bring all people — one at a time — into the literate world.

# *Foreword*

*by* Paula Tallal, PhD
Board of Governor Professor of Neuroscience
Codirector, Center for Molecular and
Behavioral Neuroscience
Rutgers University

Rarely a week goes by that we do not read or hear something in the press about the growing literacy crisis in the United States. Reading failure has been linked to many of the most pressing social issues of our time, ranging from juvenile delinquency to drug abuse, unemployment, and adult incarceration. Clearly the failure of increasing numbers of our citizens to develop adequate communication and literacy skills threatens our competitive prospects as a nation.

In *The Bridge to Literacy,* John Corcoran provides us with a well-integrated, state-of-the-art assessment of the causes, determinants, and consequences of reading failure from a very personal perspective — his own. Mr. Corcoran takes us on his own personal journey, from the child's growing despair as he comes to realize that he cannot learn like his classmates, to the teenager who learns to hide his shame behind a veneer of anger, to the harrowing experience of an increasingly successful businessperson who develops remarkable skills of deception and creativity to hide his dark secret of illiteracy from his friends, family, and associates.

*The Bridge to Literacy* begins with one man's lifelong quest to cross the bridge from the subculture of illiteracy to the dominant culture of the written word, a bridge that he struggled to cross until he finally learned to read at age 48. But this book is about much more than the life story of one man. It is about the scientific advances that provided Mr. Corcoran, and so many people like him, the key that finally unlocked the power of the written word. It is about the growing scientific understanding that there is a continuum from the spoken to the written word, a connection between the sounds inside of words and the letters that represent them. It is a tribute to the new methods and technologies, such as Lindamood-Bell and the Fast ForWord Language and Reading series, that have translated these scientific advances into educational practices that succeed where more traditional approaches have failed, even for individuals as severely challenged as John Corcoran. And finally, it is an exploration of the forces that lead so many in the educational system to resist change, even in the face of years of failure using more traditional teaching approaches and growing scientific data pointing in a new direction.

In Mr. Corcoran's own words, "The intention of this book is to gather all the tribes within literacy. I want to bring them together and convince them to agree to an armistice that will end turf battles over funding and arguments over whose program is more important. Such fighting has only polarized an effort that must be united in purpose to teach all learners, both child and adult, and to implement the decades of research that already exists."

This book is a call to action for all those who have a stake in increasing literacy in our country to work together — and isn't that everyone?

# *Preface*

When I wrote my first book, my desire was to share my life story—from the child I once was who was not taught how to read, through my years of being an adult who hid the shame of his illiteracy, and finally as an adult who learned how to read and went on to become a literacy advocate.

In many ways, my reasons for writing this second book are equally personal. Inside of me still lives a child who wanted to learn how to read but who was never taught. The child inside cannot accept the fact that what happened 60 years ago is still happening to other innocent children. Today, I must plead for their right to learn how to read and to be taught by properly trained teachers.

Inside of me also lives a college graduate who wanted to be a scholar but who did not have the basic skills to carry out his studies. In many ways, the research and writing of this book is to fulfill what that young man could not do. It is also part of my ongoing efforts to continue my education and improve my own literacy skills. I am walking the walk of a lifelong learner.

Within me is a teacher who knows that it is not enough to tell people to cross the bridge to literacy, nor is it sufficient to tell somebody else that it is his or her job to get people across. The intention of this book is to put forth a blueprint to build the bridge—high, wide, and strong—to span the chasm of illiteracy. The bridge also connects what we know and what we do. Research has shown us what works; now it's up to us to put it into practice.

My personal experience and perspective as an adult learner make me unique among advocates today and provide me with insight into both the failures of childhood education and the needs of adult literacy programs. But this book is not really about me. It is about you—whether you are a parent, teacher, policymaker, researcher, advocate, adult learner, volunteer tutor, student, business leader, or community member. To prevent illiteracy in childhood and to eradicate it in adulthood will take all of us. Our commitment needs to be fueled by the passion that comes from understanding the depth of despair of not knowing how to read. Our conviction to act must be backed by knowledge, with proven research that shows us without question that direct, systematic instruction works to teach all learners.

Over the past 20 years, I have met people from every camp, philosophy, and persuasion. During that time, I have accepted more than 600 invitations to speak, and most of my presentations have been based on my life experience: I have described how I learned to read at the age of 48 and how it transformed my life. I have enjoyed many formal discussions and informal conversations with people whose viewpoints I respect. They have given me so much support and encouragement, candid advice, and love. Some of their suggestions have been used in my speeches over the years, and they were also incorporated with appreciation into this book.

Through my travels, I have come across people whose opinions and viewpoints on literacy did not always agree with mine. And sometimes I found myself, particularly in the writing of this book, surrounded by people who did not agree with each other. I do not doubt the sincerity of any of these people, nor do I question their goals and objectives in the name of literacy. I, myself, see things through the lens of my own experiences, which are unlike anyone else's; but then again, that is true of everyone.

The intention of this book is to gather all the tribes within literacy. I want to bring them together and convince them to agree to an armistice that will end intense turf battles over funding and arguments over whose program is more important. Such fighting has only polarized an effort that must be united in purpose to teach all learners, both child and adult, and to implement the decades of research that already exists.

I have felt this way since I became a literacy advocate. In the 1990s, I was on the board of the National Institute for Literacy, which promotes adult programs. I recall times when I wanted to address childhood education. My comments were either redirected or fell on deaf ears. Board members wanted only to talk about adult literacy. At other times, I was around early childhood experts whose focus was solely on what should be done for young learners. My comment that it is as important to teach an adult to read as it is to teach a child upset some and was ignored by others. We are at a critical juncture in the reading revolution. For the past several decades, we have done the research; the next phase is for all the parties to come together to implement it on a larger scale. In the process, we must expand the understanding of how children and adults learn how to read and the importance of everyone becoming an independent reader.

Early childhood educators, classroom teachers from kindergarten to grade 12, adult literacy advocates, the universities that train our teachers, and researchers who study this field — all of them and more can come together to further the cause of a literate America. They must also be held accountable, quantifying their results and sharing their best practices. They need to see themselves as being on the same team. To do so requires that they set aside their egos and careers and move to the common agenda of helping nonreaders advance over the bridge. If we lose sight of that, then all we have is more of the same, which is not nearly enough.

I welcome everyone onto the bridge with me, those who agree and those who disagree, those who see themselves as right and others as wrong, those who are aligned and those who are opposed. Do not stand outside the debate, but rather, engage in it with the intention of working together. Doing so is the only way to redeem our failing education system and give more than just hope to those who cannot read. We know what we can do, and now it is time to act.

As for me, I have already crossed the bridge to literacy, but I keep going back to the beginning or to the middle, depending on where the people needing help and instruction are in their journeys. It is also important to be at the end to congratulate and encourage successful learners and teachers to share their stories and to inspire others. Thank you for reading this book. Please consider joining the team to build a stronger bridge to literacy in your community so that no child or adult is left behind.

John Corcoran
July, 2008

# Across the Bridge:
# One Man's Journey

Twenty years ago, I crossed the bridge from the subculture of illiteracy to the dominant culture of the written word. At that time, I celebrated the liberation and vindication that I, a 48-year-old man who had not been able to learn how to read, write, or spell before, could master literacy skills. That experience, which began in August 1986, was nothing less than miraculous; it was as if I had died and gone to heaven. I was no longer an outsider in my own native culture. I belonged.

I remember well that summer day when I drove up to the Carlsbad City, California, Library Adult Learning Center for the first time to speak to the director. I did not really believe that I could learn how to read. I asked myself: Why should this time be different, when every other attempt has failed? I had spent plenty of time in libraries and around literate people, and no literacy skills had rubbed off on me. I even went so far as to take a speed-reading course once just to see if it would work. Needless to say, I was out of the seminar in a few days. Still, I had to try again, even though I had very low expectations for success. At the learning center, I was matched up with a volunteer tutor, a 65-year-old woman named Eleanor Condit, who turned out to be the second-grade teacher I always wished I had had. After 13 months of one-on-one instruction, I was reading at about a sixth-grade level. It was a major victory for me, and later it would inspire me to become an advocate to help free those who were still shackled by their illiteracy. First, though, I would have to free myself.

After about a year of working with my tutor, I went to a diagnostic center, the Lindamood-Bell Clinic at San Luis Obispo, California, where I was honored to become a pupil of Patricia Lindamood. (I am proud to have called Pat my dear friend. Seriously ill for many months, she found the time to do an interview for this book, but, sadly, she died as the first chapters were being written.)

A battery of tests at the Lindamood-Bell Clinic revealed that the main reason behind my learning deficiencies in reading and writing was a severe auditory discrimination problem. Intensive instruction in the Lindamood Phoneme Sequencing (LiPS) Program helped me to integrate sensory information from feeling, seeing, and hearing to identify the 44 English speech sounds. Of the three senses — feeling, seeing, and hearing — the deficit for me was in hearing the sound. (To be clear, I did not have a hearing problem, but rather, difficulty in discriminating sounds.) Therefore, by concentrating on how it felt to make the sound, my brain was stimulated in a new way. This multisensory, phonics-based experience gave me the missing link to move on to intensive, direct, systematic phonics instruction and then to reading. Every breakthrough was monumental, but there was so much more to master.

It took me seven years to feel like I was really literate. It took me three more years before I could tell my wife that I didn't feel dumb anymore. By then, I was 58 years old, and I had finally taken myself out of my place of shame — the "dumb row" of second grade.

Why did it take me so long to learn how to read? Why did it take 40 years for my prayers to be answered? As a little boy, I would go to bed each night, saying, "Dear God, let me wake up in the morning and know how to read." There are no easy answers to these questions, but they must be explored — not for my sake but for those who remain in the darkness of illiteracy. My prayer now is that by exploring these questions, we will be able to turn on the light of learning for so many more children and adults.

I began to reflect on my first experiences in school. Like any other child, I went to school at the age of six with the promise and the expectation that I would learn how to read and write. As I shared in my first book, *The Teacher Who Couldn't Read: The True Story of a High School Instructor Who Triumphed Over His Illiteracy*, I had no idea that I was different from the other children. I was a good boy; I wanted to learn. By the time I was in second grade, however, the subculture had already claimed me. I was lumped together with the other nonreaders, and we knew we weren't as bright as the other students. I couldn't understand why or how that had happened.

I grew up in a family with parents who loved each other and loved their six children. My parents were educated: my father had graduated from college and was an avid reader, and my mother was also literate. At times, my parents were poor, but as my father liked to say when we complained about money, "I don't ever remember you missing a meal or not having a roof over your head." There are stereotypes people like to apply to children who cannot read, such as that they live in broken homes, are exposed to drug and alcohol abuse, or have incarcerated parents. One of the most widely believed, yet harmful, myths is that some people just aren't smart enough to learn how to read.

People may fail to learn how to read for many reasons. These include learning disabilities/deficiencies such as dyslexia. Some who have these afflictions may be highly motivated and highly intelligent. However, learning deficiencies have prevented people like me from being successful in school, because our teachers were not properly trained to teach us how to break the code. The education system failed me as it did so many others. Social promotion — the practice of passing students who are failing or have poor grades — passed me from grade to grade until I graduated from high school, receiving a diploma that I couldn't read. Over the past 50 years in America, if students showed up and behaved themselves in school, they got a diploma. It didn't matter whether the person could read or not. Committed to fulfilling my parents' expectations for me and because of an athletic scholarship, I went on to college, which demanded all of my survival skills. I became a master at finding ways to cheat as I infiltrated the collegiate literate culture.

"How could you graduate from college if you couldn't read?" is one of the frequent questions I hear. It's an understandable question that deserves an honest answer. Although I had a scholarship to play basketball — for the record, none of my coaches did any facilitating to help me pass my courses — I was a college student in desperation. I lied about a term paper being mine, I cheated off someone else's paper, and I stole answers to tests. I tried to avoid professors who gave essay exams, but when I couldn't, I had to find another way. For example, one time I painstakingly copied down four essay questions into an exam booklet and then passed it out the classroom window to a friend. While I pretended to write during the test, outside under a tree, my friend wrote out the answers for me. He didn't know I couldn't read; he thought he was helping me out in a tough course. In return, I helped him get a date to our fraternity's spring dance. I always found people to help me, and I always was on guard not to reveal my secret.

I don't want to minimize or sugarcoat what I did with a shrug and an apology that it all happened a long time ago. I was raised by my parents to be moral and honest. When I got to college, I realized I was over my head in terms of faking it. I had heard all my life that you can't make it in the world without a college degree, and I wanted to be successful. I didn't want to be in the dumb row of life, without an education or a chance, so I resorted to actions and schemes that were morally wrong. My only consolation was that, as "the Desperado" in my college years, I lived by an outlaw's code of ethics regarding what I would and would not do. In my illiterate, subculture mind-set, I could tell myself that if I broke into a professor's office in the middle of the night to steal an exam, that was all I would take. I would never even touch anyone's personal belongings. Yes, it was a skewed sense of values, but in my desperation, I did not see any other way. Looking back, I wish I could have just asked for help and received it. But whom could I ask? Not anyone at the university. Still, I acknowledge and take full responsibility for my actions.

My next decision after college — a choice that defied all logic — was to go back into the lion's cage from which I had just escaped. I chose to become a high school teacher, even though I could not read, write, or spell beyond a second-grade level. This created a huge moral dilemma for me. As a child, I was innocent, because it is up to adults to impart the skills to decode the written word. As a teacher, I hid my illiteracy. I have told this personal story so many times to teachers throughout the United States, Canada, and abroad, and it is cathartic for me each time. Teachers are supposed to be seekers of truth, yet I was a teacher and a liar. That was the most psychologically and spiritually damaging problem I ever faced.

My story makes people uncomfortable, and at times, I have faced harsh criticism. Once, while making a presentation to undergraduate and graduate education students at a university, I was challenged by a professor of ethics. He stood up in the midst of this group of 250 people, many of whom had driven a distance to this evening lecture, and said, "I think we may be listening to the wrong person." To my amazement, several of the students immediately spoke up, to the point of demanding an apology from that professor on my behalf. His point, however, was well taken: what I did in the classroom was not ethical. There I was, a teacher, telling my students to do things that I could not do. I was the hypocrite who could not read. I got away with it in the classroom by creating an oral and visual environment that functioned as my safety zone. I had "interpreters" in the classroom, students who would read aloud for the class (and for me) and who would write on the board for me (seeing themselves as my teaching assistants).

I cannot justify being in the classroom and not knowing how to read. Every teacher should be capable of teaching others to read, write, and spell. I have confessed to the literate world my deceit. As I have done many times while telling my story, I confess my sins, my crimes, and my trespasses against literate society, and I ask for forgiveness. I have also forgiven the trespasses, real and imagined, against me, particularly those done by the teachers who could not or did not teach me to read, who put me in the dumb row and eroded my self-esteem. I also need to forgive myself. The only way to do any of those things is for me to tell the truth. As the saying goes, the truth shall set you free. I have told my truth to set myself free, and by exposing the desperation of my actions, I hope to free other learners from their shame and encourage them to seek out help to learn how to read. If I can do it, anyone can. I also hope that by telling the story, the literate world is invited to explore the truth of why illiteracy persists in our schools and society.

Before I learned how to read, I relied on my intelligence, survival skills, exceptional ability in math, and social acumen, as well as being white, blond, blue-eyed, and six-foot-four, and having the sheer force of will to survive in the literate world. After teaching, I became a successful entrepreneur, builder, and real estate developer in California, running several companies, negotiating deals and contracts, and managing 20 or so employees and up to 100 subcontractors and tradespeople at times. Being the boss made it easier to expect the secretaries and clerk-typists to do any reading or writing that I requested, and if they weren't available at a business lunch meeting, I could always use an excuse like, "I forgot my reading glasses." Such are the survival skills of the subculture. For me, learning how to read, write, and spell opened up the world of the written word and also improved my oral language skills. As evidence of that fact, I have given more than 600 speeches and presentations in 44 states, Canada, and Europe, and I have testified before Congress. I was appointed to the National Institute for Literacy by President George H. W. Bush and subsequently served on the board of the institute into the term of President Bill Clinton. Learning how to read and write has also been my passport into a new world where I no longer have to hide my inadequacies and deficiencies from our society's literate culture.

When I learned how to read and write, the world that had been closed off, inaccessible to me, was now open. The secret of my illiteracy, which I had guarded so carefully, as if it were a precious jewel, was replaced by a real treasure: my ability to read. I jealously hoarded that knowledge at first, resisting all urgings and invitations to share my story of having been a nonreader. This was not a secret I was willing to share.

As a new citizen of the literate world, I could have turned my back on where I came from. I could have forgotten where I spent the first four decades of my life. I could have tried to put it all behind me. But then again, I couldn't because of all the joy I now had inside me. I was dying to tell the world what had happened to me, yet I didn't want to embarrass myself, my family, my community and school, and the university that gave me a degree. I still lived in the community in which I had been a teacher for 17 years, a teacher who could not read or write. My wife, Kathy, was happy for me and proud of what I had accomplished. However, her reply when I first approached her about telling my story was an emphatic "No!" With joy on one side and fear of exposure on the other, I was locked in a quandary.

Then one night, as I drove the five miles from the library to the house, I had a little talk with myself. All of us are multifaceted people, differentiated by the roles we play in life and aspects of our life experience. That night in the car, I called upon two of these roles, or "personalities," inside me. Keep in mind, I am not talking about multiple personalities in the clinical sense (I'm not "Sybil" or the "Three Faces of Eve"), but rather, different aspects of myself. I needed this inner reflection to help me sort through my conflicting feelings.

I got in touch with the little boy inside me, the little boy I call "Johnny the Innocent." This little boy went to school at the age of six, believing he was a winner, just as his parents saw him. It wasn't very long, however, before Johnny found out that his teachers didn't see him the way his parents did. By the time Johnny was in the second grade, he was in the dumb row. When the teacher called on Johnny or the other children in that particular row, the students would put their heads down and hope that everything would just disappear. Johnny didn't know how he got into the dumb row, because he felt pretty smart at times, and he didn't know how to get out.

He had good math skills and strong social skills. He loved recess; that was the best part of his day. He loved his family, and felt loved by them. He did his chores at home and obeyed his parents. When his mother and father went to Johnny's school for a conference, his teachers assured them that Johnny was a smart boy and a good boy—he had even mastered his roman numerals. He was having a problem with the alphabet and with reading, but his parents shouldn't worry. He would get it. He would catch up... And so it went for Johnny the Innocent through second, third, and fourth grades.

As I began to think about writing this book, I asked Johnny the Innocent, that part of me that was still connected to the experience I had as a young child in elementary school, about sharing our story. He was excited. "Go for it! Go tell the grown-ups, and then they'll teach us. Tell them, and then they'll stop hurting us."

There were, however, other voices that wanted to be heard. Johnny the Innocent had a reading problem. Johnny the fifth-grade student, however, didn't have a reading problem, although he still couldn't read. This Johnny had other problems—emotional, psychological, and discipline problems. At the age of ten or so, Johnny, knew he couldn't compete. Young boys and girls at this age know their truths; no one has to tell them that they can't read, write, or spell. They feel the shame and disappointment of failure, so they act out. They lash out because they are second-class citizens in a world that is dominated by the written word, which for them is the classroom. Not knowing the language, they have to get by somehow, survive at any cost.

As nonreaders, they are part of an oral subculture with no written language. Anthropologists tell us that a culture with no written language is "primitive." That was the culture that Johnny belonged to: the subculture in America that cannot read, write, or spell. It did not matter that Johnny was born in this country and grew up speaking English as his primary language. He was an alien in his own land. He became Johnny the Native Alien.

I approached Johnny the Native Alien, an all-American boy who in the fifth, sixth, seventh, and eighth grades knew he didn't belong. He knew he was an outsider. He had spent most of the seventh grade out in the hallways being disciplined and isolated from his classmates. He had been suspended and expelled, and once he spit on a teacher. The Native Alien would rather turn over his desk and be sent to the principal's office than be insulted in front of his peers for not being able to read a single sentence. In the school spelling bees, the Native Alien never spelled one word right. He couldn't have spelled the simplest of words correctly, because he didn't know the connection between what he spoke and what he saw on the page. He became defiant rather than show his pain and his anger. He was an outlaw. Like other children who can't read, the Native Alien acted out, disrupting the education of his classmates as well as his own.

When I asked Johnny the Native Alien about sharing the story, he answered with a string of foul language. "Don't waste your time," he said. "Don't bother with it. They don't care. They didn't care then, and they don't care now. Don't tell them anything. Don't expose us."

There were a few other subpersonalities in my early life, such as the ninth-grader who realized it was not in his best interest to be a problem, the athlete who distinguished himself on the playing field, the Desperado college student... In the end, I cut a deal with all of them. I assured Johnny the Innocent that I would tell the story for his sake because he was not to blame. He didn't have anything to do with the fact he did not learn how to read. It is the responsibility of adults to impart skills and values to children.

I told the Native Alien that he was not going to dominate my life anymore. He had gotten me into a lot of trouble as a young man and as an adult. I told him I was going to tell the story — me, the adult personality of "Mr. Corcoran." I told the Native Alien he had to behave himself, especially when Mr. Corcoran was speaking in public. But I also vowed that I would not whitewash him out. He had been betrayed, abandoned, and left without the skills to compete in the classroom and in the world, no matter how clever or smart he was. I assured the Desperado that, even though we would have to confess what we did to get by, he would not be ostracized. Instead, he would be understood and forgiven.

I would no longer let the Desperado, the Native Alien, or Johnny the Innocent dominate my life, keeping part of me always suspended in childhood, emotionally, psychologically, or spiritually. Mr. Corcoran had a story to tell and a job to do.

The first time I told my story was in front of a group of businesspeople in my community, many of whom I knew professionally — and some of them personally. They were stunned. Then they gave me a standing ovation. Since then, I have shared my story with students, volunteer and professional teachers, other businesspeople, academics, and lawmakers. I have told my story on television, radio, and in print. I'm telling it again — only this time, it isn't just my story.

As I began to improve my reading skills, I discovered that I carried a great deal of emotional baggage. I was ashamed about my inabilities and angry toward a system that I believed had let me down. I grieved lost opportunities. These emotions posed a significant barrier to my progress, until I learned that telling my story was a vital part of the healing process. But it was equally important that I continued to develop my literacy skills. I believe that most adult new readers must go through this same healing process to maximize their learning experience and, one day, go on to help each other. Each time I have the privilege of meeting a new learner, I share that person's joy even though I am aware of the pain as well. For a new reader, the emotions are mixed, but always the positive must prevail.

While my experience was intensely personal, it does not belong to me alone. I share it with millions of adults in the United States today who cannot read or write. They encompass all racial, ethnic, gender, and socioeconomic groups. My desire in writing this book is to allow others in the subculture of illiteracy, one of the largest subcultures in America, to tell their stories. Other voices need to be heard: those of literacy champions, advocates, and researchers. With their experiences, passion, and knowledge, they can bring together the essential tools to give to the people who can make a difference: the teachers who interact with students — children, teenagers, and adults — every day.

> *It is great that we are learning how to read and write. It is never too late to learn. Keep up the good work. You know that it is hard work for some of us to learn how to read and write, but the good news is that we can learn. Don't give up on yourself.*

> — Your fellow traveler, John Corcoran
> (an email sent to a new reader)

I have experienced the feelings that confront a person who emerges into literacy, from the joyful elation to the bitter anger of having been betrayed and abandoned by the system. Released from the bondage of my illiteracy, a state of second-class citizenship that I compare with enslavement, I realized how much emotional baggage I carried. Only then was I able to transition to acquiring the skills not only to become a reader but to become a leader for the cause of literacy. As one who has been on both sides of the bridge — the subculture of illiteracy and the literate world of the written word — I know my experience is no accident. The healing that has come to me is the result of dedicating and deploying my experience for the good of others.

The statistics can be and are debated: Just how many people are illiterate? What does it mean to be illiterate? What grade levels are they reading at? And so forth. All this becomes irrelevant to one who has been there. I know what it's like to fake reading in the classroom. I know what it's like to pretend to read a storybook to my own child, unable to comprehend the words on the page. Moreover, I know there are many, many adults just like me. The only relevant question we should be asking is, "How can we teach them to read?"

In today's world, it is as important to teach adults to read as it is to teach a child to read. Some of the responsibility for teaching a child to read falls on parents, and a good portion falls on the teaching profession. The lion's share of the responsibility, however, belongs to the institutions of higher learning: colleges and universities that must get on board with preservice preparation of teachers, using proven strategies and methodologies that can teach the vast majority of learners (perhaps as many as 95 percent) in the classroom. I have high respect for the teaching profession. It holds the keys to the learning that all children and adults deserve and desire. Yet teachers must be properly trained at our colleges and universities to teach all learners. Some people, no doubt, will say that environmental factors impede children from learning: poverty, broken homes, and the abuse of drugs and alcohol. These are not acceptable excuses for not teaching a child to read. If we cannot give them literacy skills, we abandon them to a substandard existence. When one part of society advances and another part — and a very large part at that — cannot, the wounds run deep. The divisiveness of illiteracy tears at the fabric of society almost the way racism once did.

In the 1960s and 1970s, I was very interested in the civil rights movement in America. Seeing the images of people, adults and children alike, who were engaged in peaceful demonstrations, being knocked down by high-powered water hoses or attacked by police dogs, awakened in me the need to understand the cause of African Americans. I was moved by the stories shared by so many people, educated and undereducated alike, who were oppressed by an unfair system that did not see them as valuable human beings or give them the respect and opportunity they deserved. This was a time when many Americans changed their hearts, minds, and behaviors and, finally, changed the discriminatory laws of this country.

I could not read at the time of the civil rights movement, so I relied on what I heard and watched. I identified strongly with the story of Frederick Douglass, who had escaped from slavery and then become an abolitionist. It was not enough for him to win his own freedom; he needed to free others. Reading an article about Douglass recently, I was struck by the role that literacy had played in his life and his determination to overcome slavery. As a child, his master's wife taught him the alphabet — until the master put a stop to it because teaching a slave to read was illegal. He then recruited neighborhood boys to be his teachers, sometimes giving away his food in exchange for lessons in reading and writing.

To Douglass, reading led to freedom, and so it is with those who are held in the bondage of illiteracy. Without acquiring reading and writing skills, they are locked in chains of shame and despair, fearing exposure and humiliation. After I overcame my own illiteracy, I became fervent in my desire to help others. In fact, my freedom from illiteracy demanded that I plead the case of my fellow travelers on the bridge to literacy and present it to the dominant culture in its own language: the written word. This book is written for those who can read it, but it is dedicated to those who cannot.

Today, I am no longer the teacher who couldn't read. I am the teacher who can read and wants to educate others about the importance of meeting the needs of all learners. I am a builder of bridges, linking those who need to learn with those who have the tools to teach them.

## CHAPTER I

# The Call to Action

*No man can sincerely try to*
*help another without helping himself.*

— Ralph Waldo Emerson

It is hard for the literate world to imagine what it is like not to be able to communicate in the written word like everyone else. Gifted with the ability to read and write, most people give little thought, if any, to their literacy when they pick up a newspaper, dash off a few lines in an email, or pass the time with a book or magazine. They read much as they breathe, unaware of the skills they acquired as children.

To the literate world, illiteracy is unfathomable and, therefore, invisible. After all, you can't look at a crowd and pick out the people who can't read or write. You certainly wouldn't have been able to look at me 20 years ago when, in my forties, I had all the trappings of monetary success but could not read or write beyond a second-grade level. You would have seen the successful California businessman with a large house on a hill and an ocean view and said, "No, not him. He's not illiterate." And you would have been wrong.

Because illiteracy is invisible, it's easy for the literate world to overlook it. Unless literate people have some connection through a child, a family member, or close friend who has struggled with reading and writing, illiteracy does not cross their minds. Without any personal connection, they shrug off illiteracy as someone else's problem: "It's not my children. It's not me. So what does it have to do with me?" They tell themselves that there's nothing they can do about it. The experts — the schools and the teachers — should be teaching people to read. It's so easy to take comfort in these beliefs, but the relief is only temporary at best, an illusion that hides the dire consequences for all society.

> *Literacy is the ability to use printed and written information to function in society, to achieve one's goals, and to develop one's knowledge and potential.*
>
> — National Assessment of Adult Literacy [1]

Illiteracy doesn't just pluck at our heartstrings; it also picks our pockets. Illiteracy thwarts the employer looking for skilled workers who can be trained to do more sophisticated jobs. It robs the community that needs productive members who can contribute time, money, and talent for the good of all. It undermines a society that must spend more resources on fixing problems rather than striving to exceed and excel. It cripples the next generation, whose parents lack the ability to introduce their children to the joy of the written word.

When a child grows up unable to read and write, but through social promotion is given a high school diploma that he cannot read, or drops out of school at 16 because he knows he cannot make the grade, what happens then? Those who are undereducated will be underemployed and unemployed, and that, in turn, results in a quantifiable cost for the literate, educated world.

According to a report from the Organization for Economic Cooperation and Development (OECD), U.S. adults who do not finish high school earn 65 percent of what high school graduates make. The OECD report also noted another shocking statistic: one-third of students don't finish high school on time — or at all.[2] If we, as a society, do not address the number of high school dropouts — kids who typically have low literacy skills — what will happen to these young people when they try to enter the workforce? Where will they go? Who will pay to house them and feed their children?

When a large portion of the population cannot be adequately trained to take on more advanced jobs in a changing U.S. economy, society will pay the price. There will be higher costs for social programs to support those who cannot make a competitive wage and for those who are incarcerated. An astounding percentage of inmates — some experts have put it as high as 75 percent — are illiterate. Moreover, experts state that prisoners have a higher proportion of learning disabilities (although I personally dislike that term) than the general population, including 75 to 90 percent of juvenile offenders.

Judge James R. Milliken, retired presiding judge of the San Diego Juvenile Court, who led the drive to offer intensive language and literacy instruction to juvenile offenders in two San Diego juvenile camps, sees a direct correlation between illiteracy, addiction, and recidivism: "If we are going to solve the problems associated with incarcerating too many people and dysfunctional families with kids in foster care because their parents are incarcerated, then we need to require people to learn how to read and to receive drug treatment during their incarceration." However, this would require providing these institutions with teachers who have actually been trained to teach students to read using the findings of scientific research in reading.

The problem of illiteracy — whether it concerns children who are not taught to read and end up in special education programs or adults who cannot read and, therefore, cannot live and work to their full potential — carries a hard-dollar cost to society. If we, as a society, do not recognize this cost and respond with a call to action, then more children will be at risk of growing up to be functionally illiterate adults who cannot fulfill their potential for themselves, their families, and their communities. The gap between the haves and have-nots — socially, psychologically, and economically — will widen. And if that is not enough to create the urgency to act, then consider the cost of programs that will be borne by the literate. Wouldn't it be easier and better and make more economic sense just to provide the services that are needed to make more people productive in their lives, in business, and in society? If we're going to pay — and pay, we will — then shouldn't it be for programs that are proactive in teaching people to read rather than for reactive measures to take care of the ills caused by illiteracy?

In a recent Editorial Observer column, the *New York Times* pointed out the high cost of not teaching reading. According to the *Times,* a growing number of families has asserted their rights under the federal Individuals with Disabilities Education Act to provide private education — at public expense — for their children who struggle with reading. "Federal disability law offers public school systems a stark choice: The schools can properly educate learning disabled children — or they can fork over the money to let private schools do the job. The instructional techniques for helping those children are well documented in federally backed research and have been available in various forms from specialized tutors and private schools for more than 50 years. Even so, few public schools actually use the best practices."[3]

For literacy programs to be truly effective against this raging epidemic, which has claimed a significant portion of adults who were once children like me, and which still threatens our children today, we must embrace a new vision to prevent and eradicate illiteracy. To address the prevention of illiteracy, the federal No Child Left Behind Act was signed into law on January 8, 2002, with a goal of ensuring that every student can read and do math at grade level or better by 2014. As of this writing, the reauthorization of the Act is about to enter the political arena in earnest. Although I maintain that literacy is an apolitical issue — meaning it is a cause that everyone can embrace, regardless of political persuasion — it is highly politicized. As we have seen in previous political fights, such as over the Reading First program — which saw its funding cut dramatically in early 2008 from $1 billion to under $400 million — things can and will turn vicious.

Regardless of what happens with No Child Left Behind in the future, I maintain that this federal legislation must be reauthorized. No matter what political battles are waged — or what power struggles occur from the hallway of the schoolhouse to the hallways of Congress — we cannot lose sight of two pillars of this law: its emphasis on research-based methodology to teach all learners how to read and the necessity of holding schools accountable for teaching children. Accountability is crucial across the literacy cycle, and especially in early childhood, to ensure that learners are being taught the fundamentals they need to acquire literacy skills. If we do not measure, how can we manage?

Our call to action in literacy is to reach all learners, wherever they are. As an adult learner, I know the importance of programs to catch those who have "fallen through the cracks" of our compulsory education system. As a literacy advocate, I have spent time with high school students, some on the verge of dropping out, who have only rudimentary reading and writing skills. And I have spoken with countless parents who are concerned that their young children are not "catching on" the way that schools promise they will. All the assurances from teachers and administrators that "students learn at different rates, in different ways, and in different styles" do nothing to quiet parents' fears that their children are falling behind their peers.

There is no magic pill to cure illiteracy. The only cure for illiteracy is literacy—and achieving it requires a scientific approach. Our efforts with young students in the critical years between kindergarten and third grade will do much to address problems among emerging learners and to decrease the size of the population of adults who lack the necessary literacy skills. The Reading First program has been hailed as "the largest, most focused, and most successful early reading initiative every undertaken in the country." Reading First applies scientifically based research and instruction tools and assessments to help teachers improve student achievement (see Chapter 6). According to the U.S. Department of Education, as of early 2007, more than 5,600 schools in 1,600 districts nationwide have participated in Reading First. State programs funded by Reading First have served approximately 1.8 million students, while more than 100,000 teachers have benefited from its professional development. Secretary of Education Margaret Spellings called Reading First's initial results "extremely promising," with students in Reading First schools demonstrating increases in reading achievement across all performance measures for the 2004–2005 school year.[4]

Reading First's federal funding was cut by 60 percent in early 2008, but the program remains alive. Whatever the future holds for Reading First—whether it gains ground again or morphs into something else—the fact remains that teachers must employ research-based tools to assess and instruct students. The science has shown us what works; now we must put it into action.

As part of the battle to eradicate illiteracy, community-based literacy programs for adults, operating in a vacuum some of the time and dependent on local support to serve its constituents, must have a greater funding commitment and accountability in order to teach more than just a few learners. While commendable, these programs, which are often staffed by dedicated volunteers, are the proverbial drops in the bucket. I make that statement at the risk of offending those who have given their time, talent, and energy for the betterment of others — and as the recipient of those services, I know how valuable they are. Yet, we must wake up to the bigger truth: literacy initiatives need a bigger, broader, and more universal vision.

A new approach is needed to share the practical application of instructional practices that are grounded in the findings of three decades of reading research. But most important of all, there must be a commitment to put the latest research-based tools into the hands of all teachers, professionals, and volunteers alike. Literacy initiatives from early childhood intervention in school districts to community-based adult programs must cooperate and communicate. A new vision of literacy requires a ceasefire in the turf battles over funding and squabbles over whose approach is better. There's a five-alarm fire going on, and there are only a hundred buckets of water. Instead of arguing over whose bucket is better or more important, we've got to stop fanning the flames of illiteracy with the "gasoline" of faulty teaching practices that started the fire in the first place. Instead we must recruit others to make the bucket brigade of effective instruction deeper and wider than ever before.

As Sharon Darling, president and CEO of the National Center for Family Literacy, remarked, "There is interconnectedness among all the programs. Don't try to pull off a piece and say, 'I'm going to solve this' because someone believes early childhood is more important, while others say adult education and others say high school.

Let's not have a zero-sum game, but see how it's all connected. There is a continuum."

Without a new vision of cooperation, communication, and the sharing of best practices; without proven, research-based curricula and methods, particularly in early childhood education; without greater accountability through the gathering and analysis of data; and without a commitment from public and private funding sources, we will be doomed by the limits of our own success. We will manage to help a few people cross the bridge to literacy, gaining mastery of the written word, and say, "Look at what we've done," but we will not be able to see how many others will be left behind. We won't be able to look because that's a truth few of us could face. While each individual who learns how to read — whether a child or an adult — is a cause to celebrate, we can't let our self-satisfaction paint a rosy pink cloud over the reality that the subculture of illiteracy isn't getting any smaller.

The purpose of this book is to provide the call to action along three distinct yet interconnected paths:

- Teachers must be equipped with research-based tools and methodologies to address the needs of all learners. According to the American Federation of Teachers, scientists estimate that 95 percent of children can be taught to read — and yet at least 20 percent of elementary school students do not read fluently enough to enjoy or engage in independent reading.

- Universities and colleges that train teachers must revamp their curricula on reading instruction consistent with the findings of scientific research that have been proven to work in the classroom — specifically instruction in phonemic awareness, phonetics, fluency, vocabulary development, and comprehension (the essential components of reading instruction). Decades of carefully conducted research has proven beyond any reasonable doubt that teaching children that written letters and combinations of letters are represented by sounds, and that to read proficiently they must be taught the alphabetic system of the English language so they can read, write, and spell. Yet, the institutions of higher learning persist in following a whole language approach that would have students memorize words, with little or no understanding of the connection between the letters of the English alphabet and the sounds they represent. Teacher-training programs should be required to align instruction with research-based practices. States must test teachers for their knowledge of the alphabetic principles and the essential components of reading instruction as a prerequisite for teacher licensure and certification.

- For those who have not mastered the skill of reading, appropriate instruction must be delivered at every point along the life cycle, from early childhood education through adult programs. Teaching children to read will reduce the number of illiterate adults. Teaching adults to read will not only help these individuals become more productive and positive members of society, but also enable them to help prepare their own children for learning. As international literacy consultant Dr. Thomas Sticht observes, "We cannot throw away the parents and try to fix children independent of the adults who cannot read."

Fortunately, forces already at work have begun the necessary revolution that will bring about sweeping change in our educational system. The No Child Left Behind legislation, although politically controversial, sets a high standard to teach all learners by 2014. Across the country, states have taken steps to end social promotion, the insidious practice of promoting students who are failing or have poor grades in order to keep them with their social peers.

These are some of the crucial pieces, but they do not solve the whole puzzle. We must have a comprehensive strategy to address illiteracy at every level of society. This means early detection and intervention for young children; instruction in reading beginning in kindergarten, first, and second grade that is based on the findings of science; intensive remediation for any children who have not mastered the skill of reading by grade three; proper training of teachers at every level in the techniques that are proven by research to work; and adult literacy programs to intervene with older students, high school dropouts, those in danger of dropping out of school, and older adults who have tried to get by in life without being able to read.

We must mobilize forces in support of literacy at every opportunity, among state and federal lawmakers, business leaders, faith-based initiatives, and service organizations. The media must also be called upon to exert its vast influence to illuminate the scope of the problem of illiteracy and the solutions that already exist. Just as the American Broadcasting Company (ABC) and the Public Broadcasting Service (PBS) in 1985 joined forces in an unprecedented alliance to establish the Project Literacy US (PLUS) campaign, the media today must commit their resources to help put an end to the epidemic of illiteracy.

Through public awareness we can reach out to those who need these skills as well as those who want to help them. As James Duffy, former president of ABC who later led the PLUS project on behalf of the network, said at the time of the founding of that campaign, "We have a plan to help do something about illiteracy through Project Literacy... It can involve every person in this room and can affect every person in our country."[5]

Today's media campaign must be more than the same old motivation of how much fun it is to read, which is a source of frustration for the parents of children who struggle with reading and also adults who have difficulty with the written word. The problem for these learners is not motivation but a lack of proper instruction. Teaching reading, writing, and spelling is a challenging job and requires more than just a good heart and a love of books. Well-meaning teachers and tutors at all levels, whether they work with children or adults, must have the research-based tools and methodologies that have been proven to work. After decades of scientific research, we know that instruction must be grounded in phonetics and emphasize comprehension, fluency, and vocabulary building.

The media awareness campaign this time must not only shed light on the entrenched problem of illiteracy in America, but also bring home the point that there is ample scientific evidence backing how to teach people to read. There is, however, a persistent gap between what we know and what we do at all levels, including in our elementary schools, where the prevention of illiteracy must be a top priority.

We must recognize and encourage the beneficial chain reaction of teaching all learners. In Appalachia, children who learned how to read in school introduced their parents to the written word, and soon families were starting to read together. In California, Ramón Gómez, who came to the United States from Mexico at the age of thirteen, learned how to read and write English as an adult.

Today he speaks publicly on behalf of the library-based program where he is a learner and he is a real-world inspiration to his three children to stay in high school or pursue a diploma through an alternative program.

Ramón's mastery of reading brought one more person across the bridge, but his story is bigger than that. He is a living example of the importance of family literacy, particularly for minority communities, where the lack of education and the ability to get a job splinters the family unit that is so important to society. Family literacy strengthens generational ties, creating strong bonds between parents and children, as well as bonding families to their communities. As America grapples with immigration issues, Ramón's experience challenges us to teach those who come to this country, providing them — and their children who are born here — with the resources they need to read, write, and speak English.

"They don't see me as an immigrant now. They see me as a person in a community. That makes me feel good when people speak to me with respect," Ramón observed. "This is the opportunity that we didn't have in our native country. This is the gold we're digging for, and we're going to keep going."

*Widening the coverage and effectiveness of basic education can have a powerfully preventive role in reducing human insecurity of nearly every kind.*[6]

— Amaratya Sen,
2003 Nobel Prize–winning economist

## The Subculture of Illiteracy

The subculture of illiteracy is larger than anyone on the outside would ever believe. The National Assessment of Adult Literacy (NAAL) conducted a study of illiteracy among adults in the United States in 2003, results of which were released in December 2005. NAAL found that 43 percent of the total population aged 16 and older — or some 93 million people — ranked at the below-basic or basic level in their reading skills. Fourteen percent of the adult population had below-basic skills in reading and understanding prose texts — a percentage that was unchanged from 1992, when the first NAAL report was released. At the below-basic level, these adults ranged from those considered nonliterate in English to those having some limited ability, which NAAL described as "locating easily identifiable information in short, commonplace prose texts." Another 29 percent of the population, the NAAL study found, had basic skills "necessary to perform simple and everyday literacy activities," such as "reading and understanding information in short, commonplace prose texts."[7]

The higher levels of reading skills are defined as intermediate and proficient. *Intermediate* is "reading and understanding moderately dense, less-commonplace prose texts as well as summarizing, making simple inferences, determining cause and effect, and recognizing the author's purpose." *Proficient* means "reading lengthy, complex, abstract prose texts as well as synthesizing information and making complex inferences."[8]

The gap between the 43 percent at below-basic and basic prose literacy and the 57 percent at intermediate and proficient raises the question: How can those at lower levels compete in a world that demands increasing literacy skills? Not surprisingly, the NAAL study found that among adults with below-basic prose literacy, 51 percent were not in the labor force.[9] Dr. Sandra Baxter, director of the National Institute for Literacy (NILF), a federal organization that addresses literacy across the lifespan and across federal agency programs, commented, "The 2003 NAAL results suggest we have a very serious situation on our hands. The United States cannot afford to have this many adults whose skills are at basic or below-basic levels and expect to remain competitive in a global economy. This is an urgent problem that we need to focus on now." The statistics on the subculture of illiteracy are sobering, but the real tragedy goes beyond the numbers. The sad truth is that the gap between those who have mastered literacy and those who have not is not closing.

The late Pat Lindamood spent more than 40 years working first as a speech pathologist and later as a pioneer in literacy. In a conversation a few months before she died, Pat shared the perspective that illiteracy is a problem of the haves and the have-nots. People who were taught how to decode the English writing system were able to grasp reading and writing easily as children. They are the haves in the literate world, the people for whom reading is as natural as speaking, because they were taught to read using scientifically valid instructional methods.

"The haves actually have no appreciation of the problem. They have no way to understand that other people do not get the information that they get when they see the wholeness of a word. The haves can repeat the wholeness of the word and also tell you the individual sounds within it," Pat explained. "The have-nots, however, have no clue that there are people who get information from that word—information that hasn't registered in their brains. The have-nots begin to assume that the haves are smarter than they are."

If the have-nots are not given the type of instruction they need as children, they are at risk of becoming high school students who drop out or who graduate without obtaining the literacy skills they need to live and compete in the world.

Kevin B. is a highly intelligent, articulate man in his forties who, for reasons that still escape him, although he suspects he is dyslexic, did not learn how to read in school. After a pattern of frustration and acting out in school, he dropped out at 16 or 17. He recalled, "I was always in the same basic reading class with the same people. I knew then, without anyone telling me, what they thought: 'You're not as sharp as the rest of the kids. You're not measuring up or competing.' I have no fond memories of school."

Even though he found professional success with his high level of mechanical ability, Kevin always felt a hunger to learn how to read, which eventually led him to a library-based adult literacy program where he was matched with a tutor. He also pursued his General

Education Development (GED) high school equivalency diploma. "I just wanted to read my son a bedtime story," Kevin explained. "I knew that if I didn't seek help for myself, I would not be able to help my son. He was going to follow in my footsteps, and I didn't want him to be caught in that same cycle."

## The Call to Action

*As part of their everyday lives, adults in the United States interact with a variety of printed and other written materials to perform a multitude of tasks. A comprehensive list... would include activities such as balancing a checkbook, following directions on a prescription medicine bottle, filling out a job application, consulting a bus schedule, correctly interpreting a chart in the newspaper, and using written instructions to operate a voting machine.*

— National Assessment of Adult Literacy[10]

In a world dominated by technology and the Internet, the written word cannot be avoided. Email, Internet searches, blogs, and instant messages are tools of the literate. The printed media is a great vehicle of mass communication, but what value is it to those who cannot read? Once again, the subculture of illiteracy is left behind.

The ability to read requires the same body of knowledge about the English phonetic system in every real-life application. If someone has been taught to read by a properly trained teacher using scientifically proven methods, then that person can read anything. As Dr. Baxter observed, "Reading is important in all the contexts in which adults must function: at work, at home, in the community. And the level of skill an adult has acquired has important implications. For example, we know that adults with higher-level literacy skills are more likely to be employed full time and more likely to earn a higher income."

When more than 40 percent of adults in the United States cannot read and write with proficiency, it is the epitome of a broken promise. The United States prides itself on compulsory education. Our standard is that every child must attend school. Without a firm commitment to teach all children to read, that standard is reduced to a farce that would seem to indicate that children who attend school do not necessarily have to learn how to read and write. When they are old enough, which in most states is age 16, they can leave school — without a high school diploma and without the basic skills to get a job in this country. Is this what American public education stands for?

As the federal education reform No Child Left Behind goes before Congress for reauthorization, we must stay the course for accountability and research-based reading instruction. As Education Secretary Spellings noted, "The No Child Left Behind Act recognizes what truly makes a difference in providing a quality education. It calls for a highly qualified teacher in the core subjects in every classroom; the use of proven, research-based instructional methods; and timely information and options for parents. Schools that underperform are held accountable, providing their students with free tutoring or transfer to a better-performing public school. In other words, children's education needs are placed first — where they belong.[11]

*People are the common denominator of progress.*
*So ... no improvement is possible with unimproved*
*people, and advance is certain when people are liberated*
*and educated ... Conquest of illiteracy comes first.*

—John Kenneth Galbraith
*The Affluent Society* (1958)[12]

## The Right to Read

All children in this country have the right to learn how to read and write. They are our children. Denying them the right to learn how to read is a form of child abuse and child neglect. It's traumatizing to grow up knowing you cannot read. Nothing that anyone does for you seems to work. Something must be wrong with your brain, or so you tell yourself. You go underground with your secret and begin living the lie that will color the rest of your life. For me, it happened in third grade. That was the time in my life when I knew that I was different from the other children, those who could read and write. It was obvious that I wasn't keeping up with the rest of the group. I didn't understand the markings on the page. I didn't know the logic of the words. The written word of my own native language was completely foreign to me.

I've spoken to many people who grew up like me. Third grade, they told me, was the stage at which they, too, realized that they were illiterate. Third grade is like a gateway into a higher level of literacy and expanded subject matter, which for too many students becomes a closed door unless they receive intensive intervention. By third grade, students should be able to transition to advanced phonics and word study. For those who have not mastered basic phonics, intensive intervention and direct instruction are necessary to prepare them for the greater reading demands of the higher grades.

Without that intervention, even these young students know what's next. Sadly, they will realize, as I did, that if they don't know how to read by fifth grade, the odds will be against them ever learning how to read — at least in school. The educational system has been driven by the curriculum, and as many adult nonreaders found out the hard way, by about the fifth grade, the window of opportunity for learning how to read has shut. As a society, we must make a commitment to teach everyone to read, write, and spell — no matter where they are or what age they are. It is never too late to learn how to read.

When children do not learn how to read in school, fear takes root, making them believe they will never be able to read. They see themselves as outsiders, inhabiting a shadowy world where they always have to be on guard, fearing judgment and ridicule from the dominant, literate culture. They feel alone and abandoned in that existence, as if they are the only ones experiencing the anger and the shame. They have no idea how many millions of people are like them.

Not knowing how to read or not believing that learning how to read will ever be possible may cause a person to become locked in the second or third grade. I know from my own experience that illiteracy suspended me in childhood — emotionally, intellectually, psychologically, and spiritually. It doesn't matter what one accomplishes elsewhere in life, whether running a multimillion-dollar company, as I did, or becoming distinguished in sports or entertainment, as others have. We know that we can't do something that a child can do: read. The shame of illiteracy branded each of us with a mark we tried desperately to hide from the dominant, literate culture that has all the power.

Among the broad population of all learners — both children and adults — about 30 percent will have challenges learning how to read unless they are taught directly and systematically, according to the late Pat Lindamood. From 2 to 3 percent of this group of children have physiological difficulties. Some children have what Pat termed "language-processing difficulties." These learners do not possess the gift of language processing that other people have. It has nothing to do with intelligence; rather, they do not have an inborn gift that other people do — just as some people have perfect pitch while others are tone-deaf.

I always knew that I had a problem pronouncing words, but I did not link that to my inability to learn to read. I had an auditory discrimination problem, which meant I could not distinguish the difference between certain sounds. That problem was at the root of my learning deficiencies in reading, writing, and spelling. I prefer to use the term *learning deficiency* or *reading deficiency,* because I believe those terms are the most accurate and descriptive. The word *deficiency* is defined as lacking something necessary. The terms *learning deficiency* and *reading deficiency* reflect the fact that a person has a lack or need in these particular areas, which research has shown and personal experience has demonstrated can be overcome with proper instruction. I know now that if I had been given the proper diagnostic assessment when I was at the early stages of being taught to read and then had received instruction that was systematic, direct, and based on the findings of reading research, I would never have been left behind and unable to read until I was in my forties.

Although the terms *learning disabled* and *learning disability* are widely used, I believe these labels are inaccurate. Being disabled means that someone is "not able" — in this context, not able to learn. On the contrary, we are able to learn! I was able to learn how to read. Labels such as learning disability reflect an all-too-pervasive mind-set in schools and throughout society that individuals with certain deficiencies are not able to learn. Sadly, many people who are illiterate also believe that about themselves. Having tried before without success, they give up on themselves; they allow themselves to be convinced that they are not able.

I am a living, breathing example of what specialized tutors and private instruction can do for someone who went through 12 years of school and 4 years of college and still had not learned how to read, write, and spell. Fortunately, I could afford the time and money to travel to San Luis Obispo to become a student in the famed Lindamood-Bell Clinic, where I gained greater mastery of reading skills. More than money, I also invested hundreds of hours and tremendous effort.

Finally, I could read! I was liberated from a cruel imprisonment that had crushed my spirit every day. Then my triumph turned to sadness. Yes, I could read. At the age of 48, having spent so much of my time and effort trying to prove myself to everyone — on the athletic field and in business — I had accomplished what some children in elementary school can do with little effort at all. Why had it taken me so long? Why weren't these skills imparted to me sooner? I have come to peace with these questions, although they do linger in my mind. I know the answers intellectually, but they do not correct what felt like an injustice for so many years.

I know for many new learners, it might seem impossible to make the necessary commitment and sacrifices to learn how to read. Adults have many competing demands on their time, including families and employers. Still, those who struggle with literacy must try, for there are occasions in life when the choices made alter not only one person's life for the better but also the lives of others. Improved reading skills may mean a better job, a happier family, and immense personal satisfaction. If nonreaders are asked to make these investments of time, money, and effort, then the literate world must respond by providing effective adult learning centers; properly trained teachers and tutors; and the moral, ethical, financial, and political commitment to support their efforts.

## Jason's Story

Jason was a young man in a very deep hole. Although this 22-year-old had graduated from high school in Maryland, he was functionally illiterate. "I couldn't even read the basic information in a newspaper about a movie," he explained. He recalled the night when he felt the most isolated and alone, miserable about what he didn't have—especially the ability to read and write. "I kind of broke down that night. I believe it was God trying to get my attention," Jason said.

Jason and his father began searching for tools and programs to help him to learn how to read. In time and after a few false starts, this led him to a highly trained tutor who was an expert in scientifically based techniques. After some evaluation and one-on-one instruction, it was determined that Jason was an excellent candidate for a computer-based program to improve his word decoding and reading skills, along with continued tutor support. One consideration for him, as an adult with a job, was his commitment to be an independent learner. He took to the online program immediately. It was a breakthrough for him. He began to see results right away, motivating him to work harder. Four months later, through working on the program every day, he is now able to decode and is challenging himself with more difficult words.

"I'm reading better than I ever imagined after three or four months," he said proudly. "Who knows where I'm going to be when I finish this program."

Jason's newfound passion for reading contrasts with the story he told of not being taught in school. "By the time I was in fifth grade, they stopped teaching me. That's what it felt like to me. Instead, they read everything to me, and then they wrote down what I dictated. I passed, but I couldn't read."

Now a devout Christian, he says the Bible is his favorite book, and he is thinking about perhaps going to Bible school and becoming a missionary one day. What's made the difference, clearly, is Jason's ability to read and write, gaining mastery of fundamental literacy skills that opened up an entire world of possibilities to him. Moreover, he looks at himself in a more positive light, which is also reflected in his interactions with others. "I can't go back and blame those people who didn't teach me before because I can't dwell on that my whole life," Jason said. "My only concern now is, are they letting kids pass school who don't have the knowledge to live in the world? Without written language, you don't have anything."

## The Myths of Illiteracy

As a functionally illiterate adult able to survive in the professional world, I was fortunate. I do not consider myself separate, however, from those who lack reading and writing skills and are economically disadvantaged. In fact, my success in spite of my illiteracy affirms my conviction to work as an advocate on behalf of others. I know how difficult it was for me, facing more and more papers from permits to zoning ordinances, to get by without reading and writing — and without letting anyone know my secret. I know what it's like to be enslaved by the shame and fear, as well as my deficiency with the written language.

Out of its own fear and ignorance, literate culture imposes stereotypes on the subculture, creating myths and false beliefs that anyone who cannot read lacks intelligence, a functional family, or the desire to learn. My own story defies those stereotypes, as do the stories of others whose voices are heard in this book. While the details of my story are unique, I have heard this same theme echoed over and over again.

Donna Archer, widow of golf great and former Masters champion George Archer, revealed in the March/April 2006 issue of *Golf for Women* the secret that the couple had hidden from the public. "Despite years of effort, he [George Archer] never learned how to read beyond a rudimentary level, and he never could write more than a few crude sentences."[13]

She described her husband's anxiety over trying to hide his illiteracy, especially from potential sponsors who might want him to read a speech or write a few words: "George was an honest man, and I knew that if anybody had confronted him about his literacy problem, he would have told the truth. Fortunately, no one ever asked."[14]

Jacques Demers, the head coach of the 1993 Stanley Cup champion Montreal Canadiens, had his wife read news articles to him. He relied on his staff to sum up reports. When someone would ask him to read something, he would say that he forgot his glasses. Demers was illiterate. As writer Mitch Albom wrote in a *Parade* magazine article, Demers was "scared to death...[that] if anyone found out, he'd be finished." He continued, "The number of people who are functionally illiterate in this country—and the rest of the world—might stagger you. Studies show that as many as one in seven American adults may be unable to comprehend a job application or a newspaper's front page."[15]

## Illiteracy in Literate Terms

Over the years, I have attempted to divide my illiterate and literate worlds into two components. By focusing my attention on them separately, I believed I could increase my awareness of each and experience a deeper level of transformation from the phases of being illiterate, functionally illiterate, developing literate, to literate. I coined the phrase "developing literate" to bridge the gap psychologically between having been functionally illiterate and becoming literate. In the process, I gave myself permission to move into another stage and to reduce the tension, rigidity, and pressure that most functionally illiterate people experience. As a developing literate, I freed myself from the stresses that afflicted me as a functional illiterate. By defining where I was, I gained the freedom to claim my space in the literate world and occupy it.

To survive as an illiterate and even as a functional illiterate, I used precise skills of observation and perception. I had to learn English by hearing it. I could not read it, and my mind's eye was blind to the written word most of my life. Instead, I came to rely on my 20/20 vision to explore people, places, and things, whether close-up or at a distance. I needed my own language for thinking. I used my sensory receptivity to give me information and a context in which to assess, analyze, and understand the people, situations, and events around me. As my sensory receptivity sharpened, my spoken language improved. At each stage of inner awareness, I gained power and confidence in the literate world.

I still use these skills that I developed as an illiterate, from my intuition to my physical senses, which provide me with information. Over the past 20 years, I have also gained proficiency and confidence with the written word. I have found that writing is a very good means to focus my attention. I am cognizant of the fact that I speak more clearly and my mind is quieting. Now I am deploying the skills of the illiterate and literate worlds the way a person who is fluent in two or more languages might translate foreign text into content that others can understand. As a literate adult, I can communicate in the written word to the dominant culture, trying to make real for them what it is like to function as an illiterate.

I believe that a greater understanding of the illiterate world is essential if we are to strengthen our nation and live up to our ideals and our creed. If we, as a nation, want to preserve our way of life, our rights and freedoms, we must recognize our obligation to teach all learners how to read and write. To do this requires a revamping of our educational system, tossing out old perceptions and bringing in new ideas. Change is never easy, and the more entrenched the institution, the more difficult that becomes. This approach requires that teachers be taught at colleges and universities how to teach children to read using the latest and best research. Colleges and universities need to equip all teachers — regardless of their grade-level or content specialty — with the fundamentals of reading instruction. Teacher credentials and licensing requirements need to be raised so that the best and brightest are attracted to this profession, made accountable for their results, and then paid what they deserve.

Addressing illiteracy means we need to take a hard look at how we educate children. The status quo clearly isn't working — not with 43 percent of adults at below-basic reading levels. As the furor over high school exit exams has shown (as will be addressed in Chapter 3) a significant percentage of students have gone through 12 years of school and still lack the ability to read and write at grade level. Special education programs are full of students with normal or above-normal intelligence whose only deficiency is their inability to read. If these are the problems, then isn't the solution painfully obvious? We must teach all learners how to read. Best practices must be shared across literary programs and venues. Whether in the school district or the privately funded program, data must be measured and results quantified.

"We need to focus on assessment and intervention as early as possible to correct the problem for as many individuals as possible," agreed Dr. Baxter. She added that intensive programs in the elementary and secondary schools, alone, will not negate the need for adult literacy intervention. Indeed, conquering illiteracy requires a multifaceted approach. Nonetheless, early intervention — before the gap among learners has widened too far and before students see themselves as unable to learn — is key to stopping illiteracy from claiming a new generation.

We must have the right tools available — especially in our elementary school classrooms — to identify deficiencies early on through diagnostic testing and to begin proper instruction immediately, putting the latest research into action. That responsibility rests with the universities and colleges that train teachers. They must make it imperative that all teachers are properly trained to teach all learners.

In a statement issued in March 2002 in support of the No Child Left Behind Act, First Lady Laura Bush highlighted the need for better training for teachers at the university level. "We heard from education experts who said that over the next decade, American schools will need more than two million new teachers," said Mrs. Bush, who is a former elementary school teacher and librarian. "And all teachers, whether new or tenured, must have better training and resources to succeed." [16]

In her statement, Mrs. Bush highlighted the need for teachers to have thorough and up-to-date knowledge of teaching skills and subject content, as well as the ability to assess student needs and use the most effective instructional methods and materials so that students make the greatest academic gains.

Illiteracy is not a problem that will go away on its own, nor does it affect only one type of student or group of individuals. The solutions we provide must transcend boundaries and categories, reaching out to everyone who lacks adequate literacy skills.

The purpose of this book is to illustrate the depth and magnitude of the problem; to put a human face on a societal issue; and to help the dominant, literate world to relate to the illiterate subculture. Understanding the problem, however, is only half the task. We must identify, analyze, and articulate the problem to find the solution. Wherever illiteracy exists, the best resources must be deployed to eradicate it. Millions of dollars have been spent on research into the problem of illiteracy. Now the research must be turned into action.

We have been in denial in this country. We have kept the secret that we as a society have failed to teach millions of people how to read, write, and spell. When we fail them, we fail ourselves. In a country that talks about equal opportunity, there are still millions of adults who are illiterate. For the child or adult who cannot read, there is no equal opportunity, not in the classroom or in the workforce. The only cure for illiteracy is literacy.

As each nonreader crosses the bridge, all of society benefits. When literate society reaches out to include all the children and adults, empowering them to read and write, we invite them to be full citizens. Our culture has done so much in other endeavors, it gives us hope for this challenge. In 1961, President John F. Kennedy gave our country a vision: man in space. As he said at that time, "I believe this nation should commit itself to achieving the goal before this decade is out of landing a man on the Moon and returning him safely to Earth." Those of us who are old enough remember that charge and what it did to this country: it electrified us with hope and purpose, right down to the individual on the street. We rose to the challenge, in our universities and laboratories, among our scientists and engineers, and by the end of the decade, Neil Armstrong stepped on the moon.

Solving illiteracy in America, I would argue, is less complex than it was for this country to go from a relatively low level of space technology to a manned Moon landing and return. Yes, using the tools and resources to tackle illiteracy will take a strong commitment, time, and the allocation of sufficient money across the literacy continuum, from the elementary school classrooms where children are taught, to the community programs that cater to adults, to the universities where teachers are trained. We have those tools and resources, and that is more than half the battle. We cannot allow fights over funding to disrupt our goal of teaching anyone who wants to learn how to read.

Ralph Waldo Emerson wrote, "No man can sincerely try to help another without helping himself." I believe the inverse is also true:

no man can sincerely try to help himself without helping another. I know that this is my job now: to go back into the subculture of illiteracy to help those who are invisible to literate society. Ensuring that everyone becomes literate is a noble cause. It inspires a sense of moral obligation for those who are able to read proficiently in the culture to share their precious gift with those who don't have it. Adults and children who have not been taught to read cannot simply pick themselves up by their proverbial bootstraps. I couldn't teach myself to read, no matter how many books, magazines, and newspapers I looked at. I needed someone to teach me, and thank God I found that someone.

The printed word is the greatest source of information. Knowing how to read — decoding and understanding the printed word — can give the masses access to information, knowledge, and enlightenment. The printed word can change or confirm new and old ideas. As Thomas Jefferson said, "If a nation expects to be ignorant and free, it expects what never was and never will be."

No sane person in literate society believes it is bad or wrong to teach others to read and write. This is a cause that all of us can support. The dominant literate culture, however, must make the first move, crossing the bridge into a subculture it would rather ignore. For the sake of those left behind, we must be willing to make the journey again and again, no matter how long it takes.

## CHAPTER 2

# The Epidemic of Nonreaders

To an outsider, we looked nothing alike. There I was, a 68-year-old white male in business attire addressing an audience of teenagers, predominantly Hispanic and African-American as reflected the demographics of the community surrounding the high school. To me, however, it was like looking in a mirror. In some of their faces, I saw traces of Johnny the Innocent, the blameless child I had once been, who through no fault of his own had not learned how to read. In many, many more, I saw the Native Alien, angry, betrayed, and ready to lash out in frustration and defensiveness.

As I drove down to the southern California high school, I knew that I would tell my story as I have so many times and in front of so many people: teachers, educators, policymakers, civic groups, corporations, students, prison inmates, librarians, and volunteer literacy providers. After hundreds of presentations in 44 states, as well as in Europe and Canada, I knew that my story would forge a connection with the audience as it always did — this time an audience of 14- to 16-year-old high school students in a special education program. My message would resonate with them: I know what it's like not to be able to read like other people.

After nearly 20 years of making these presentations, I was also aware that the joy and happiness of having made a connection with these young people wouldn't last very long. Soon, I'd face the feelings of sadness and despair that always come up after I meet people who remain in the subculture of illiteracy, the place I had escaped from as a 48-year-old man.

As I looked out at the faces of the teenagers in the audience on this particular day — some looking back at me, others with their eyes cast down — I knew what I had to say. "We are not dumb," I told these students. "We are not dumb."

Having spent more than four decades in the subculture of illiteracy — in the dumb row in second grade, exiled to the hallway as a junior high discipline problem, and sneaking through teachers' filing cabinets as a desperate college student — I could use the word *we* when I spoke to these high school students. I had the same experiences in my life that they were going through, and I wasn't talking down to them. I wasn't giving them words of encouragement from a mountaintop.

I had been where they were, and I knew all too well the challenges they faced in the outside world, which is dominated by the culture of the written word. I had suffered from the debilitating symptoms of the epidemic of illiteracy in America, which society tries to ignore and which too many policymakers do not recognize as a crisis. Sadder still, it is an epidemic we know how to stop. The cure is putting the right tools into the hands of teachers who have been properly trained by colleges and universities.

In three sessions at the high school that day, I spoke to approximately 90 students who were reading at about the third- to fifth-grade level. About a third of the students were familiar with my personal story. The teacher who had invited me to speak had read my first book and shared it with her class. All of the students had watched a tape of my interview with Oprah, which also gave them an introduction to my story. This was enough to establish our common ground from the start. They knew that I had been like them: young, illiterate, and ready to pass from high school into whatever came next. Miraculously, what followed high school for me was college, even though it had taken drastic and desperate measures for me to graduate. For these young people, I feared the worst for what was ahead of them.

"Don't give up on yourselves," I told them. "You can do it. It's never too late to learn how to read."

I say these words every time I can to nonreaders, because I know they were true in my life and in the lives of many others. For an increasing number of children, young people, and adults, however, these words are only half-truths. Like Johnny the Innocent and even the Native Alien, kids can just keep trying, believe in themselves, stay in school, and behave themselves. But that alone won't teach them to read. Their desire is not enough to break through the barriers that keep them from processing language, decoding words, and comprehending what they read. The statistics of the epidemic of illiteracy prove that point.

Robert Sweet, Jr., president and cofounder of the National Right to Read Foundation (NRRF), retired professional staff member of the U.S. House of Representatives, and former acting director for the National Institute for Education, minced no words on the topic of illiteracy in America. "This is a fight to enable America's children to be able to reach their full potential," he said. "There has been an inability to recognize the problem of illiteracy and its root causes. When a literacy report comes out, there are headlines for a few weeks. 'Millions and millions of Americans can't read at all, or very well, or proficiently.' All the newspapers cover it, and all the reporters write about it, and people say, 'That is just terrible.

How can it be?' Even most of those who do get it don't know what to do about it."

Dr. G. Reid Lyon, a preeminent research scientist who studies how children and adults acquire the skill of reading, stated, "Failure to develop basic reading skills by age nine predicts a lifetime of illiteracy. Unless these children receive the appropriate instruction, over 70 percent of the children entering first grade who are at risk for reading failure will continue to have reading problems into adulthood."

In this statement, from his March 2001 testimony before the House Subcommittee on Education Reform, Dr. Lyon, who was chief of the Child Development and Behavior Branch, National Institute of Child Health and Human Development, National Institutes of Health, offered this solution: "On the other hand, the early identification of children at risk for reading failure coupled with the provision of comprehensive early reading interventions can reduce the percentage of children reading below the basic level in the fourth grade (e.g., 38 percent) to 6 percent or less."[1]

> *Your life taught me to not fear my difficulty.*
> *Also, what I learned from your book is that*
> *even though you have problems in your life,*
> *you can always overcome them with hard work.*
>
> — Paul, a high school student

Children who have difficulty learning how to read and write need proper instruction. Proper instruction requires properly trained teachers. Looking at the three teachers and six teachers' aides in the audience at the high school that day, I delivered the words that are the heart and soul of the message of this book: children cannot learn how to read unless they have proper instruction from properly trained teachers. That is the truth as I have experienced it personally and as I have heard it time and again from researchers, many educators, and literacy advocates.

"You have to believe that every child can learn how to read. Reading comprehension is the key to all other academic areas," said Dr. Joyce Bales, a nationally recognized school superintendent who led a dramatic turnaround in academic achievement in the Pueblo School District in Colorado (see Chapter 5).

The sad truth is that too many of our children are not learning to read in school, and much of the blame lies in the instruction they are receiving. "Over the decades, millions of children in America have been denied the opportunity to learn to read," the U.S. Department of Education stated. "Popular but misguided learning fads caught on in many school districts, which were not held accountable for results."[2]

"Not teaching a child to read is the worst thing we can do to children. And it's not the fault of the child. It's because of the adults who have not been able to teach that child," added Dr. Bales, who at the time of her interview was starting her first year as superintendent of the Vista (California) School District, where she was implementing a program of assessment and intensive intervention with the support of the school board and teachers.

Certainly, some children have language-processing deficiencies as I did. And, yes, these problems require a series of critical steps, including early diagnosis, to determine if there are any physiological barriers to learning to read and, if so, appropriate intervention with research-based instructional methods. Most importantly, schools must offer reading and writing curricula that teach all children early and quickly the decoding skills that are included in a comprehensive approach to reading instruction, thus ensuring that every child and adult who has not learned to read has the opportunity to do so.

Each of these programs has a common denominator: an understanding of just how big the epidemic of illiteracy is. Illiteracy does not just affect some other people's children. Reading and writing at the most basic level is not the problem of people who lack intelligence, drive, or the ability to learn. Illiteracy is an epidemic that crosses racial, ethnic, gender, and socioeconomic backgrounds. Currently, this epidemic has claimed 43 percent of the adult population, those who read at the basic or below-basic levels, according to the National Assessment of Adult Literacy (NAAL).

"It is critical for individuals to attain a level of literacy that allows them to contribute to family, work, and community in a way that is meaningful and productive for them and for our larger society," commented Dr. Sandra Baxter, director of the National Institute for Literacy (NILF). "Literacy is a significant national asset. It is an important factor in our nation's ability to maintain a competitive edge in the global marketplace and a high quality of life for the members of our society."

The epidemic of illiteracy is not confined to the United States. Adult literacy is a global problem, including in developed countries, according to the Organization for Economic Cooperation and Development (OECD), which issued a report based on the International Adult Literacy and Life Skills Survey conducted in a selection of OECD countries and regions: Canada, Italy, the Mexican state of Nuevo León, Norway, Switzerland, and the United States. Focusing on the ability to understand and use information in a written text, the survey found that two-thirds of Norwegians, for example, had at least the necessary skill to perform this task. "But the figure falls to around 60 percent of people in Bermuda and Canada, a little over 50 percent in Switzerland and the United States, and around 20 percent in Italy, and 11 percent in Nuevo León. So there are clearly inequalities not only between, but also within countries."[3]

Literacy and economic strength go hand in hand, not only for the individual but for the country as a whole. When a significant portion of the population lacks the adequate skills to perform required tasks and to take on increasingly complex jobs, there simply are not enough workers to fill the needs of employers. In the United States, where the aging of the population is already creating an experience gap in the workforce, illiteracy is a bottom-line, hard-dollar issue. People who worry about jobs being outsourced at every level from low-level manufacturing to high-level technology, in particular, should give more thought to the importance of having a literate workforce at home that is able to take on these jobs. Business owners are eager to hire employees who can read, write, and spell. The future is bright for those who can, bleak indeed for those who cannot.

Too often, the discussion about the epidemic of illiteracy gets lost in the semantics. For example, critics like to point out that someone who has basic literacy skills can read a newspaper and write basic sentences; therefore, this person is not illiterate. As someone who once functioned at a second-grade literacy level, I can tell you that I did not feel very literate. I was sorely aware at the time of my lack of competency in reading and writing. It does not take a researcher to quantify that basic literacy skills are inadequate for competing in the modern workplace.

"Think about changes in our society in terms of technology—it has changed how we work and how we communicate in our personal lives. There was a point in our history when if you had a high school diploma, you were pretty well set in life," Dr. Baxter explained. "Technology is advancing so quickly that you must be able to grasp and master new skills constantly."

The link between literacy and competitiveness may not strike many people as a burning societal issue on par with a national disaster. They understand that if someone cannot read or write, that person won't have a job — or at least a very good one. But literate America does not see that it is undermining itself when a large percentage of the population lacks the basic reading and writing skills to perform the duties and tasks that, in most jobs, involve computers to some extent. This is hardly a new revelation.

In 1995, when I was on the advisory board of the National Institute for Literacy (NIFL), the institute issued a statement in reference to the first International Adult Literacy Survey (IALS), noting, "This groundbreaking study sounds an alert about the hurdles the U.S. must overcome to compete successfully in a world increasingly dependent on information."

As Andrew Hartman, who was then director of the NIFL, said in the statement, "The IALS shows once and for all that adult literacy is not an isolated educational concern, but a fundamental issue of human resource development. The study lends a new urgency to the NIFL's focus on the literacy needs of welfare recipients, clients of job training programs, and parents of preschool and school-age children."[4]

The statistics, the news headlines, and the governmental reports will only go so far in raising America's consciousness about illiteracy. Even the most startling data cannot put a human face on the numbers or rivet the literate reader's attention to the invisible demoralization of the nonreader's soul and hopes for learning and life. For that to happen, one needs to spend a day in a classroom as I did in California, eye to eye with the next generation of students who — without an intensive level of intervention — may graduate from high school without adequate reading and writing skills. Or they may drop out, or even be pushed out, without achieving the literacy level they need to compete in the workplace. This can happen behind the scenes, because educators have figured out how to manipulate the dropout numbers to distort the dropout rate.

The high school students I spoke to were not young children like Johnny the Innocent. They no longer believed that, one of these days, the magic would happen and they would wake up knowing how to read. They were aware of how far behind their peers they were; they knew the extent of their reading and writing difficulties. They struggled to read their history and science textbooks, and now they faced exit exams they knew they couldn't pass, and they wanted it all to be different.

"I know that everybody in this room at one time or another — all you Innocents and Native Aliens — you prayed or you dreamed or you hoped or you wished that you could read at the high school level." When I said this, there was silence in the room. The only communication was the knowing looks, the eyes that met mine and then were cast down.

Here is the cold, unemotional fact: children who are not taught to read by the fourth or fifth grade will most likely become young adults who still cannot read in special education programs, and later on adults who lack all but the most basic literacy skills. Even those who are of average or above-average intelligence will suffer the same fate, unless teachers have the diagnostic tools and teaching resources to help them. Although I remain firm in my conviction that we must reach out to learners at every age and grade level and even into adulthood, clearly the prevention of illiteracy starts with the youngest of students. Like Johnny the Innocent, these young learners want to read, and they cannot understand why they are different from those who take to the written word like a new friend.

Teachers, especially, need to understand that the key to teaching students who struggle is not to tell them to try harder, or to focus, or to study extra. These admonitions won't solve illiteracy. Children who fail to learn how to read are often trying particularly hard, as even brain scans have documented. Children who are among the approximately 30 percent of the population that has some degree of difficulty learning how to read and write need a different approach than is typically used in the classroom. They need small-group instruction, or if that doesn't work, they must work one-on-one with properly trained teachers who use research-based instruction, who know how to identify deficiencies and gain the child's trust, and who can give the child hope with a plan of action for learning. The teacher must take on the responsibility of finding the right way of teaching children a concept, rather than the children feeling that it is they who have failed to learn a concept.

When teachers and administrators are present in the audience when I speak, I know that I run the risk of offending someone, but I feel compelled to share how so many nonreaders feel about their illiteracy. In doing this, I must mention that there are some philosophical debates regarding how reading should be taught. Nonreaders need direct, systematic instruction and lots of practice to become automatic readers. Some teachers fear that this approach will "drill and kill" a young child's interest in reading. Instead, these teachers must realize that the lack of skills kills. Lack of skills frustrates nonreaders. They soon learn that no matter how hard they try, they cannot understand what looks to them like scribbles on the page. Lack of skills can kill their desire even to try to learn how to read, often resulting in the demoralizing learning disabled (LD) label. Many students soon learn that it is easier to be called lazy for not trying to do the work than to try, fail, and be labeled as dumb.

When students, whatever their age, learn the secret of the written code, a light illuminates the darkness at the very core of their being. Once learners link the oral language to the printed word, the light goes on. Their posture straightens. Their eyes, which previously evoked pools of doom, begin to sparkle with hope as they learn each link in the alphabetic sound-symbol chain — a chain that no longer binds them in sorrow but allows them to pull themselves out of the despair of their subculture of illiteracy onto the bridge to literacy and success.

Science tells us that the best time to teach our children the alphabetic code is in the early years of school. This is when the teaching of sounds and symbols can be done with music, nursery rhymes, games, and other fun in a structured and systematic way to build strong, core basic skills. Young children take pleasure in repetition and becoming successful as they learn new skills. Early measurement in kindergarten of a child's language skills (or any learner's skills as that person starts literacy instruction) is an important initial screening to predict with great accuracy whether the child will have future reading difficulties. This timing is critical, because young children remediate faster. With early screening, we can prevent reading failure.

It's not that teachers don't care — they do care, and they want to teach students to read. The problem, however, is that in most colleges of education and teacher-training programs at universities, students are not given the instruction in teaching a child how to read based on the latest science (see Chapter 7). They don't know how to teach children who can see each of the letters in c-a-t but can't make the connection with the oral description of a cat and can't picture in their minds a small, furry mammal with pointy ears and whiskers. And because these children are not being taught to read proficiently, the epidemic of illiteracy will spread, and all the while the American public turns a blind eye and a deaf ear to doing something about it.

Before reading any further, ask yourself what assumptions you have about people — children and adults — who cannot read. Do you assume that they are mentally handicapped, that they have low IQs that prevent them from learning how to read and write? What if the students who can't read are in a special education program — do you think that this points out some underlying cause for their inability to read and write on the level with their peers? Do you think they are learning disabled, meaning that they are not able to learn how to read and write? Do you think everyone can learn how to read, or do you believe that some can never learn? Who are they?

Most of the students who were in the audience at that California high school were in a special education program only because they read at a third- to fifth-grade level. Most were of average intelligence; some may have had above-average intelligence, but like me, they had difficulty processing language, which impeded their ability to learn how to read and write in the same way as other learners. This isn't surprising at all, given the national statistics on children in special education who have deficiencies learning how to read.

According to the President's Commission on Excellence in Special Education, which was created in October 2001, of the 6 million children in special education, almost half had been identified as having a "specific learning disability." This group that has grown more than 300 percent since 1976.

"Of those with 'specific learning disabilities,' 80 percent are there simply because they haven't learned how to read," the commission stated in its July 2002 report. "Thus, many children receiving special education — up to 40 percent — are there because they weren't taught to read. The reading difficulties may not be their only area of difficulty; but it is the area that resulted in their placement in special education. Sadly, few children placed in special education close the achievement gap to a point where they can read and learn like their peers."[5]

Using the California high school students as an example, what if everyone had been taught to read from square one, including those who needed additional and specialized instruction like I finally had with Lindamood-Bell? What if the teachers had been trained before they entered the classroom to teach all students to read, including those with auditory-processing deficiencies? It's probable that most of them would not have been in that special education class at all, listening to me with their eyes cast down as I talked about not giving up hope.

When children don't learn how to read, the system breaks down — as it has repeatedly and continually — for decades. At the risk of oversimplifying, here's the ideal scenario: children who are taught to read, write, comprehend, and spell grow up to be literate adults, who can teach and help the next generation of children to read, write, comprehend, and spell. Critics will argue that this is too simple a vision, that there are myriad reasons it is difficult for some children to learn how to read and many reasons teenagers drop out of high school without having grasped the basic literacy skills. I know that, too. I also know that an alarming percentage of high school and even college graduates lack the necessary levels of literacy to compete in an increasingly complex and competitive world.

Dolores Perin, a reading expert at Columbia University Teachers College, was quoted in a recent *Washington Post* article: "There is a tremendous literacy problem among high school graduates that is not talked about. It's a little bit depressing. The colleges are left holding the bag, trying to teach students who have challenges."[6]

I was one of those students with challenges, who received a college degree but could read and write only on a second-grade level (although I could fool everyone because of my oral and visual comprehension, plus speaking abilities). Those high school students I spoke to that day also knew that part of my story. They, like so many people I've spoken to, wanted to know how I managed to beat the system. I can point to social promotion, which passed me from grade to grade until I got a high school diploma. I can admit to the desperation of cheating to get through college. The truth, however, is that I never beat the system. The system beat me every day of my life when I could not read, just as it was beating those high school students I addressed that day.

People who cannot read and write to the standards of the literate world are second-class citizens. Although part of me celebrates that I made it — I crossed the bridge from illiteracy into the dominant literate culture that had intimidated me for so many years — I am still saddened that it took me four decades to become a first-class citizen. My heart breaks when I think about how many adults and children are left behind and lost in the desperation of the subculture.

People who can read — and in particular those who learned easily as children, taking to the written word the way birds learn to fly — underestimate their precious gift. They cannot connect with the pain and frustration that we nonreaders experience. Yes, we are a nation that has made a commitment to universal literacy, but the epidemic of illiteracy continues to rage because the "vaccine" has only recently been released from the laboratory. The National Reading Panel Report (NRP), which was released in 2000, was subsequently sent to every school in America. (The report is currently available online at the NIFL website, *www.nifl.gov,* the National Institute of Child Health and Human Development website, *www. nichd.nih.gov,* and the U.S. Department of Education website, *www.ed.gov.*) This "prescription" comes from more than 30 years of research, giving us a way to solve illiteracy in America and in English-speaking nations around the world.

"By putting in place well-designed, evidence-based early-identification, prevention, and early-intervention programs in our public schools, our data strongly show that the 20 million children today suffering from reading failure could be reduced by approximately two-thirds," Dr. Lyon said in his testimony. "While still a totally unacceptable rate of reading failure, such a reduction would allow us to provide services to the children who are in genuine need of special education services with substantially greater focus and intensity."[7]

My purpose in writing this book is not to shame anyone. Shame produces no good — none at all — for student, teacher, parent, professor, researcher, or anyone else who is involved in the battle for literacy. I believe that we are all, ultimately, on the same side, just not on the same page. As I experienced the emotional and spiritual healing that came from having learned how to read and write, I no longer saw the good guys and the bad guys in this fight. Before I could read, I usually saw the literates as my jailers, the gatekeepers who kept me out. After I learned how to read, however, it became clear to me that illiteracy was really the enemy, and not only my enemy but society's adversary as well. Recognizing this, I believe everyone is on the same side. We just need to be pulling in the same direction.

Is this is a personal issue for me? You bet. And so it should be for you. When we as a society have classrooms like those I visited, with some tenth graders who are reading at a third-grade to fifth-grade level, we get a big, fat F. Schools have had years to detect and prevent illiteracy among these students, yet they have failed to give many learners what they need in the all-important primary and elementary years. I have to include myself in that failure, because I have crossed the bridge and I am now part — and an active part, at that — in the dominant literate culture. When I wrote my autobiography, *The Teacher Who Couldn't Read*, these high school students were in kindergarten. I came clean with my story, hoping to shed light on a problem and inspire others, yet here we are, more than a decade later, and not much has changed, particularly for those students.

The 2003 NAAL report states the facts: there was virtually no improvement in percentages of adults at the basic and below-basic literacy levels from the first study in 1992. Now there is another generation of students in grade schools, junior high and middle schools, and high schools, and their fates will determine whether change will happen in the next 10 or 20 years.

Most literacy initiatives today are like grains of sand moving to build a beachhead. Despite a lot of effort, there is not much to show for it. Although the NAAL statistics showed no meaningful improvement overall in adult literacy between 1992 and 2003, should we stop? Of course not. For the sake of those grains of sand, we have to continue our efforts — and then get a bigger shovel and do some real excavating. Then we can put in the footings to build bigger bridges to literacy. "There is an unprecedented amount of knowledge about the most effective way to teach reading that has been presented in the last fifteen years. This is not a mystery. This is something we can do," observes Robert Sweet.

Unfortunately, many have made learning to read a politically charged issue, although it is certainly not. Two of the biggest controversies, which will be explored in more detail in later chapters, have been the Bush administration's No Child Left Behind policy, which it has called a blueprint for education reforms, and, in my home state of California and other states, exit exams given to high school seniors.

Familiar arguments are waged on all fronts about whether students are being treated fairly, standards are too high and should be lowered, our educational system is being scrutinized too much, teachers are being punished, and so forth. The arguments cloud the central issue at the heart of these and all matters surrounding literacy: children need to be taught to read, write, comprehend, and spell in the elementary grades, no matter what it takes. Once students get into high school, teaching them to read is a much greater challenge. High school teachers, for the most part, do not think it should be their job to teach students to read when those students should already have been taught in previous grades. By then, the students have given up on themselves, and for the most part, so has the educational system. Students do not learn how to read for many reasons, but an elaborate structure of excuses must not become a wall imprisoning children in the subculture of illiteracy.

*A six-year-old is only six once. If we don't reach these youngsters now, we can't come back fifteen years later and make it right. It is time for action.*

— Representative Anne M. Northup (R-KY)[8]

Perhaps most importantly, there needs to be a commitment on behalf of all of us — especially teachers and those who educate them — based on the knowledge that virtually all children can learn how to read. For some, success may take more effort or a different approach. But children in school today, whether in the regular classroom, a special education program, or other learning environment (with the possible exception of those with severe handicaps), can be taught to read. Without commitment to this principle, the children who cannot read will grow up to be adults who cannot read and who cannot help their children learn how to read. The cycle is as vicious as poverty, for it robs the spirit and erodes the soul. I know. I have been there.

Adult literacy programs are an important link to bridging the literacy gap. I am proud to be the product of a library-based adult literacy program, and I strongly support these programs. There is no denying, however, that adult literacy programs are reaching only a small number of people who need help to cross the bridge out of illiteracy into the dominant culture of the written word. That is not to take away from anything that these heroic tutors and brave students have accomplished. Every single adult who learns how to read has achieved a monumental accomplishment. There just needs to be more of them.

For example, Jose Cruz, CEO of the San Diego Council on Literacy, estimates that in California more than 6 million adults — 23 percent of the adult population in the state — are at the below-basic literacy level as defined by the NAAL report. Each year, only about 10,000 adults who lack literacy skills receive services from library-based programs in Southern California. "We are serving more people than ever, and we have more awareness than ever, but it's still not enough," Mr. Cruz admitted. "The reason we are able to do what we do is we have very dedicated people in this area, people who are very motivated. We give a lot of credit to the students. For them, it takes real sacrifice and real courage."

For Mr. Cruz, 10,000 adults per year receiving literacy services from library-based programs out of a population of 3.7 million adults who need help in southern California may seem like the proverbial drop in the bucket. Yet he and other literacy program leaders, teachers, and advocates persist because they believe in the positive chain reaction that results from adult literacy. Although these programs often rely on volunteers and are woefully underfunded, they attack illiteracy on two levels: first, they teach adults to read; second, they promote family literacy, creating home environments to promote reading. (One excuse often given by teachers and other educators for the failure of the system to teach some children how to read is the inability or failure of the parent to be involved in the child's education — an issue that will be discussed in Chapters 6 and 7.)

## From Street Skills to Reading Skills

When I was a small child, I thought I was smart because my mother and father told me so. After I had been in school for a while, I became confused and began to question whether I was smart. I had above-average skills in math, but I struggled in reading. I also had good playground and survival skills. I became cunning and resourceful; being a survivor earns a diploma all its own. Those California high school students I spoke to could relate to that. In the questions they asked me and the few stories they shared, they showed their resourcefulness and ability to get by — survival skills of the street. The street today, however, is a harsher place than it was 40 years ago when I was an angry young man. Today, the street can be a one-way ticket to drug addiction, crime, incarceration, and even death. Fortunately, from the White House to the house next door, passionate literacy advocates understand that not teaching a child to read is neglect or abuse — a travesty, especially in an affluent, resource-rich society like ours.

In this universe of passionate advocates, two of the shining stars are Gloria and Stoney DeMent, who, as literacy directors for The Dyslexia Foundation, work tirelessly on behalf of individuals with dyslexia. Retired educators themselves, the DeMents have made it their life purpose and passion to educate others about the truth of dyslexia: that it is a language-processing disorder and not a deficiency that makes someone less intelligent. (In fact, many dyslexics are of above-average intelligence.) Among the DeMents's pet projects is the Language Literacy Link, a division of The Dyslexia Foundation, which promotes awareness of the importance of early oral language development from birth through preschool. A conversation with the DeMents reveals what it takes to be effective in the literacy movement today: knowledge of the latest, peer-reviewed, replicated, effective research; compassion for those whom they help; and an unshakeable faith in what is possible.

*Too many children in America are segregated*
*by low expectations, illiteracy, and self-doubt.*
*In a constantly changing world that is demanding*
*increasingly complex skills from its workforce,*
*children are literally being left behind.*

— President George W. Bush,
Foreword to No Child Left Behind [9]

Since I wrote my first book, I have made advocating for literacy a big part of my life. The John Corcoran Foundation created a tutoring program, including software packages, and developed online solutions to try to help children everywhere. My creed is a statement of values and beliefs about literacy, which continues to guide my actions:

- America is a global, proactive model for universal literacy.

- Improving and developing literacy skills and values is a lifelong process.

- It is never too late to learn how to read, write, comprehend, and spell or to improve those skills.

- It is as important to teach an adult how to read as it is to teach a child how to read.

- The key to teaching everyone to read, write, comprehend, and spell, is proper instruction.

- The key to proper instruction is properly trained teachers.

- Phonemic awareness and systematic, explicit phonics instruction are critical components of teaching reading.

- The only cure for illiteracy is learning how to read.

- Literacy skills are predictors of our economic, social, and personal well-being.

- Imparting basic skills empowers the individual more effectively than accommodation.

- The integrity of the individual learner must be valued.

- Promoting literacy is our essential duty and an investment in America's future. Teaching children and adults to read, write, comprehend, and spell is prudent and economically expedient. It is also an act of love.

My work is enormously gratifying on the one hand but discouraging on the other. So much needs to be done. For every child who gets the help she needs, dozens more are left behind in the Death Valley of illiteracy with its dark secrets and hidden shame.

"How many of you tell your friends outside of this room that you can only read on a third-, fourth-, or fifth-grade level?" I asked the students in that California high school.

I think I surprised my audience with that question, but then again, they might have expected it from one of their own — someone who knows the subculture from the inside. I knew the answer without hearing their responses. These young people long ago had learned to hide the fact that they were different.

I asked them, "When you're with your friends outside of school, do you tell them that you're in special education?"

Then came the smirks and low murmurs. "No way," they told me. "I don't want anyone to know."

Other children and adults with reading deficiencies can get away with it, too. After all, they don't look any different, act any different, or sound any different from others. Their deficiency in reading and writing is hidden, invisible to the outside world. It turns out that this is a mixed blessing. As a child and, later, a teenager who felt like an outsider and desperately wanted to fit in, I was glad that no one could tell by looking at me that I couldn't read, write, or spell. This was crucial in college, where I was a blond-haired, blue-eyed, all-American, athletic type. No way did I want someone to know that I couldn't read and write the simplest phrases. Not even my college girlfriend knew.

The problem with masking this hidden deficiency is that it further obscures the magnitude of the problem. Unless a parent has a child with a learning deficiency or someone has a close friend or relative who has struggled with literacy issues, they don't know how many people around them have difficulties with the written word. People don't recognize a problem that they can't see and don't know firsthand. They don't know that an epidemic is raging around them.

"Our children don't have outside deformities. They don't make good poster kids because they're so 'normal' looking. They don't pull at your heart strings like a child in a wheelchair or with leg braces or hooked up to IVs," commented Fran Thompson, a literacy advocate in British Columbia and the mother of an adult daughter who has faced reading deficiencies, including dyslexia and a severe spelling disorder. "Their problems are invisible."

Because literacy problems are invisible, it is easier to hide them behind a smoke screen of excuses and ploys. Hiding, however, makes people want to be invisible, as well, to put as much distance as they can between the literate world that intimidates and enslaves them and the subculture of illiteracy where they know how to survive.

"Why didn't you quit school?" one of the teacher's aides at the high school asked me. Later she told me she asked that question on behalf of two young men who were on the verge of quitting school — one with his parents' permission.

I didn't quit because I didn't want to disappoint my parents, I told her. My mother and father told me all of my life that I was smart, and they valued education and expected me to graduate, and I bought into it. The other explanation was that I had been defiant all my life, had a sense of fair play, and instinctively knew that teachers underestimated and discounted me. I wanted to prove them wrong. I knew I had a problem with reading, and I wanted to fix it. Somehow, I thought I could fix it by staying in school.

I still want to fix the problem; this time, the problem is institutionalized illiteracy. And so I tell my story, which fascinated these students in California, who identified with my pain, my anger, and my survival skills. I told the story about disconnecting a little spring inside our rotary telephone to keep my mother from talking to the teacher when she called our house, which was always around seven in the morning. I'd fiddle with the phone, and when my mother picked up the receiver, the line would disconnect.

A young man in the audience raised his hand tentatively. "I disconnect the phone, too," he told me, our eyes locking on each other like those of two coconspirators.

Later one of the teachers told me that this was the first time she had ever heard that young man speak in public or share anything in a group discussion. I was elated that we had made a connection, that he felt safe enough to share his story with me as I had with him. As two Native Aliens, we had found each other.

Although we connected, the fact remains that today I can read, write, comprehend, and spell. I found the solution that would fix my problem, and I took the actions I needed to master the written word. But what will happen to this student, especially if he drops out as he plans? What will become of a 16-year-old high school dropout who can read and write at only a third-grade level? Would you hire him?

I drove home from the high school, my head swirling with thoughts. Yes, I would follow up with the teachers as they requested and look into the resources that were available to them. A few more grains of sand would end up on the beachhead. But how many classrooms are like that in America (not to mention in Canada and Europe)? How many students are approaching the age at which they can drop out of school or somehow manage to graduate from high school without having the necessary level of literacy skills?

Speaking at the high school put me back in a place that I love — and that I hate. As the teacher I once was and am by nature, I sincerely enjoy being around young people. I love listening to them and talking with them. When I can make even a small contribution to them, I feel that I am doing something very important. But it also submerged me once again in the subculture of illiteracy, and my heart ached to see so many children trapped there.

We already have ample research into the field of literacy. Even if people disagree on what approach is best, the fact remains that many scientific, research-based programs exist that can benefit learners. The good news is that advocates and teachers, who are real heroes, are waging war on the epidemic of illiteracy — not looking for someone to blame but focusing on fixing the problem.

The purpose of this book is to spotlight those who are trying and to give a platform to the voices that must be heard. Otherwise, we abandon a significant portion of our society to the darkness and shame of illiteracy, betraying them and damaging ourselves.

CHAPTER 3

# No More Social Promotion

Social promotion is a dangerously addictive educational behavior. Many students, and even some of their parents, have come to expect that 12 years of "seat time" in class, without any serious behavior problems, entitles them to be passed from grade to grade until they graduate. At the same time, it's considered demoralizing and counterproductive for students to repeat a grade. As a result, many schools have deemed it better to socially promote these students — meaning they are passed along with their social peers even though they are failing or have poor grades — rather than dig into the core issues of why they lack the basic skills in reading, writing, and math.

Sadly, our dependence on social promotion has led to hundreds of thousands of high school students across the nation graduating each year without essential literacy skills. According to a May 1999 report from the U.S. Department of Education, "research indicates that from 10 to 15 percent of young adults who graduate from high school and have not gone further — up to 340,000 high school graduates — cannot balance a checkbook or write a letter to a credit card company to explain an error on a bill. If one examines national assessments of student performance, upwards of a third of students score below the basic level of proficiency."[1]

Like any addiction, social promotion has serious side effects. Promoting students who have not acquired the necessary literacy skills does not raise their self-esteem by making them think they have met the grade. These students know they are failing and have probably adopted an antischool attitude. They are convinced of their own inadequacies, because everyone has given up on teaching them; instead, they're just pushed along with the crowd.

On the other hand, grade retention — the practice of requiring a failing student to repeat a grade — also has serious drawbacks. According to the National Association of School Psychologists (NASP), research does not support the efficacy of grade retention — even though this practice has increased over the past 25 years. NASP estimated that as many as 15 percent of American students are held back each year, and 30 to 50 percent are retained at least once more before ninth grade. "Evidence from research and practice highlights the importance of seeking alternatives that will promote social and cognitive competence of children and enhance educational outcomes," NASP states.[2]

On the surface, it's easy to see why the rallying cry of "No more social promotion!" is a noble one. It's brimming with passion and conviction that we — as parents, teachers, administrators, policy makers, and society in general — no longer think it's permissible just to push students through the system without really educating them and meeting their needs for life. However, we cannot think that a student who failed a grade the first time will automatically grasp the material the second time, especially if it is presented in the same way. At every grade level, students who have learning and reading deficiencies must be assessed and their needs met by properly trained teachers. This is particularly critical in fifth grade and beyond when, as the saying goes, children go from learning how to read to reading to learn.

> *Along with ending the practice of social promotion,*
> *we must provide extra help for children after school*
> *and in the summer so that we don't just identify*
> *children as failures, but instead say, we're going*
> *to give you more help until you succeed.*
>
> — President Bill Clinton, July 1998[3]

We must stop social promotion; of that, I have no doubt. But we also must proceed on this mission with our eyes open and be fully aware of the pitfalls along the way. Undoing what we've done for more than 50 years will create problems, some that we can foresee and others that we probably cannot. We must be prepared for a transition period, which will require triage at the higher grades and intensive intervention at the lower grades. If we underestimate the impact of ending social promotion, then more students will be at risk of dropping out of high school.

These students will quickly realize that all the showing up, trying their best, and good behavior won't earn them a diploma. Discouraged, beaten up by a system that does not serve them, and without the outcome that they've been counting on, these students will have no incentive to stay through grade 12. By dropping out, they will increase an already embarrassingly high dropout rate that is estimated to be around 30 percent. This is a shameful statistic for the United States, which prides itself on compulsory public education yet falls short of delivering on the promise to many of our young people.

School districts across the country are already taking the bold and brave steps to end social promotion. In New York City, for example, the practice of social promotion was ended for seventh-grade students as of the 2005–06 school year, as it was in prior years for third- and fifth-grade students. In a July 2005 announcement, Mayor Michael Bloomberg noted, "Maintaining the status quo is simply not an option. It doesn't do anyone any favor to send unprepared students up the line to the next grade. Those days are over. Instead, we're going to give our students the attention they need, and hold them to the standards they must meet."

Bloomberg called ending social promotion in seventh grade "an enormous challenge," adding, "In the lower grades, struggling students may be only a little behind their peers. But by [seventh] grade, the effects of their having been socially promoted in the lower grades may mean that some students now lag further behind."[4]

Putting an end to social promotion does not mean our job is done; in fact, it is only the beginning. The decision to end social promotion must be grounded in a genuine commitment to provide a safety net for the students who will be doubly at risk for dropping out of school. Taking away social promotion will pull the proverbial rug out from under these students. The hurt, anger, and abandonment that they've harbored because they have not been taught how to read, write, spell, and do math like everyone else will become outrage. They will be condemned by the system that has already failed them.

We cannot expect these students to overcome their problems on their own. Those who have deficiencies, whether in math, reading, or another area, must be given the support and intervention they need. Unfortunately, middle school and high school teachers concentrate on teaching specific curricula; they do not think it is their job to teach students basic skills, such as reading and writing. All classroom teachers must know the reading competency level of their students so they can identify those who can read a textbook and answer essay questions and those who cannot. When students with reading or other learning deficiencies are identified, teachers must act and school districts must be prepared to provide the resources they need.

One model to draw from is the Individual Education Plan (IEP) that is developed for every special education student. The idea of all students — not just those in special education — having an IEP based on an assessment of their individual needs is an appealing concept. The student's IEP then establishes the baseline of the proper instruction and remediation they need to address their particular deficiencies.

Without targeted intervention, the students with deficiencies, who are on the border between completing school and dropping out, will become the collateral damage in our fight to end social promotion. If that happens, then we have only traded one ill for another. If we end social promotion without helping our students to succeed, we will have adopted the attitude (unspoken, to be sure) that it's OK for those with deficiencies in reading and/or math to leave school at age 16 without a high school diploma. If that is the result of ending social promotion, then we have only widened the gap between the haves and the have-nots, condemning a bigger percentage of young people to a life of subsistence.

Where can uneducated teenagers without a high school diploma get jobs? They may be able to perform some menial task or do physical labor, but how many more will slide into a life that consists of little more than hanging out? It doesn't take much imagination to connect the dotted lines between dropping out of high school and crime, drug use, teen pregnancy, and a host of other societal problems. As these undereducated young people become parents — including teenage moms who lack the educational skills and family support for their own lives, let alone those of their children — how prepared will the next generation be for school? Parents and families play a vital role in literacy, introducing children at a young age to the joy and the power of the written word. When families lack the resources — educational, financial, and social — to do this for their children, others must fill the gap, especially those who provide services through schools and community programs.

## The Failure of Social Promotion

Pretty, shy, and soft spoken, Nyla Henry recalls making herself invisible in the classroom by sitting in the front, knowing that teachers usually focus on the students in the back of the room.

Cooperative and eager to please, she also learned how to win over teachers who passed her along — even though her grades were mostly Ds and Fs, with the exception of art, where she excelled.

"They kept passing me along through elementary school, junior high, and then high school," Nyla said. "Then they realized that I couldn't pass the proficiency tests. When I was a senior in high school, they put me in special ed."

She described her special education teachers as "great," recalling how they also recognized her artistic talent and even praised her when, unable to write out an assignment, she decided to draw instead. Nyla's experience is but one of many examples of the failure of special education, which must change from merely being a holding tank for students with learning deficiencies, particularly in reading, to a comprehensive program that serves the individual needs of students.

After 12 years of social promotion, Nyla was functionally illiterate when she graduated in 1982. "I felt I couldn't go anywhere. That's when I met my first husband and had my kids. I knew I could be a good mom, except I couldn't cook. I couldn't read the recipes."

With courage and conviction, Nyla eventually made a life for herself, including ending an abusive first marriage, establishing a career as a property manager with bosses who believed in her ability, marrying a loving and supportive man, and achieving the ability to read as an adult learner. "I'm not ashamed of how I was. I am not the only one," Nyla explained. "I wanted more for my kids. I wanted them to be successful, and now I have a grandchild and I want him to be successful. You have to break that chain."

Nyla's story is a powerful example of how America has unintentionally institutionalized illiteracy in our public schools. Parents and educators have collaborated in the implementation and perpetration of social promotion for more than 50 years. Because of social promotion, too many students keep being pushed through without learning. Some stay in school, get promoted grade to grade, and are given diplomas. Some hang on only until they reach the age at which they can drop out or are pushed out.

In all of these cases — whether kids do the time to graduate or quit at age 16 — they are not provided what they need for life. "To pass students along in school when they are unprepared or retain them without addressing their needs denies students access to opportunities at the next level of schooling, in postsecondary education, and in the workplace," the U.S. Department of Education said in the 1999 report. "Both policies send a message to students that little is expected from them, that they have little worth, and that they do not warrant the time and effort it would take to help them be successful in school."[5]

Stopping social promotion will trigger resistance among parents, students, and educators. Yet we must be willing to admit that a high school diploma for a student who does not meet the minimum education requirements in reading and math isn't worth the paper it's printed on. The high school diploma also needs to mean something to an employer who hires a high school graduate assuming that the employee has at least basic reading and math skills.

I have great empathy for students who are socially promoted through a tortuous school experience of failure, low self-esteem, and acting out against the system. But social promotion is nothing more than avoidance and denial. It holds only empty promises and leads to far greater problems later on, because the students do not have the literacy skills that will enable them to pursue higher education and get a job in today's technology-driven economy. Thus, when I hear the comment made by a high school student that it "doesn't hurt anyone" to give a student who doesn't have adequate math and/or reading skills a diploma, my immediate reply is, "Yes, it does hurt someone. It hurts you."

Ending social promotion and implementing higher education standards, including exit exams for graduates, are part of the greater expectations we must have for students, for teachers, for schools, and for ourselves. To do this, we must abandon the blame game that we use to pacify ourselves (e.g., teachers blame the kids and parents for the children's failure in school, kids blame their parents and teachers, and so forth). The blame game stops at the classroom door. Because of compulsory education in this country, I believe that more than half of responsibility for teaching children falls on the education system, which in turn must have properly trained teachers in place.

## The California Debate

Social promotion hit the national spotlight in the midst of the California high school exit exam controversy of 2006. Here's a short recap of what has happened as of this writing. Across the state, 46,700 students were ineligible for high school graduation because they did not pass the exit exam. The exit exam was temporarily blocked when an Alameda County Supreme Court judge issued a ruling in mid-May 2006 that would have prevented school districts from denying students a diploma if they failed to pass the exit exam.

The California Supreme Court overturned that ruling on May 24, putting the high school exit exam back into effect.

The California exit exam controversy remains a highly emotional topic, with tearful and angry students and parents on one side and state education officials with the resolve to do what they feel is right on the other. Commenting on the California Supreme Court ruling that backed the exit exam, State Superintendent of Public Instruction Jack O'Connell called it "a clear victory for public education... The students who have worked very hard to pass this exam will be given a diploma that signifies their mastery of essential skills in reading and math." Further, Governor Arnold Schwarzenegger said in a statement, "The exit exam ensures that our schools are living up to their responsibility by giving our students the skills and the knowledge they need to succeed in college and in the workplace."[6]

On the other side of the issue, Arturo Gonzalez, a San Francisco attorney who filed a lawsuit on behalf of students to block the exam, issued a statement criticizing the ruling, "If the constitutional rights of our children are violated, we cannot punish them further by depriving them of a diploma that they have rightfully earned by passing all required courses." A high school senior in Oakland told a local television station, "Other people... they went to school for a long time, and then just one test is going to stop them from graduating, from getting their diploma; and I think that's wrong."[7]

The California exit exam has national implications in what the Los Angeles Times called "a crucial test," as many states are moving forward with or developing their own exit exams.[8] The court's decision to uphold the California exit exam is a victory for teachers, who now have a firm foundation on which to base their education policies and practices. Too often, teachers go through the roller coaster of having a program put in place and being asked to jump through hoops to implement it — only to have it all changed a year or two later with a so-called better idea, which might be changed again. What's really at stake here—in California and in every state—is the long-time problem of students who are passed from grade to grade until they are allowed to graduate, even though they lack the necessary literacy skills.

Make no mistake about it: I am a proponent of the exit exam—a bitter irony, perhaps, since 50 years ago I never would have been able to graduate high school had this requirement been in effect. By the time I reached high school, I had learned to play the system. After the Native Alien acted out in the seventh and eighth grades—with more detentions than anyone could count and numerous suspensions—Johnny, the high school student, got smart. I learned how to get by, get along, and get a passing grade, even though I still could not read or write much better than I could when I was in the dumb row in second grade. Students like me who weren't book-smart became street-smart. I figured out, for example, that helping out the high school drama club by working backstage earned me enough brownie points with my English teacher that I passed the course. I got other kids to help me with everything from homework to term papers.

Finally, I made it! I celebrated with my classmates and friends and proudly went to my high school graduation. I crossed the stage when my name was called, shook the principal's hand, and took my diploma. Inside, it was blank. I was shocked! No one had told me or my parents that I was lacking one class to graduate, although the high school did allow me to go through the motions of graduating. I was devastated—just like all those students who today are not being allowed to graduate in California because they did not pass the exit exam. I felt angry and betrayed. In my case, I was able to make up the class in summer school by cheating again. I received my diploma. Yet having a high school diploma hadn't given me anything other than a piece of paper. I still lacked the skills I would need in college and in life.

Because of my personal experience, I know better than most the emotions that run high on both sides of this issue. I have deep empathy for the students who do not have the adequate literacy skills to pass the exit exam and their parents who fear for their future. Yet I believe the bigger issue is creating and upholding standards in compulsory education, not only in California but also across our nation. One of the fundamental standards in mandated education is that all young people must be taught to read and write. Otherwise, what is the purpose of compulsory education? Students must possess the essential reading and writing skills that will enable them to function as adults and compete in college and the workplace. Anything less than meeting that standard is a complete failure on the part of our schools, a breach of trust with our students, and the undermining of our country's most precious resource: its young people.

The exit exam is neither the cure nor the sickness (depending upon your point of view, pro or con). Rather, the examination—which in California tests students' ability to perform eighth- and ninth-grade math and read at a tenth-grade level—points to the glaring need for a comprehensive strategy to identify and meet the needs of all learners. What I'm suggesting is not an educational utopia but a viable, real-world solution. In this country in which education in most states is mandatory until age 16, we need to do more than pass kids through the system by social promotion.

## The Truth About the High School Dropout Rate

When ending social promotion, school administrators, teachers, and parents also must open their eyes to the truth about the high school dropout rate. Ask the average person what the high school dropout rate is nationally, and the estimate is likely to be very low. Ten percent? Maybe 15 percent? Jay P. Greene, PhD, a senior fellow at the Manhattan Institute for Policy Research, has estimated that the national public school graduation rate in 1998 was 71 percent, adding that "public schools' graduation rates are lower than is commonly reported." He further stated that while the national graduation rate for the class of 1998 was 71 percent, the rate was 78 percent for white students, 56 percent for African-American students, and 54 percent for Latino students.[9]

Dr. Greene's estimate of a 71 percent graduation rate — which implies a 29 percent dropout rate — is not the only dire picture of secondary education in America. As *Time* magazine noted, "an increasing number of researchers are saying that nearly one out of three public high school students won't graduate... For Latinos and African Americans, the rate approaches an alarming 50 percent. Virtually no community, small or large, rural or urban, has escaped the problem."[10]

The National Center for Educational Statistics (NCES), meanwhile, reported a national high school completion rate of 86 percent for the class of 1998. "The discrepancy between the NCES' finding and this report's finding of a 71 percent rate is largely caused by NCES' counting of General Educational Development (GED) graduates and others with alternative credentials as high school graduates, and by its reliance on a methodology that is likely to undercount dropouts," Greene noted.[11]

The truth is that it's difficult to get a handle on the dropout rate, at least partly because school districts have found and used a loophole in the reporting procedure chronically to underestimate the number of students who leave high school before graduation. In the simplest terms, here's how it can be done. A school district, say, in California, is told that a student is transferring to another high school, say, one in Texas. The California school district reports the student as a transfer — not a dropout. But there is little or no confirmation in most school districts that the student really did register in Texas or if the student dropped out. These practices are an intentional, inexcusable manipulation of numbers on the part of school districts to deceive the public and themselves about the size of the dropout rate. Requiring districts to report these students as dropouts until they receive a request for transfer of records and confirmation of transfer would take care of the problem and give us more consistent, accurate dropout rates.

It is not difficult to track dropouts; they are either in your school or out of your school. In the past, those districts that have told the truth about their dropout rate have been penalized for appearing to have such a dramatic problem compared with those that are actually underreporting their numbers. More accurate and consistent reporting will equalize the system.

In an interview with *Time*, Secretary of Education Margaret Spellings said that much is being done to get better data on dropouts. "She points to the National Governors Association's resolution last year to set, for the first time, a common definition of a dropout that all states will use to report graduation rates to the federal government," the magazine reported.[12]

Until we have accurate estimates of the dropout rate, however, society is duped into thinking our students are better off than they really are. Waking up to the truth about social promotion, the dropout rate, and the pervasiveness of illiteracy in this country is a shock, but we have to face these tough truths to make the right decisions.

As it is enforced, the federal No Child Left Behind legislation, which has set the goal of every child learning at grade level by 2014, may help with the accuracy of our statistics on dropouts and the number of students reaching grade-level standards. Admittedly, No

Child Left Behind is controversial, and critics believe it will only punish school districts in poorer neighborhoods and schools that have a large population of special education students. Nonetheless, this breakthrough federal education policy points to the bigger societal and economic issue that affects all of us: our children — regardless of their abilities or deficiencies — must be taught to read, write, spell, and do math.

In a speech given in April 2006, Secretary Spellings said the higher standards and accountability of the No Child Left Behind law were working. She cited statistics that over the past five years, nine-year-old students made more progress in reading than in the previous 28 years combined. Scores for African-American and Hispanic students were also at all-time highs. Yet much still needs to be done. Secretary Spellings said, "We have a saying in Texas, 'If all you ever do is all you've ever done, then all you'll ever get is all you've ever got.' And in my experience, if you just put more money for the same old things in the same old system, it usually means you'll get the same old results. Until every child can read and do math on grade-level, the same old thing won't be enough. Not by a long shot. If we're serious about our 2014 goal — and I know we are — then we've got to change some things."[13]

Ken Noonan, superintendent of schools in Oceanside, California, and a member of the California State Board of Education, commented, "I think most of the No Child Left Behind legislation has been extremely helpful in keeping the focus on standards and making sure that every child is held to the same high standards. That has been a benefit." Mr. Noonan has received praise on the state and national level for his leadership of a districtwide commitment to excellence in schools, despite demographics that would seem to make success unlikely. About 85 percent of students in the district's Del Rio Elementary School are minorities, and more than half of the students are enrolled in programs for those whose first language is not English.

Despite being one of Oceanside's poorest schools, Del Rio Elementary became a high-performing campus, according to California Department of Education reports based on the results of standardized tests. Del Rio achieved an Academic Performance Index of 801 based on students' test scores — surpassing the 800 mark to become a high-performing school.

This is an incredible achievement for Del Rio and a real statement about what is possible when schools have high expectations for students, then implement the necessary programs to help young people succeed. Although it has a very large minority population, including many Spanish-speaking students, Del Rio teaches in English. Mr. Noonan praises the teachers and staff at Oceanside, where the district's English-immersion program replaced a previous policy of bilingual education. "Our job is to make sure every child becomes literate in English and fluent in English," Mr. Noonan explained, adding that he believes it is the parents' responsibility to ensure that the child also retains the ability to speak the family's native language.

His district accomplished this not by throwing kids who speak another language — predominantly Spanish — into an English-speaking classroom and expecting them to get by. Rather, the district has English-immersion teachers who are specially trained to teach language development. "We've been teaching kids in English since 1998, and the parents don't apply for waivers [to request bilingual education]," Mr. Noonan added. "The parents want their children to read and write and speak in English."

For me, there is an indisputable link among these themes: ending bilingual education by providing English immersion; eliminating social promotion; and making a committed effort to teach all students to read, write, and spell in English. If we do not impart these skills to children, we are robbing them of a future. We can't let fear of being politically incorrect keep us from doing the right thing for all children. This takes courage, commitment, and vision, but to do anything less is to violate our belief in equality in this country. If we truly believe in equal rights — regardless of race, ethnicity, gender, creed, or national origin — then we must carry over this philosophy into education and teach all students to be literate in the written word and fluent in the spoken word in English.

## From Commitment to Action

As social promotion comes to an end, it must be replaced by a comprehensive program to assess and intervene, teaching students regardless of grade level how to read, write, and spell. Educators and researchers will state, accurately, that it is easier and preferable to teach children to read when they are in the lower grades. However, older students can be taught, too. The late Pat Lindamood said that, based on her more than 30 years of clinical and classroom experience, age is not a deterrent in teaching a person to read.

> *We cannot proceed with the noble notion,*
> *Of no more social promotion,*
> *Until we are willing to concede,*
> *That we must teach our children to read.*
>
> —John Corcoran, *No More Social Promotion*

Granted, Oceanside schools are in my backyard, so they garner a lot of my attention. But this district's willingness to implement innovative programs serves as an example to our state and to our nation. Two exemplary programs are Oceanside's Academic Recovery Center and the Dropout Recovery Program. The Academic Recovery Center is a dedicated facility for high school students, particularly juniors and seniors, who have failed two or more classes. This program, which operates 210 days a year instead of the school year's regular 180 days, provides remediation and intensive instruction in English-language arts and math to help the students attain the credits they need to graduate.

"We take them out of the pressure cooker of the mainstream program where they are failing and get them caught up. Then we put them back into the mainstream," Mr. Noonan explained. "This is essential for those students who are academically behind. They are at risk of not making it and then just disappearing one day."

The Dropout Recovery Program allows students who have dropped out of high school to earn a high school diploma without re-enrolling in high school. This is particularly appealing for older students, who may feel embarrassed about going to classes with freshmen who are four, five, or even six years younger than they are. "We find those students and recruit them, letting them complete their work here and get a high school diploma. They can do a lot of their work at home — after all, some of them have jobs and children. We'll offer weekend sessions." Mr. Noonan added, "Our goal is to get those students back into school, on track, and help them to get a diploma in a year, or maybe two."

As the Oceanside programs illustrate, schools can neither discount those who are on the brink of dropping out nor forget about those who have. We must make sincere and repeated efforts to reach out to those who are struggling or who have given up on themselves. Every student who stays in school and receives the instruction he needs, every dropout who enrolls in an alternative program to get her diploma, is a victory. Mastering literacy not only helps the individual, but in a very important way, it benefits the generation to follow.

## The Family Connection

Parents are a child's first teachers. Many parents, however, may not have adequate literacy skills themselves, or due to other domestic problems are not capable or able to help their children learn how to read. Schools, therefore, must accept this reality and assume the responsibility to become proactive with students whose parents lack the education, parenting skills, or ability to engender an interest in reading and writing in their children. Even when parents are able to promote literacy, a partnership must be forged between parents and educators. Neither party is as effective when working alone.

Jenny Wilk, who lives in Illinois, is the mother of five children; each one is remarkable in his or her own way. For example, her daughter, Christine, who has cerebral palsy, has become an advocate and champion for students with disabilities. Her third son, Brad, has become literally a poster child for what students with learning deficiencies can accomplish. Brad's story of overcoming his learning deficiency is also Jenny's story of advocating for her son.

The story begins when Brad was three and Jenny was concerned that her son wasn't learning his colors. She had him tested but was told there was nothing wrong with him physically — that he was a late bloomer. "I knew that there was something amiss," Jenny recalled. "I didn't know what it was. It wasn't something I could see. After all, learning deficiencies are invisible."

By the time Brad had entered first grade, Jenny was working part-time outside the home. She still kept a close watch on her son's development, although she was careful not to say too much for fear of being viewed as an interfering parent. Finally, midway through first grade, the school suggested that Brad be tested. Jenny breathed a sigh of relief; this is what she had wanted all along. The diagnosis was that Brad had a learning disability based on the discrepancy between his IQ and where he was functioning in school. In Brad's case, his IQ was above average at 112, yet he was functioning well below average. Based on this assessment, it was determined that Brad needed special education, and a resource program was implemented for him, including an hour a day with a resource teacher. By the end of first grade, however, Brad had made no progress.

"I was freaking out," Jenny recalled. "Since I was working part-time at the library, I started researching learning disabilities myself. I gained a lot of information about how the brain processes information, but I wasn't getting information about how to teach my son to read, write, and spell."

Second grade also brought no improvement, and by the time Brad was in third grade, he was still completely illiterate — except for a few simple words such as *and, if, the,* and *but,* plus a few words that reflected his passion for sports, *football, baseball,* and *soccer.* The resource teacher with whom Brad was working was dedicated to the students but did not have the proper training to teach Brad to read. Countless meetings with teachers and school administrators followed. Then one night, working at the library, Jenny came across a copy of my book, *The Teacher Who Couldn't Read,* and checked it out. When she called me, she poured out the whole story about Brad, leading up to a meeting with the school principal. He had told her that Brad might never read above the second-grade level.

I told her, "If you are asking for my opinion, then based on what you've said and my own personal experience, I believe that proper instruction is the key to your son's reading problems. Continue to follow your instincts." I agreed to help her any way I could, and it just so happened that I was coming to Chicago to speak. She arranged for me to meet with officials in her school district. The result of those meetings was that Brad's fourth-grade resource teacher was trained in the Lindamood-Bell program, which had been the saving grace I had needed as I struggled to become literate.

Tears came to Jenny's eyes as she recalled the heartbreak of seeing her son, whom she knew was intellectually gifted, not able to read. "I would read to him and do what I could at home. I would try to get him to pick out words that he could read. He'd take the book and fling it against the wall. And then I would get up, pick up the book, and tell him that I understood he was frustrated, but that he wasn't going to give up."

Most importantly, Jenny wasn't going to give up. No matter what she had been told over the years — that he was a late bloomer who would catch up, or that he would never be able to read — Jenny was determined that her son would be literate. She started a support group for parents and children with physical disabilities or learning deficiencies. She became the spokesperson for families in her community whose children had disabilities. There were many battles along the way, such as when Jenny advocated that Brad be excused from taking mandatory Spanish classes in fifth grade because he had not yet mastered English, his native language.

As a result of her sheer will, courage, and determination, when Brad was in fourth grade, he began receiving intensive training in the Lindamood-Bell program. Ten months later, his reading jumped two grade levels. Three months after that — at the end of the fourth grade — he was reading at grade level, and his vocabulary was above the seventh-grade level. By the time he was in sixth grade, he was no longer receiving resource education.

When Brad was in seventh grade, the family moved out of the school district after his father changed jobs. He was in special education, but only for monitoring, with a case manager who checked on him once a month. In his regular classes, Brad was functioning, getting Cs and then Bs on his own. "That was phenomenal. It really was," Jenny said proudly.

After graduating from high school, Brad, a star football player, attracted the attention of several colleges. In the end, he decided he would attend a small school in Wisconsin called Lakeland College. A brochure for Lakeland features a picture of Brad on the cover. "We call him the Lakeland poster boy," Jenny laughed.

Advocating for Brad had taught Jenny many important lessons, which she readily shares with other parents, such as focusing on what one's child needs and not getting caught up in the emotion of the battle. "The whole idea of advocating for your child is to get what the child needs, not to push the school district around. So many times I've seen that happen, when the focus was lost and it was all about the fight and the power struggle, and who was going to come out the winner," she commented. "I knew in my case that I would end up in a due-process hearing and that no one would win. That would be frustrating for me as a parent. I understand what the parents are feeling and what they are going through, but I've also seen very clearly that you have to keep your focus."

As the saying goes, it takes a village to raise a child. In the case of children like Brad—who are intelligent yet, because of a language-processing deficiency, have difficulty learning how to read and write—it takes a dedicated and committed community to teach them.

Brad's story is one of victory over adversity and what happens when a parent is able to convince a school district to provide the necessary resources. Too often, however, children fall through the cracks in the system. Their parents cannot advocate for them, and they never get the resources they need. For every Brad who makes it, countless others do not.

## A Brave and Better World

As a society, we are on the brink of what will be a brave and better world for the next generation. The research has shown what can be done, and the desire is there in the hearts of most teachers — certainly the vast majority of those with whom I come into contact. Now we need to move beyond the talking stage and into implementation and action.

We must end social promotion and implement innovative programs that target students who are at risk of dropping out. We must also reach out to those students who have dropped out and draw them into these programs. We must devote time and energy to assess younger students and, based on those assessments, provide the instruction they need to bring them up to grade level. Early intervention will prevent problems later on. For students in the middle — between the vulnerable new learners and the critical cases of those who are about to drop out — additional opportunities must be provided for them to get the help they need.

Dr. Sandra Baxter, director of the National Institute for Literacy, calls each of these phases "literacy touch points," from the early years when children need the foundational skills all the way through elementary and secondary schools and even post–high school with adult learners (as will be addressed in Chapter 6). "At every step, we want to make sure every person has what he/she needs to progress to the next step," she added.

This is a far better approach than social promotion, which is nothing more than denial. Social promotion takes children who cannot read and write in third grade and makes them into someone else's problem in fourth and fifth grade, all the while hoping that someone in sixth grade can do something. I know what that feels like, and I know how futile it is and how damaging it feels. Social promotion is an ill that must be stopped immediately. In its place, we must have a plan of action — and the courage to put it in place.

*We can't wait, can't continue to debate,*
*Can't capitulate, we must articulate.*
*So focus, focus,*
*No more hocus-pocus.*
*To eliminate social promotion and diploma mills,*
*It will take basic literacy skills.*
*Oh, what a thrill!*
*That little, basic skill.*

—John Corcoran,
*No More Social Promotion*

# CHAPTER 4

# Subculture of Survival

For the nonreader, the written word is the childhood bully that continues to taunt him. It's in black and white, it's on every page; it's in the courtroom, in the textbook, in a novel, a newspaper, or a magazine. It's on every job application form. It's more important than the spoken word. The printed word is the currency for reading and learning, the vehicle for mass communication, and it enriches the lives of literate people every day.

To survive in the dominant culture of the written word, the nonreader must acquire skills that literate people do not even think about. Nonreaders learn to rely on pictures — whether on a menu or on a restroom door — to acquire and process information. It takes a special talent to get to some place unfamiliar when you can't write down an address or read a street sign and must always look for landmarks. And then there's the need to outsmart the bureaucracy of forms and paperwork. Worse than the everyday inconveniences is the stigma attached to the words *illiterate* or *learning disabled*.

Adult learners who have crossed the bridge or who are still in transit speak with candor, humor, and even some remorse about what they've done to survive in a world in which the written word made little or no sense. No wonder Luvena, a gentle and soft-spoken woman who is still acquiring literacy skills, boasts with a hard-won conviction: "I may not have a high school diploma or a college degree, but what I have inside me could match a person with a master's degree."

For the newly literate, learning how to read, write, and spell means admission into the fullness of society, citizenship, and her own personhood. The ability to read even the simplest words brings wholeness and healing, both emotional and spiritual. What has been denied is finally attained. Past wrongs, real and imagined, are righted. The needs of the child inside are finally met. For an adult learner, looking in the mirror is a reason to smile.

"Talking to adult learners, you hear the terms they use: 'freed of shackles,' 'no longer imprisoned,' and 'no longer afraid.' Learning how to read increases their self-confidence and sense of self-worth," commented Peter Waite, executive director of ProLiteracy Worldwide. Formed in 2002 by the merger of Laubach Literacy International and Literacy Volunteers of America Inc., today ProLiteracy is the oldest and largest nongovernmental literacy organization in the world. It represents 1,200 community-based volunteer and adult basic education affiliates in all 50 states and the District of Columbia.

Studies on the motivation of adult learners are equally enlightening. The reasons cited include wanting to improve their chances of employment or to get a better job, wanting to read to their children, and wanting to become more involved in the community and to vote. "While all those were strong motivators, the primary reason — and the one that most people indicated above all others — was they wanted to feel better about themselves," Mr. Waite added.

As an adult learner, I wanted to read for all those reasons and more, including my desire to prove something to myself and to the literate world that had excluded me for so long. The motivations have to be strong to sustain the adult reader throughout the long journey across the bridge. It is a gradual process: first understanding the letters and the sounds they make, then joining letters into words and combining words into sentences. As literacy skills are mastered, longer words and longer sentences follow. With them comes the ability to read newspapers, magazines, and books.

When I was a new learner, I couldn't imagine why anyone would want to read for anything but information. It was so much work to read, it just didn't make sense that someone would have anything but a pragmatic reason to tackle the printed page. Then I read a novel for the first time: J. D. Salinger's *Catcher in the Rye*. I loved those characters and their stories so much, I didn't want the book to end. I could finally understand why literate people have their noses in books all the time.

"I always envied people sitting by the seashore, reading a book," admitted Danny Bauer, a former high school dropout who could not read but who now, in his mid-fifties, is able to read for pleasure.

> *Very few adult learners come into the program*
> *to learn to read for pleasure. They come for survival.*
>
> — Lynda Jones, Founding Coordinator,
> Adult Learning Program, Carlsbad City Library

Adult learners like Danny—and several others who willingly and graciously shared their stories—hungered for years to learn how to read. They went to school with the same expectations as their peers—expecting to learn—but they could not. Then, out of anger, frustration, or escape, they acted out, acted up, or just plain acted. They bided their time until they eventually dropped out or else were socially promoted and given a diploma that was all but meaningless without the ability to read and write. They found jobs that didn't require much reading. They relied on other people — usually spouses or friends — to fill out the forms, do the paperwork, handle the bank account, and even take the written tests for them.

"I needed to take a written exam in order to get a job, so I sent a friend of mine instead. This was in the days before you needed to show an ID. My friend scored 98 percent, and I got the job," Danny recalled.

Outwitting the literate world becomes a kind of sport. Each time nonreaders manage to get by — hiding their illiteracy or finding a way to make up for the fact they cannot read or write — they score one in their favor. But this is a game that illiterate adults always lose, because in the end, they still can't read or write. More than anything, they long to be able to pick up a piece of paper and read for themselves. They don't want to be dependent on others to translate for them.

The average adult learners who come to a volunteer-based literacy program are in their thirties and forties. Most have jobs, perhaps a part-time job or one that pays minimum wage. They have a car or access to public transportation and a telephone — which are indicators that the learner will be able to make the two-day-a-week tutoring commitment.

"We don't target people in their twenties. Their school experiences are too recent," said Lynda Jones, founding coordinator of the adult learning program at the Carlsbad City Library in California. "People come to us after they realize that they are never going to be independent, or they start to have children and they don't want their children to suffer like they did. By age 40, people have come to terms with themselves. They know they have to get past this façade of being a nonreader. They have already been turned down for job promotions. They have kids in school, and they can't help with homework."

For adult learners, there is the inevitable moment when — either on their own or at the encouragement of someone else — they decide to learn how to read. Learners can identify these moments in their lives, when even their fear of yet another failure couldn't keep them from trying something else. Looking back, these moments may seem like a stroke of luck, a coincidence, or divine intervention.

Kevin B. was looking up a different number in the phone book when he came across a listing for the adult learning program. "I didn't call it right away, but I bookmarked it. I went about my business for a while, but then I came back to it. I called and made an appointment," Kevin recalled. "I really wasn't sure what I was expecting, but I was optimistic that I would find somebody who could help me. I decided to call and see what happened."

Danny was in a movie theater, watching the credits roll by at the end of the film, trying to see the name of a musician who had played on the soundtrack. The credits were nothing but a blur to Dan, exaggerating just how much the printed word frustrated him. "I walked out of that theater and went next door to the library. I asked them, 'Do you have a reading program?' They said, 'Yes, we do.'" Danny signed up, and despite some stops and starts due to job responsibilities and health concerns, he is still reading and working with a tutor.

Looking back, Danny wondered what would have happened if he had gone to a different movie or if he had been at the theater with a date. Would he have missed his chance, or would there have been another opportunity? One thing is certain: the library-based literacy program wasn't the first time that Danny had reached out for help. When he was in high school, a friend's mother who was also a teacher had tried to teach him to read. But after a few months, distractions and the peer pressure of teenage life took him in another direction. The day he walked out of that movie theater, however, Danny was firm in his conviction.

## The New Joy of Reading

Often when adult learners share their stories, whether publicly or privately, tears flow freely. Many times, they don't know why they're crying, except that something very deep has opened up, allowing years of frustration, anger, sadness, and mourning finally to escape. Their tears are joyful, too, reflecting that what they've tried so hard to attain is now firmly in their grasp. For five or six years after I learned how to read, I would cry all the time. I would cry when I gave speeches, usually at the same point in the story I had told over and over again. Thinking that I was crying on cue, a few people have accused me of faking it. The tears shed by adult learners are real; sometimes we just don't know why we're crying.

In the midst of a group of new learners, it's easy to get caught up in the joy of reading, in the healing of the hurt child and the angry teenager inside and in the liberation and empowerment of the adult. Achieving literacy is so much more than a feel-good, happy ending, though. For the adult learner, literacy has required the sacrifice of countless hours and tremendous effort by the student and a dedicated volunteer tutor. Or learning how to read may have meant spending large sums of money for private tutoring, which has been worth every dime. For the learner's family, there are also sacrifices: not having the learner at home two days or evenings a week; not having the learner available during those times to help with transportation, child care, cooking, and so forth; and even having to forego certain social outings (such as going to the movies) because the learner is at lessons.

According to research conducted by John Comings, a Harvard Graduate School of Education (HGSE) senior research associate and director of the National Center for the Study of Adult Learning and Literacy, there is a shortage of education programs to help adult learners. State and federally funded programs serve only about 3 million adults. Moreover, of the adults who enroll in literacy and basic skills program, Comings's research found only a small number complete the program. "Unlike K–12 students, adults are under no obligation to stay in school," Dr. Comings said in an *HGSE News* interview.[1] The demands of course work, family obligations, and jobs are often more than adults can handle.

This reality raises the need, Dr. Comings added, for programs to design curricula and train teachers to help students persist. Important factors in promoting persistence include goal setting to motivate learners and support from family and friends to encourage them to continue when they want to drop out. "If instructors are trained to help their students identify goals and to foster sponsoring relationships, I believe more students will stay the course," Dr. Comings said.[2]

Adult literacy programs also need policy makers and champions on their side — just like the late Senator Paul Simon of Illinois or Barbara Bush when she was First Lady. Peter Waite of ProLiteracy said, "We have no one on Capitol Hill to champion us."

As I will explore later in the book (see Chapters 6 and 9), adult literacy needs to be taken seriously in Washington, reflecting the commitment given to young students through the No Child Left Behind education reform legislation. Moreover, adult literacy programs need to think beyond the boundaries of their communities to see the bigger picture — not only about the needs of 93 million adults with only basic or below-basic literacy skills but also about how these programs can share best practices with others. Adult literacy is linked to childhood literacy in myriad ways, from helping children to be better prepared for school to modeling good reading behaviors. The more this link is understood and is broadcast to the literate world, the more people will truly understand what I mean when I say, "It is as important to teach an adult to read as it is to teach a child." Moreover, I want others to embrace this language — I want these words on the lips of every literacy advocate.

## A Personal and Sometimes Costly Battle

On the personal level, overcoming illiteracy is a victory that comes after a long and costly battle in which there are casualties. Friendships, relationships, and even marriages may become strained or end because the adult learner has shifted the power base, becoming no longer completely dependent on others. One man confided that his wife, who was the one who found the adult literacy program and encouraged him to enroll, left him as soon as he became literate enough to handle their bank accounts. A woman said that, although she knows her marriage is strong, she worries that as she becomes more independent, her relationship with her husband will change. Despite this pain and personal cost, it is still worth it, learners say. For their sakes, for their children's sakes, they would do it all again.

"The education that I have accumulated in these past 20 years has caused me to be more assertive and outspoken," Luvena said with pride. "When I didn't have anybody to turn to, I wouldn't speak up to anybody, not even my husband. He would call me stupid, and I would feel stupid. Now, I can write my own checks and I can read. I won't accept it now if he calls me stupid. I know how I feel inside."

The biggest change for adult learners is how they feel about themselves, deep inside. They know — as I did — that they're not dumb, they're not stupid, and there's nothing wrong with their brains. They can learn.

> *A recent study... of adult literacy learners*
> *in Tennessee found a variety of outcomes in*
> *learners' lives, including an increased rate*
> *of employment, increased self-esteem, and*
> *increased community participation.*
>
> — National Center for the Study
> of Adult Learning and Literacy[3]

Adult learners never forget how far they've come. When they tell their stories, they go back through it all, the pain of feeling left out and abandoned by schools and sometimes by families. They remember all the coping skills it took to get by and all the subversive things they did in school to get back at an unfair system. Their stories may be funny at times, but the anger and the sadness linger just below the surface.

## Acting Out

By the time Danny had reached fifth grade, he knew he wasn't making the grade. When he had started school, no one suspected that he had a language-processing disorder that would prevent him from learning how to read in the classroom — even with well-meaning teachers who wanted to teach but did not have the skills and training to teach learners like him. As he got older, the gap between Danny and the other students widened. "By fifth grade, the peer pressure had already started, and so I started acting out. I had a real attitude because I was having a hard time," he recalled.

*Success is like a vitamin…*
*If you don't get enough of it growing up,*
*you'll suffer a very severe deficiency that*
*could have long-term impacts in your life.*

— Mel Levine, MD[4]

Labeled a slow learner with a behavior problem, Danny was sent to another school, where he encountered a hostile crowd. He managed to make it through fifth grade in that school by acting tough and being the outsider, then went back to his own school only to find out that he was being placed in seventh grade to keep up with his peers. Danny panicked. If he couldn't keep up in the fifth grade, it would only get worse if he skipped a grade and went on to seventh. This was social promotion at its worst.

Nonreaders who are socially promoted feel as if they are being pushed out of a system that doesn't want them. No matter what the system says, the meaning of its actions is clear. Students who act up and act out — who are labeled as lazy, troublemakers, and behavior problems — are not welcome.

For Danny, junior high meant more acting out and getting into trouble. "I started to cut school, and girls were coming into play. I could do all those things well and socialize with the crowd. But reading just wasn't cutting it for me," Danny admitted.

Still desperate to learn how to read, in high school Danny signed himself up for special education class, thinking that would help. He registered by forging his mother's signature. What he found, however, was that the class was made up of students who had severe developmental and physical handicaps. The program was not suited for someone with a reading deficiency as he had. Frustration and anger perpetuated a cycle of acting out and getting suspended.

It's a little hard to imagine Danny as a teenage rebel; he is now a quiet man who does yoga and loves landscaping and gardening. But you can't miss the gleam in his eye as he recalls which rules he had to break—wearing his hair a little too long or wearing a shirt without a pocket—to escape the classroom with a trip to the principal's office. There were other, more serious infractions, too, such as mouthing off to a teacher or using foul language. He even knew how to make a game out of being suspended. He'd start kicking the little swinging door that separated the waiting area in the main office from the secretary's desk. Finally, the secretary would jump out of her chair and threaten to get the principal to sign his suspension notice.

"I'd say, 'Send it in the mail. I'm out of here.' I was just gone," Danny said.

Pretty soon, Danny was gone for good from the school system, a teenage dropout who could not read or write but who managed to find an odd job washing dishes and then a better job working maintenance. At work, he had to cover up his lack of literacy, often getting his girlfriends to do the paperwork for him. Danny got by, slipping into a world of hanging out, having fun, and working with his hands. He found his calling in landscaping, his true talent and passion, but always the hunger to read remained.

For Kevin B., by the time he was in second or third grade, he knew he had been left behind. Even at that young age, he said, "I accepted it and learned to deal with it." For a short time, in sixth or seventh grade, he was tutored, until the woman he worked with had to relocate. "School was always a struggle. I hated school," Kevin explained. "I was the class clown. I was very popular with other kids, and I was one of the biggest kids. But I had such a fear of reading and writing."

Knowing he worked well with his hands, Kevin enrolled in a vocational program and got involved in automotive work. He admitted that he also got involved in drugs, hoping to escape from his life, including the pain of not being able to read or write. His desire to learn, however, never left him, and like many learners, he was willing to try anything. He paid $500 to a teacher his father had met who said he had developed a program to help children who had difficulty reading. After a few sessions, the teacher decided he couldn't help Kevin, although he kept his money.

A hard worker, Kevin knew his mechanical abilities afforded him a good living, and he sometimes earned more than $100,000 a year as a team leader. He tried to convince himself that he didn't need a piece of paper to prove he was intelligent; he knew how smart he was. Yet as soon as he signed up at his local adult literacy center, he did take the program coordinator's advice to enroll in a GED program next door. "I didn't feel like a whole person without that education and the ability to read. If I had achieved that, I believe I could have been anybody I wanted to be," Kevin said. "I'm a goal achiever. That's one thing about myself that I admire. If I can think it and see it in my mind, I know I can achieve it."

## Becoming Invisible

The mirror opposite to acting out is playing the role of the good boy or the good girl to win over teachers, to be quiet and invisible, and to be the one whom teachers want to help by passing along through social promotion. "I sat up front, close to the teacher, because they focus on the kids in the back," explained Nyla Henry who, now in her forties, is an adult learner. "I didn't socialize when I was in school. I didn't want anybody to know that I couldn't read. When I was called on, I stuttered through it, until the teacher moved on to the next person. I felt out of place. I didn't belong. I was an outsider."

Always for Nyla, her artistic talent and her creativity impressed her teachers and brought her positive attention. In fact, she was accepted at a school in Texas for art, but her illiteracy and her mother being ill kept her from pursuing the opportunity. After high school, Nyla married young and pursued her dream of being a mother, thinking that she could find her purpose and meaning in caring for a family. What she discovered, however, was that she couldn't help her children with even the simplest schoolwork, which frightened her. Her first husband was emotionally abusive, never offering any help or encouragement. When they separated, Nyla got a job working as a teacher's aide with preschool students. When the teacher discovered that Nyla couldn't read, Nyla managed to keep the job and worked on arts-and-crafts projects with the children instead.

It always amazes me how many nonreading adults end up working in schools: as custodians, cafeteria workers, teachers' aides, and, in my case, as teachers. One can only wonder what their motivations are. Perhaps they want to taunt the beast that intimidated them as students. My theory, however, is that they hope that by being in the learning environment, something will rub off.

Nyla's job ended after her estranged husband falsely told the school district that she was a drug user and had a felony record. Although her reputation was cleared of these unfair and cruel accusations, the humiliation was too much for Nyla. She quit the job and went back to being the outsider who didn't belong—especially in school.

"You get stuck in a cycle, like you're in a tunnel. I thought it was my fault because there was something wrong with me, so I thought it was okay for me to be treated that way," Nyla explained. "I didn't even think I was a second-class citizen. I was a nobody. My focus was on how to get through the next day, just surviving.

I was always scared that somebody was going to find out, so I had to put up that front."

## At Work: From Hiding to Success

Having a job as a nonreader requires another set of skills, both to hide the lack of literacy and to make up for this deficiency. Many adult learners take jobs that involve physical labor, or they learn to apply a particular talent, such as Danny in landscaping or Kevin with his mechanical ability.

No matter how hard someone works or how good they are, there is always the inevitable trap: paperwork. Forms need to be filled out — time sheets, requisition forms, a request for a day off. To the literate person, paperwork is a nuisance or maybe a headache. To the nonreader, paperwork is a nightmare.

Ramón Gómez, who came to the United States the first time on his own at age 13, has always managed to get a job. He laughed as he told a story about a job he had at McDonald's, working as a cook and following instructions that had been given to him verbally. Then one day, he was called to work the counter; the store was shorthanded, and they needed help up front. The only problem was, Ramón couldn't read the words on the wrappers to put the orders together. So Big Macs were put in double-cheeseburger wrappers, and cheeseburgers ended up in McChicken wrappers. "The manager said to me, 'Don't you see what you are doing? Why are you putting Big Macs in with the Quarter Pounders?' I told him that I didn't know how to read or write."

The manager took Ramón aside and helped him memorize the names on the wrappers. Ramón learned to survive by acquiring skills as he needed them. Hardworking and personable, his ability to speak English and his natural leadership qualities always caught the boss's attention. Working in landscaping or construction, Ramón was the one the bosses wanted to make foreperson. Since that would mean paperwork, he always had to turn down the promotion or quit.

It was a vicious cycle of working hard, getting offered a promotion, and then having to quit. One day, Ramón had to come clean about his lack of literacy, just as he had done at McDonald's years before. His boss asked him if he could drive a truck to bring materials to a job or to deliver supplies. Ramón said yes, he could; after all, he had been driving since 1978. What Ramón didn't say — nor did his boss ask — was that he didn't have a driver's license. Getting a driver's license would require him to read, which he couldn't do.

"I would be driving like this, always looking around," Ramón laughed, mimicking himself at the wheel, constantly on the lookout. "When I would see a police car, I would pull into a shopping center as if that was where I wanted to go. I would hide out there, and then pull back out again."

When his boss asked him for a copy of his driver's license for insurance purposes, Ramón knew he had to admit the truth. "I said to him, 'Maybe today is my last day on the job.' When he asked me why, I told him that I didn't have a driver's license," Ramón recalled. "He said, 'What! You don't have a license!' I told him, 'You never asked.' I was in the [adult literacy] program by that time and so my goal became getting a driver's license."

Ramón took the written test to get his driver's license, missing only two questions. He was particularly proud of that accomplishment, since his tutor had gotten many more wrong when he had taken the written test.

Ramón (whose story as an adult learner continues in Chapter 6) remains in the adult literacy program. As his literacy skills have improved, so has his ability to speak English — a common experience among native speakers as well as those who come to the United

States from non-English-speaking countries. Ramón has learned to use a computer and surprised his daughter, Maribel, with an email.

"I read everything—the street signs, the advertisements, everything," he said. "I am so happy that I can read now. Just last week I pulled up to a McDonald's. Before, I could only order by picture and number. But right there I saw the words *Dollar Menu,* and I could read everything on that menu. So I said, 'You have a double-cheeseburger for a dollar?' They said, 'Yes, we do.' So I said I would have that. 'You also have McChicken sandwich for a dollar?' 'Yes, we do.' And I said I would have that, too. 'And also apple pie for a dollar.' I ordered everything because I could read it! And you know what? It was good!"

For Luvena, after years of doing housekeeping, becoming a nurse's aide was a fulfillment of a dream and a good use of her talent as a compassionate and caring woman. With the support and help of her tutor, Luvena set a goal of becoming a certified nurse's aide. It was a big goal for Luvena, who had left school at age 13 and, until she enrolled in an adult literacy program, was functionally illiterate.

Luvena's tutor helped her understand the text she had to study by breaking down the sentences and words into simpler terms. It was up to Luvena, however, to take and pass the test on her own, which she did. "My instructor said to me, 'You are amazing, to come in with the education you had and to pass that test,' " she said proudly. "I had my tutor behind me, which I needed, because the words were so long—some of them had 15 letters in them—and all the scientific terms. After I became a certified nurse's aide, I started to make so much money. I was just so happy and thanking God. I didn't think I could do any more, but I would like to go further."

*We should not falter in insisting that the mission*
*of adult education and literacy is grounded*
*on the highest national principles. That is*
*the irreducible rock on which to build.*

— Forrest P. Chisman, Council for
Advancement of Adult Literacy[5]

After leaving the teacher's aide job she loved because her first husband spoiled the opportunity for her, Nyla worked as a janitor for ten years and then became a property manager. "I finally found a job that I love, something that I have a passion for," she explained.

To make up for the fact that she could not read or write, she asked her second husband, Floyd, to take care of the paperwork. Then the property she was managing changed owners, and the new owners demanded that she provide a detailed report of what she did each day. "I felt ashamed of myself to ask Floyd to do that for me, so I went in and told my boss that I couldn't read and write. He and his wife talked about it, and then he told me about the adult literacy program," Nyla explained. "They even moved my schedule around so I could go to the program."

When the property sold again, Nyla had to tell another set of new owners that she was an adult learner. They, too, have been very supportive. Although it's hard for her to accept the compliment — low self-esteem shadows many adult learners, making them feel they have to do more to prove themselves — it's obvious that her bosses see in her a valuable employee who will be able to do so much more as her literacy skills improve.

Now working in landscaping, Ramón has the support of his boss, who will accommodate his sessions with his tutor. For him, that means getting up at 5:00 AM, being on the job from 6:00 AM to 7:45 AM, working with a tutor from 8:00 AM to 9:30 AM, and then going back to landscaping until 5:30 or 6:00 PM. "My boss said, 'Go ahead, as long as I see you putting in eight hours.' I am working so hard now so that boss will see what I'm doing. I have to work even harder so he sees me."

Kevin B., who recently was recognized as a top employee by the property and housing company he works for, says he's reached the point now where if he's asked to read something to a group — for example, as part of a safety meeting — he can do it as long as he can read it through first. "All the other managers are college graduates. If they hand me something and ask me to read it to the group, I'm as stiff as a board. But I can read it as long as I don't let the anxiety level get to me."

Reading unlocks opportunities even for those — like Dan, Kevin, Nyla, Luvena, and Ramón — who have managed to get and keep jobs without having adequate literacy skills. Yes, being able to read and write allows them to take on new tasks and responsibilities, but it goes beyond that. Literacy brings self-confidence and a peace of mind that enables them to be more productive and to achieve even more. The fear of being caught — having someone find out that they can't read, they can't write, or they don't have a driver's license — saps a person's energy. Reading releases that burden, taking away the anxiety and leaving in its place the self-confidence that one can do anything.

## The Family Circle

Adult learners are rarely motivated by just one thing. Yes, getting and keeping a good job is a powerful incentive. Everyone wants to succeed in life and show what they can do. But there are other reasons adults put in the huge amount of time and the tremendous effort to learn how to read — their children.

Nyla recalled the panic she felt when her children were young and couldn't read and she couldn't help them. "I felt crushed. I felt totally helpless. I can't describe the feelings because so many emotions go into it. I wanted better for them," she explained.

Her daughter, she said, sailed through school, recently graduated from college, and has been accepted into a master's program to become a teacher. Her son, however, struggled and hated school. Her worry for him was noticeable as she spoke, although she was proud to say he does have a good job.

Kevin B. can read Harry Potter books now for pleasure, but he recalled when, as a new learner, he took his son to the library where the little boy would always pick out books on dinosaurs. Reading books with words like *Tyrannosaurus rex* and *Apatosaurus* was a struggle and a frustration for Kevin, yet he kept going to the library every week. "I wanted to encourage him. I wanted him to the have the opportunities that I didn't have," he explained.

Kevin took his advocacy for his son a step further, insisting that the school test him for learning deficiencies. "I was adamant about that for him. His teachers kept telling me that he was struggling in reading but his vocabulary was very good. He was struggling just like I struggled." Eventually his son received the intervention he needed and is doing well in school. "I broke the cycle," Kevin stated. "Now my son is 12, and he's at the age where it's up to him. But he has all the support he needs."

Ramón's teenaged children listened as he told his story of never going to school in Mexico because he was too poor and needed to work and of not receiving any education in the United States other than three months in high school. His insistence on learning how to become literate in English has been an inspiration for his children to stay in school or return to school to get their high school diplomas.

"When my baby was born premature, I didn't think I would go back to school. Then my dad would call me and ask, 'When are you going to get your high school diploma?'" Ramón's daughter, Maribel, related. "When I was walking with my cap and gown on my graduation day — my husband and my son were there, and I could see my dad — I knew then that it's never too late. My husband is in college now, and when he's done — because moneywise we both can't go — I have college in my future plans."

## The Words on the Page

There is no substitute for literacy. Even though it takes some of us longer than others, when we reach the goal of being able to read, it is such a victory. It is pure joy to read the words on the page that used to baffle us. We can understand the instructions on a box. We can read a label on a prescription bottle. We can get information from a newspaper or magazine. And we can become absorbed in the story written in a book.

Danny was a little nervous when a friend asked him to read aloud in front of a few people who knew he was a new reader. He hesitated at first, not wanting to be put on the spot, but he didn't refuse. Clearly he had come a long way from the teenage rebel who defied a teacher who had called on him to read, telling him, "I'd rather take an F."

Danny opened the book to the first page and scanned the words. He started to read, slowly at first, pausing at one word for a moment, then reading more fluently as he gained confidence. As Danny read, his listeners were moved, not so much because of the story but because he was reading it.

When he got to the end of the page, Danny closed the book. Then he smiled.

CHAPTER 5

# The Pueblo, Colorado, Story

School District 60 in Pueblo, Colorado, was in trouble. Colorado standardized tests given to fourth graders in 1997 showed that the district's schools were far below the state's proficiency criteria. In response, an intensive districtwide intervention program was put in place, with a research-based reading model at the center. Within just a few years, District 60 had turned around, earning praise and recognition from the state capitol to Washington, D.C.

Although District 60 school board members, administrators, teachers, parents, and students deserve much praise for what they have done, to focus only on the happy ending at Pueblo would miss the bigger point. District 60 and its nearly 18,000 students cannot be viewed as an amazing, magical Cinderella story. The real message of the story of Pueblo, an urban, multicultural school district, is that what was accomplished there can be done in other school districts as well — provided they are willing to do the tough work to retrain teachers and change the way that children are taught. For that reason, the Pueblo story, which has already captured headlines on the state and national levels, deserves retelling here. My purpose is to provide both inspiration and practical advice for other school districts that are struggling with the same problems of low student achievement; poorly deployed resources; ineffective professional development for teachers; and a growing feeling of desperation that, despite all the talk, nothing is really changing.

Admittedly, the fact that the setting of this story is Pueblo, Colorado, does add to the drama. District 60 has a large minority population, many monolingual Spanish-speaking families, and a large percentage of families that rank below the federal poverty level. According to District 60 statistics, about 58 percent of Pueblo's students were minorities, and 54 percent qualified for free or reduced lunches. At one of its schools in particular — Bessemer Elementary School — 88 percent of its 212 students were minority children, including 76 percent who were Hispanic; and 84 percent of its students qualified for free or reduced lunches according to federal Title I poverty guidelines.

> *I don't see income; I see children.*
>
> — District 60 teacher

Therefore, having access to ample resources — such as one might imagine in places like Beverly Hills, California, or Greenwich, Connecticut — was not the key to success. Throwing more money at an entrenched problem was not the solution. District 60 pulled itself out of the doldrums to reach a high level of achievement because of the commitment of its school board, the leadership of its administration, and the willingness of teachers — spearheaded by a few pioneers — to try a new approach. Existing resources were redeployed, attitudes shifted, and behaviors changed.

In a recent conversation, Dr. Joyce Bales, who was superintendent of District 60 from August 1999 (when she was first appointed on an interim basis) through June 2006, was quick to point out that Pueblo's success reflects the commitment of the entire community.

And here is the lesson: for a school district to achieve the kind of results that were realized in Pueblo — to go from the bottom rung to the top of achievement — everyone must embrace the belief that all children can learn how to read. At the same time, strong, visionary leadership is needed to put in place the programs and recruit the right people to make change happen.

Change, however, does not come easily or automatically. Human beings by nature are change-resistant, and most of us to some degree find change uncomfortable or even threatening. Because of politics and personalities, school districts are especially change-resistant. The status quo is comfortable. The unknown — a program that may or may not work — is not looked upon favorably. It usually takes a powerful catalyst to spark the kind of fundamental change that occurred in Pueblo. For District 60, that catalyst was the Colorado Student Assessment Program (CSAP) results for fourth graders who were tested for the first time in the 1997–98 school year.

For District 60 as a whole, the 1997 CSAP results showed that Pueblo students in general were below the state average, with more than half of the district's students scoring in the unsatisfactory or partially proficient range. At Bessemer, the results were even worse. Of the fourth-grade students who were tested at Bessemer, only 12 percent were rated at or above the proficient level in reading, and a mere 2 percent ranked at or above proficient in writing. "It was CSAP shock," Dr. Bales recalled. The next year, District 60's third graders faced the same testing, which found that 472 were below the proficient level. State standards in Colorado mandated that students must read at the third-grade level to be promoted to fourth grade. District 60 was facing a crisis.

Luckily, even before the CSAP results, other forces of change had been gathering. Mary Lou Jackson, who served on the District 60 school board from 1990 through 2004, was among a group of concerned people who were troubled by Pueblo's poor track record in reading. The challenge, she knew, was that in District 60 — as in school districts everywhere — there were pockets of entrenched resistance even to facing the problem, let alone addressing it.

"People didn't want to hear it. They didn't want to know that teachers didn't really know how to teach reading, and that was the problem," Ms. Jackson recalled.

Even the district leadership at the time was reluctant to change any programs or implement new methodologies to address the literacy problem in Pueblo. Rather, the hope was that by continuing to create an "enriched environment" — giving children access to books to make up for a lack of reading material in their homes — students would somehow become inspired and able to read. (As I shared in the introduction, I was around literate people all my young life and spent hours in libraries, but just being around books will not teach a person how to read.)

Even before the CSAP results were released, Ms. Jackson had been among those investigating ways in which to address the literacy problem in the district. Also at this time, she had been part of the Governor's Youth Crime Prevention and Intervention Board, which led her to examine grants to address the links between literacy and juvenile crime. Through her friendship with a Colorado teacher, Marianne Arling, who had been trained in the Lindamood-Bell program, Ms. Jackson was introduced to Lindamood-Bell to promote phonemic awareness and teach children how to read. (Separately, Ms. Arling also started an afterschool program for students in Pueblo who needed extra help with reading, using Lindamood-Bell methods.) Ms. Jackson knew she had found a valuable resource that was worth investigating to address Pueblo's need for a research-based reading program. At Ms. Arling's suggestion, Ms. Jackson contacted me, asking if I would visit Pueblo in June 1998 to address

CHAPTER 5: The Pueblo, Colorado, Story

an audience of teachers, administrators, and community members. I agreed to go, but not everyone in Pueblo wanted me there.

The district superintendent at the time was hesitant to have me as a guest speaker, particularly to address teachers. His fear was that instead of being motivational, my story would be upsetting to them. I am always honored when I am invited to speak to teachers, but it is often a challenge to motivate them because, in general, they often feel they are being told they are not doing a good job. Then I come along and tell them that illiteracy is a form of child neglect and child abuse and that the key to teaching people how to read is to have properly trained teachers. Plus, I bring along my baggage of having been a teacher who could not read and didn't learn how to read until I was 48 years old. Understandably, not everyone would want to roll out the red carpet for me.

In the end, at the urging of Mary Lou Jackson and Dr. Joyce Bales (who was deputy superintendent at the time), District 60 did invite me to speak to a group of community leaders. My reception there was warm and welcoming—even though a newspaper article about my personal story did raise a few eyebrows. The message that Pueblo took away from that night was that all learners can read and programs exist to provide teachers with the tools and resources they need to teach all children. District 60 was ready to take the first steps toward improving student achievement and, in the process, become a recognized leader in long overdue educational reform in Colorado and in the nation.

District 60's school board supported the drive to focus on reading, even at the expense of other programs and expenditures that had to be cut back or eliminated. The board's commitment was crucial to holding onto the vision of what was possible, authorizing the program changes, and keeping the district accountable.

Based on her experiences as a board member, Mary Lou Jackson says school districts that face problems similar to Pueblo's challenges need to have boards that are willing to make reading the top priority. "The board needs to say, 'We are going to put all of our efforts and all our focus on reading and get rid of the peripheral stuff. We're going to focus our dollars on that effort, even if we have to give up some other things for a while.' Students need to be able to read; after that, everything else will follow," she commented.

*The dollars follow whatever objective a board sets as its focus. It takes commitment from the board.*

— Mary Lou Jackson,
former District 60 School Board Member

## Pueblo's Total Commitment to Literacy

District 60 did not have to start from square one in the wake of the CSAP results. Dr. Bales, as deputy superintendent, had been putting state and federal standards into place in the district's math and reading programs, particularly a new reading-based curriculum. However, with the CSAP results came a heightened sense of urgency about the need for overall change of instructional practices. Pueblo was committed to change, including in how teachers were trained and how children were taught. While Pueblo opted for the Lindamood-Bell instructional processes, there are other recognized research-based models. Whatever approaches districts choose, one important feature must be the early diagnosis of children to identify their specific needs and areas of development, followed by intensive intervention to meet those needs.

From the beginning, District 60 administrators were able to work closely with teachers who supported the drive to increase student achievement. That commitment proved crucial, particularly in Pueblo, which was a strong union town where unionized teachers needed to back the new initiatives. Dr. Bales recalled that after the CSAP results for fourth graders were released, she received a note from a teacher at Bessemer Elementary where student achievement was at the lowest level districtwide. Bessemer was also the third lowest performing elementary school in Colorado. "Her note said, 'Joyce, we're better than this. Please help us.' I picked up the phone and said, 'Don't send me notes. Let's talk.' I told her I have to have teacher support in order to make this work."

To assess the problem, Dr. Bales spent time in classrooms observing children. She saw, firsthand, how many kindergartners were speaking only in words or phrases, not complete sentences. They were coming to school behind in their language development, a deficit that would only get wider without specific interventions. In time, the district established a preschool for four-year-olds.

As she dug deeper, Dr. Bales found that instruction time was not always put to the best use. For example, there were multiple centers on specific topics — from weather to dinosaurs — with children spending about 20 minutes at each center doing some sort of activity. "They were having fun cutting, coloring, and pasting, and completing the self-selected activities at each center, but there was no direct instruction," Dr. Bales explained. "The students were not engaged in activities that followed the state academic content standards to allow them to demonstrate knowledge and understanding."

For Bessemer students from monolingual Spanish-speaking families, the lack of direct instruction put them at an immediate disadvantage to become fluent in spoken English and to master literacy as well. "The worst thing we can do to children is not teach them to read," Dr. Bales observed. "When that happens, it's not because of the child; it's the fault of the adult. Adults know how important reading is."

District 60 focused on the elementary school with the highest poverty population — Bessemer Elementary — to lead its literacy drive. For those districts that believe steps like these could never be taken without a large grant or an infusion of new funding, District 60's experience holds another powerful lesson. The first year of the "Bessemer Crisis Plan," the district spent about $86,000 on the school — all from existing Title I funding that was redeployed. "It was not about getting more money, but about professional development giving teachers new skills and beliefs," Dr. Bales said.

The rollout of the reading intervention was not without some pushback and confrontation. There was a change of leadership in the school district and at Bessemer, and the principal and one teacher did leave. When the Title I funds were redeployed to establish a reading clinic and roll out a new reading process, 50 teachers' assistants were released districtwide. The district did offer to secure scholarships for the teaching assistants who wanted to go to a local university to become certified teachers; only one person, however, chose to enroll.

The first phase of the Bessemer Crisis Plan included evaluating current teaching practices, restructuring class time, decreasing student movement throughout the day, and focusing on standards. Favorite projects that did not achieve desired results were excluded. With increased time devoted to literacy, the school also integrated its Reading and Writing Across the Curriculum process. Also at this time, the Lindamood-Bell Learning Process was adopted in the district, with Bessemer targeted as a pilot project school.

The District 60 demographics, the low level of its 1997 student achievement scores, and its decision to implement a research-based reading model made Pueblo an extremely interesting test case. For these reasons, District 60 was also the focus of a study by Texas A&M University, with results published in the *American Educational Research Journal* in spring 2006.

At the time, District 60 was focused on improving the achievement of its students by turning around a school district in crisis. In the process, the district became a kind of laboratory and proving ground for research-based reading models and the value of direct instruction. "Despite the ongoing national debate about improving reading achievement in schools, reading research has produced very few studies of the effects of specific instructional programs on student achievement scores on current large-scale assessments," authors of the Texas A&M study wrote.[1]

At Pueblo, the Texas A&M researchers were given the unique opportunity to examine "the effects of gradually implementing a theoretically based reading program over a period of six years in the elementary and middle grades of a heavily multicultural school district."[2]

## Rolling Out a Research-Based Reading Program

District 60's first reading clinic was set up in an old annex building at Bessemer, staffed by eight of the district's best teachers who had been trained in the Lindamood-Bell program. Third-grade children throughout the district who were not reading at proficient levels were bused to the reading clinic, along with their teachers, who could observe the sessions and learn how to implement strategies in their own classrooms.

Over time, the district gradually expanded the reading clinic concept. By 2002–03, the reading clinic concept and the Lindamood-Bell Learning Process were implemented in 20 elementary schools, 6 middle schools, 4 high schools, and 1 alternative high school.

In addition to the intensive instruction provided to students, the reading clinic concept reflected the district's commitment to intensive and meaningful teacher training to give educators the research-based skills and tools they needed to impart the necessary literacy skills. Consultants don't teach children; administrators don't teach children. Teachers do — and they are the ones who need intensive intervention first for real change to occur at the classroom level.

*Our teachers are eager learners themselves.*

— Dr. Joyce Bales

Several factors made the reading clinic concept successful. The first was the use of diagnostic tests to determine the specific needs of individual students. Based on the results of the diagnostic tests, strategies were implemented on the individual level — and students with similar needs were put together in small instruction groups. Second, instruction was based on a research-based reading model. Ample research has been conducted into how to teach children how to read, and many methodologies based on that research have been developed and can be implemented by school districts.

In addition, the first clinic was established as a separate facility instead of a virtual clinic that delivers services to students in the back of a classroom or at a table in the school library. This location created a specialized environment in which reading was the primary focus. Teachers worked with small groups of five or six students seated at tables placed in a semicircle. Students, in general, received an hour or an hour and a half of intensive instruction. This block of time was needed to bridge the gap and bring the students up to grade level.

Answering concerns and criticism that the reading clinics took away from other instruction time, Dr. Bales noted that without reading skills, students could not be expected to read science and social studies textbooks or understand word problems in math. Without grade-level reading skills, the students would fall farther and farther behind.

The goals and objectives of the reading program were aligned with educational standards. Expectations were established that each student had to meet to exit a particular grade level. Those same expectations were also the entrance requirements for the next grade level. Schools were held accountable for assessing how well students — on a quarter-by-quarter basis — were progressing toward attaining those exit requirements.

The reading program, utilizing the Lindamood-Bell methodology, was truly multisensory, engaging the students through a sensory-cognitive process to gain word mastery. The students would "air write," using their fingers to write the word in the air. With each activity, the students were being mentally stimulated and gaining essential language-processing skills.

As the Texas A&M study noted, the reading program and curriculum enhancement at District 60 demonstrated the needed criteria for comprehensive school reform.[3] Specific elements included the following:

- Effective teaching, learning, and management practices
- Coordination of management of instruction, assessment, and professional development
- High-quality staff development
- Measurable goals and benchmarks
- Broad teacher and staff support
- Shared ownership and responsibility
- Parent and community involvement

Other factors were quality external technical support, annual evaluation to gauge success, external financial support, and use of scientifically researched methods.

## Leadership and Professional Development

Professional development at District 60 also focused on administrators with an emphasis on accountability for every child in the district. School principals were charged with becoming the instructional leaders of their schools. "I told my principals, 'You are the CEO of your school. If you were in charge of a business, you would be asked to give quarterly reports. And if things weren't working, would you keep doing the same thing?'" Dr. Bales commented.

The lesson for other school districts is that change of this magnitude can only happen when it is championed at the top. In addition, the beliefs and behaviors must be modeled by everyone from the superintendent to administrators to teachers and even support staff—with the support and direction of the school board. Honoring the Pueblo achievement, Colorado Governor Bill Owens stated that the district's "strong and positive leadership is a model for educators throughout America."[4]

Like business leaders who rely on quarterly financial statements and reports from their operations, the principals in District 60 adopted the same reliance on data. Too often, when standardized tests are administered, school principals and administrators receive data and detailed results that sit on the shelf—literally—in a three-ring binder, instead of being analyzed. In fact, Dr. Bales believes that the two key components in a program such as the one she implemented in District 60 are a research-based reading model and data assessment.

School principals were also given the responsibility of writing grants to apply for newly available funding for professional development and raising student proficiency in reading. Even though she encountered resistance at first—including some principals who initially declined her "invitation" to participate in a grant-writing session — Dr. Bales impressed upon all administrators the need to take ownership of their part in the process to apply for new funds. As a result, every District 60 school wrote a grant — and every one received monies for reading and/or professional development.

In time, the reading-based program became a unifying mission districtwide, with supporters enrolled from every rank. Custodians and bus drivers read with children. A nutritional worker in the cafeteria worked with a little Ukrainian girl, tutoring her in English. At Bessemer, Spanish-speaking parents of children in the reading clinic were learning how to read along with their children. There were many other anecdotal signs of success. As students became engaged in their work and gained more confidence and proficiency, absenteeism rates went down. Teacher absences also declined, a reflection no doubt of reduced frustration and greater satisfaction. A favorite statistic offered by Dr. Bales is that in one district elementary school, students went from checking out approximately 2,200 books per year to checking out more than 86,000 books in a year.

## Focusing on All Learners

The District 60 turnaround was a comprehensive program for all learners, including those with special needs. One such student was Arianne Lane. A premature baby, Arianne eventually caught up and had a normal life, until one day she woke up paralyzed due to a spinal cord tumor. Chemotherapy and radiation treatments damaged her brain cells, making learning difficult. As a special needs child, Arianne initially was not considered eligible for the reading clinic. Working in partnership with Arianne's mother, however, District 60 opened the reading clinic to Arianne and other special needs and special education students. Arianne became such a successful reader that by the time she reached eighth grade, she was being bused to the high school for advanced science classes.

Another student, Aaron Levinson, who was diagnosed as dyspraic and autistic, had an amazing verbal vocabulary but could not read because of his language-processing problems and learning deficiencies. His mother wanted to enroll him in the reading clinic but was told at first that he wasn't eligible because he was a special education student. District 60's commitment, however, was that Aaron, like every child, had the right to learn how to read and the school had the obligation to teach him. Aaron, like Arianne, went to the reading clinic and became a reader.

"I know that when people struggle with language they are labeled. The only thing that should be labeled as far as I'm concerned is cans. People do the wrong things to children with labels. It's really an adult issue by not having diagnosed the problem and providing intensive instruction," Dr. Bales commented.

All of District 60's special education teachers were also trained in the Lindamood-Bell Learning Process to meet the needs of their students. In time, with intensive intervention in decoding and language processing, many students mastered the necessary reading skills to leave the special education program altogether. The reading curriculum may have been implemented districtwide, but it was delivered one child at a time. In special education departments, where students languish simply because they have not been properly taught to read, each child who is liberated represents a major victory.

District 60's commitment to all learners serves as a model for schools everywhere. All students have needs and strengths to varying degrees. Instead of grouping children by what they cannot do, educators need to view children through the lens of what they can do. Thus, instead of having special education programs that are little more than holding tanks or babysitting programs, schools everywhere need to provide meaningful, individualized instruction for all learners.

*Learning should be the constant,*
*and time should be the variable.*

— Dr. Joyce Bales

The District 60 experience underscores the need for early diagnosis and assessment of all learners, even before they enter first grade. As research and practical experience continues to show, the earlier the intervention, the sooner the child can catch up. Waiting until a child is in a higher grade so that the deficiency is more pronounced and easier to assess means the gap has widened that much farther. Children who are eager learners in the lower grades eventually become discouraged, believing it is impossible for them to learn how to read and write.

"Every child should grow at least one academic year each year. If they are behind, they have to grow by 110 or 115 percent or more in order to catch up. By middle or high school, it is a much more intensive process," Dr. Bales explained. "We needed to address readiness opportunities with our young children. If you miss that opportunity, it takes a lot more effort to go back and make sure they get those skills. Reading is a key that is sequential."

Pueblo's solution was to assess and intervene at the earliest possible age, including with a preschool program for four-year-olds established at every elementary school in the district, thanks to a grant from the Piton Foundation. District 60 found that of those children who were enrolled in the preschool, 70 percent were proficient in reading by the end of third grade — a percentage that rose as high as 81 percent and has held stable at around 80 percent since then.

## District 60 Declares Victory

The proof is in the numbers. The same test data that sounded the alarm also rang the victory bells. For Bessemer in particular, CSAP reading test results showed that 64 percent of students were at or above proficient in 1998, compared with only 12 percent in 1997. That percentage rose to 74 percent in 1999. In writing, 48 percent of Bessemer's students were at or above the proficient level in 1998, compared with only 2 percent in 1997; that percentage that held roughly steady at 47 percent in 1999.

"Bessemer made the greatest gains in the state of Colorado," Dr. Bales said proudly. "Everyone in the state said, 'If they can, so can we.' There is nothing that catches on like success. It was so joyful."

The Texas A&M study also confirmed the results, noting, "The analyses across grades 3 through 5 support the conclusion that the [District 60] schools, on average, outperformed comparable Colorado schools on the CSAP tests of reading comprehension, and this was true both for all schools and for Title 1 schools considered separately. Moreover, the level at which [District 60] schools outperformed these comparable schools increased over the years of intervention."[5]

## A Model for Others

National and state recognition for Pueblo's schools put District 60 on the map. Its Bessemer and Beulah Heights Elementary Schools, for example, were named National Title I District Schools. District 60's motto, "Leave No Child Behind," which was first adopted in 1997, was later adopted by President Bush in the 2001 federal education legislation. (Meeting President Bush at Baylor University, Dr. Bales told him she was a big supporter of No Child Left Behind but reminded him that the work — and the slogan — had started in Pueblo.)

The positive ripple effect of the Pueblo story continues to influence others. When asked by other school administrators for advice, Dr. Bales graciously shares her own experiences. As the Pueblo story was publicized, District 60 received more than 7,000 visitors, among them many administrators and staff from other school districts wanting to learn and observe.

Among those who have been inspired by the District 60 story is Judge James R. Milliken, now-retired presiding judge of the San Diego Juvenile Court. He was in Denver for a wedding when he picked up a newspaper and read about Pueblo. His first thought was, if this can be done in Colorado, then why not in San Diego? "Pueblo stands out. Even though 70 percent of its learners are below the poverty line, they are well in excess of 70 percent proficient," observed Judge Milliken, whose own literacy crusade brought help and support to juvenile offenders to learn how to read and to stay sober (see Chapter 8).

He further believes that the District 60 success story illustrates the fallacy of labeling students who simply have not learned how to read as being learning disabled. "It's not a learning disability that these kids have, but an instructional disability that we have," Judge Milliken commented. "They can all learn. It's just a question of what they need."

As for Dr. Bales, after the 2005–06 school year—when the students who were in kindergarten when she arrived in 1994 were graduating seniors—she left Pueblo for a new assignment. Starting with the 2006–07 school year, she became the district superintendent in Vista, California. Among her first tasks was to examine literacy data in the district with the goal of raising standardized test scores and student comprehension. Early on, she asked district personnel to prepare quarterly reports to track progress toward specific goals set by the school board.

The community is different, but the drive to improve literacy is the same. It was still summer vacation when Dr. Bales arrived in Vista amid hundreds of boxes to be unpacked, a household to set up, and an office to establish. Staff meetings were already scheduled, and her reputation as a leader had preceded her.

For me, visiting Dr. Bales in a new location was a real treat. I had seen firsthand what her leadership had done in Pueblo, and now I can observe her in action in Vista, which is near where I live. More than that, it is a fitting ending for the District 60 turnaround story. What was accomplished in Pueblo is notable and deserves all the praise that has been lavished upon the district. But the real story is that what happened in Pueblo — made all the more dramatic by its demographics — can be done elsewhere. School districts that think data assessment and standardized tests are meaningless, that refuse to rethink their educational programs, that continue to do the same things and get the same results, or that do not believe that teacher training is the key to more effective instruction must take note. Pueblo is not just an example; it is a revolution waiting to happen everywhere.

CHAPTER 6

# The Cycle of Intervention

Ramón Gómez never intended to become a spokesperson for adult literacy. All he wanted to do was learn how to read and write English so he could pass a written driver's test. Ramón got his driver's license — and so much more. As he continues to work on his literacy skills with a tutor through the adult learning program at the Carlsbad (California) City Library, Ramón has become an advocate for the local adult literacy program. As his story (told in Chapter 4) relates, he has also inspired his three children either to stay in school or return to school to get their high school diplomas. Now he reads to his grandson, which not only models the importance of reading for the child but also forges important generational ties.

All that happened because Ramón Gómez learned how to read as an adult, becoming one more solitary learner who crossed the bridge to literacy. While his achievement is a personal victory, he's not the only one who benefits. His family, his employer, and society in general are all better off because Ramón learned how to read.

When one learner masters literacy, the benefits spread out in a ripple effect. Every child who learns how to read is one less adult in the future who cannot get a good job because of a lack of literacy skills. Every adult who learns how to read is one more parent or family member who can help a child become prepared for school. English as a second language (ESL) students who learn how to read and write open the door to literacy for their parents.

These images don't just make us feel good. They also tell us something very significant about the battle against illiteracy. It must be fought on all fronts — in the preschool and the kindergarten classroom, where children must be tested; in the elementary grades, where the intensive direct instruction found in research-based programs can prevent the gap from developing; and in middle schools and high schools, where all teachers must be trained to detect reading deficiencies and where, if the students' decoding skills have been thoroughly learned, then vocabulary-building is a critical success factor. Closing the gap completely in the K–12 learning environment could take decades, if it happens at all, because some school districts resist implementing the research that so plainly shows what works to teach children how to read. Therefore, adult literacy and family literacy programs also need funding and support to provide a safety net for those who reach adulthood without being able to read. To be most effective, adult literacy and family literacy programs need to embrace the latest research-based tools and be held to a greater degree of accountability by achieving and reporting results in exchange for the monies they receive.

To help as many people as possible to cross the bridge, literacy intervention must be delivered at every possible point along the life cycle, from preschool through adulthood, by properly trained teachers and tutors. No single intervention point along the cradle-to-grave continuum is more important than another. It is as important to teach an adult to read as to teach a child (and vice versa). A literate family is a stronger family, which is becoming critical in our multicultural society.

After hearing a brief synopsis of Ramón Gómez's story, Sharon Darling, president and CEO of the National Center for Family Literacy (NCFL), called it a "great example" of what is needed not only in adult and family literacy but also in specific communities within our society. Hispanic and other immigrant families have some of the lowest literacy skills today. To address that deficit, the NCFL has launched new initiatives, including using a $3.2 million grant from Toyota to establish model family literacy programs in five cities with significant or quickly growing Hispanic populations. The goal of the model programs is to help parents in at-risk Hispanic and other immigrant families improve their English, education, work, and parenting skills, while helping their children succeed in school.

The NCFL has focused on the Hispanic community for intervention, because this group represents America's most rapidly growing population. NCFL cited Census 2000 statistics showing that 35.3 million Hispanics live in the United States, 14 million of whom are foreign-born. "Parents in many recently immigrated Hispanic families speak little to no English, possess low literacy skills in their native language due to limited education, and frequently struggle to assist their children's English language development," NCFL said in a statement.[1]

Other statistics show that while the high school dropout rate is about 30 percent in the United States overall, for Hispanic students, the percentage is closer to 56 percent. These statistics point to the potential for a huge unskilled labor pool to develop in America, because we cannot meet the needs of our children — including those who are born here. If this happens, the result could greatly undermine the Hispanic community, which is known for having a strong work ethic, strong religious faith, and an intact family system. "Within ten years, that could disappear," Ms. Darling said. "We are not capitalizing on the strength of this population;

instead, we are systematically taking that strength away, although no one is doing that intentionally."

As the example of literacy programs for the Hispanic community shows, our efforts to impart reading skills need to be increased and intensified with specific groups, such as ESL students, high school students at risk of dropping out because of low literacy levels, young children who need diagnosis and intervention as early as kindergarten, parents with only basic or below-basic literacy skills who need intervention as well as help working with their children, and many more.

> *If we can preserve the family system, we are*
> *going to be better off as a nation. If you can*
> *affect one life, you can affect many lives.*
>
> — Sharon Darling, President and CEO,
> National Center for Family Literacy

Literacy must be promoted through every possible means of delivery. We must continue to reach out in the community, in the workplace, in schools, and through private organizations to all learners. At the same time, however, these channels cannot operate separately, like a river that flows only one way. Rather, these streams of learning must be brought together like a vast ocean of resources that can be tapped for knowledge, expertise, and best practices. And, in today's economic and political environment in which funding sources are never assured, by banding together, the literacy movement can do a better job of educating the public and attracting more public and private support.

Admittedly, literacy programs, which tend to think and act locally, will need some change in perspective. A community-based program is designed to meet the needs of its local community, not learners in some other city or state. A national program has its own agenda through its particular affiliates. Those who focus on adult literacy have different issues than those who are dedicated to early childhood programs. Despite these differences, the literacy movement cannot divide itself into smaller and smaller pieces, with everyone carving out a piece of turf to serve and defend. By coming together along the common overarching vision of preventing and eradicating illiteracy, the whole is truly greater than the sum of its parts!

To illustrate, international literacy consultant Dr. Thomas Sticht recited an ironic argument of how it is perceived to be "too late" to intervene and address the problem of adult and child illiteracy. By the time a nonreader has reached high school, most people think it's too late and turn to the middle schools to find out why students are being sent to high school without having learned how to read. In middle school, it's too late to do much because these students should have learned how to read in elementary school. In the primary grades, they say, it's already too late because these children should have been prepared with preschool programs. Then they say that preschool is too late because they need earlier programs than that. And even then they say it's too late, because literacy begins at birth.

"And then the problem is that birth is too late because we must get into the heads of those who are going to have children!" added Dr. Sticht, a UNESCO Mahatma Gandhi Medal Laureate, whose distinguished career includes being president and senior scientist for Applied Behavioral & Cognitive Sciences Inc., associate director of the National Institute of Education, visiting professor at the Harvard Graduate School of Education, research professor of industrial psychology at the U.S. Naval Postgraduate School, and visiting noted scholar at the University of British Columbia.

Dr. Sticht's comments appear to run contrary to the belief that adult illiteracy will be solved once the K–12 school system is fixed.

In a perfect world that will, indeed, be the case. We can prevent illiteracy by teaching all children how to read in the primary grades using proven, research-based methods. However, elementary education in America exists in a very imperfect world, where there is a war going on between those who cling to the whole language philosophy, which no research supports (see Chapter 8), and those who know what truly works.

There is a great need to deliver literacy along the life cycle continuum. Teaching adults who are already parents or will become ones how to read can have an effect on multiple life cycles — their own and those of their children. The purpose of this chapter is to further understanding by all parties — parents, teachers, researchers, literacy advocates, business leaders, policy makers, and society in general — of how the movement to restore scientifically based reading instruction has been progressing and what can be done to bring about a final victory.

## Early Childhood Education

Early childhood diagnosis and intervention is important for so many reasons. There is the obvious desire to give young children a strong foundation in the basics of education, which is rooted in scientifically based reading instruction. The first and most important step is for teachers to have an understanding of the essential components of reading instruction and how that instruction should be provided to all students. By the end of first grade, students who need additional assistance and those who may have some deficiencies should be evident. To identify such students most effectively, all children must be assessed regularly on their oral reading skills and be given diagnostic assessments to identify their strengths as well as their weaknesses. Children in kindergarten should be assessed for their reading readiness based on such things as their verbal language skills (e.g., are they speaking in sentences or a few words at a time?). The earlier difficulties with reading are detected, the sooner intervention can begin for those who need more help. Detection should take place before the gap becomes very great or children have begun to give up on themselves, when achieving literacy becomes much more difficult for them.

As the National Center for Learning Disabilities noted in a March 2007 report, while transition to kindergarten is key for all children, parents, and educators, it is of particular significance for new learners who struggle. "Many children follow a typical developmental pattern, but others struggle to learn," the center stated. "About 5 percent of the school-age population will be identified with specific learning disabilities characterized by unexpected underachievement despite adequate learning opportunities and at least average cognitive potential. The nature of these children's learning difficulties may mean that problems are not fully manifested, easily identified, or understood until the early grades. For example, while speech and language difficulties may be recognizable in the preschool period, specific learning disabilities in reading (e.g., dyslexia) may not be identifiable until second or third grade." We must keep in mind, though, that if appropriate research-based reading instruction is offered from day one to all students, we will have taken a giant step towards reducing the number of older students and adults who need remediation.[2]

Canadian volunteer literacy advocate Fran Thompson also champions early diagnosis and intervention as a means, as she sees it, to put resources to work where the most good can be accomplished. "That means giving kindergarten and first-grade teachers the training and evidenced-based screening tools and resources they need to teach a diverse spectrum of learners the foundational skills of reading, then building fluency, vocabulary, and comprehension skills throughout elementary school," added Fran, who is also a past president of the British Columbia Branch of the International

Dyslexia Association (IDA) and a past liaison for nine American branches of the IDA's National Branch Council.

Increasing public awareness to drive demand and supply of evidenced-based instruction has always been the impetus behind Ms. Thompson's volunteer work. During her tenure, the British Columbia Branch was successful in partnering with provincial and national funders, media, and education and literacy organizations to expand awareness of evidence-based identification and instruction through the development of seminars, conferences, webcasts, and television public service announcements (*www.knowledgenetwork.ca/literacy/*). In fall 2007, Ms. Thompson was a fundraiser and content advisor for and participant in the production of British Columbia's public broadcaster Knowledge Network's one-hour television documentary and web cast entitled *Deciphering Dyslexia*. (Both are available at *www.knowledgenetwork.ca/dyslexia/*; the documentary highlights published early intervention and instruction research by Drs. Linda Siegel and Nonie Lesaux.)

Fran Thompson's drive to promote early intervention is based on her experience as a parent of two children with dyslexia. It has taken her to the halls of provincial government in British Columbia to promote the necessary change in thinking that will allow needed resources to be made available. She has also developed partnerships with researchers to promote knowledge in her community — and encourages other parents to do the same. In British Columbia, elected officials listened to presentations by noted researcher Dr. Frank Wood of Wake Forest University, and the Select Standing Committee on Education invited him to speak in early fall of 2006. (Ms. Thompson facilitated the meetings and credits Dr. Wood as the one who convinced provincial elected officials to recommend early childhood identification and intervention.) On January 27, 2007, the province subsequently allocated $27 million to literacy projects — thanks to the efforts of countless committed leaders, educators, and volunteers working together to bridge the gap in literacy achievements across the age spectrum.

The goal in British Columbia is to make that region "the most literate jurisdiction in North America by 2015." Noting a growing economy, competition for skilled workers, the aging of the workforce, and low school enrollments, a provincial report stated: "British Columbia has long worked to increase literacy levels in the province, but the need for such training has become more important than ever in recent years."[3] (Meanwhile, the Canadian Council on Learning is working across the provinces to promote the use of predictive assessment tools to improve literacy.)

The desire to promote and build literacy in any region must include a strong early childhood component, although this should not be the only component. The greater number of children who learn how to read in school, the higher percentage of literate citizens will enter society in the future — adults who will be able to compete in the workforce and help prepare their children for learning one day.

Reading First, which has been a component of No Child Left Behind, addresses the needs of young learners by providing funding to states to implement scientifically based reading instruction, while holding states accountable for student achievement. Reading First has its share of critics, including a few school districts that have given up funding rather than change their whole language-based curricula, even though it lacks a scientific research basis (see Chapter 7).

The strongest arguments in favor of Reading First have been the statistics of achievement. According to the U.S. Department of Education, in the 2004–05 school year, students in Reading First schools demonstrated increases in reading achievement across all performance measures. Second graders who met or exceeded proficiency in reading on Reading First outcome measures of fluency increased from 33 percent in 2003–04 to 39 percent in 2004–05 for economically disadvantaged students, from 27 to 32 percent for limited English proficient (LEP) students, from 34 to 37 percent for African-American students, from 30 to 39 percent for Hispanic students, and from 17 to 23 percent for students with disabilities.[4]

What made Reading First successful was its intense focus on research-based instruction before the critical third-grade threshold. Elementary education must continue to make proven, scientific research a cornerstone of instructional programs for young learners. As the Reading First program states, "Research shows that students who fall behind in reading in the earliest grades rarely make up this deficit, and have more difficulty with schoolwork in general."[5]

The first step in educating young children is to understand that all children learn to read the English language in essentially the same way. They need to be taught the same decoding skills, learn and expand their English vocabulary, and be taught to read what they can talk about and understand. For those who fall in the category of having learning deficiencies, additional help must be provided in a timely manner.

Dr. Frank Wood, a professor of neuropsychology in the Wake Forest University School of Medicine and a leader in early school diagnostic research, explained that in a typical elementary school, children who rank near the bottom 10 percent of learners might well require instruction with a resource teacher or reading special-ist outside the regular classroom. This could involve small-group and one-on-one instruction to gain an additional spoken vocabu-lary through oral storytelling and being read to by the teacher. As their spoken vocabulary is expanded, these students should system-atically and explicitly be taught the skill of reading. Students in the 15th to 35th percentile, while considered low achievers on stan-dardized tests, could most likely benefit from better teaching by the main classroom teacher in the classroom setting and, once they have mastered the basic decoding skills, teaching that focuses on reading fluency, vocabulary, and comprehension. "Most students in this 15th to 35th percentile can get what they need from upgraded whole-class teaching," added Dr. Wood, who is also chair of the Scientific Advisory Board of the Dyslexia Foundation.

To determine the level of instruction that students need, schools need to utilize diagnostic testing as early as kindergarten to assess oral language skills and reading readiness. It is important to continue this assessment of oral reading skills through third grade as well. "Let's not be afraid to assess our students' skill profile and their development or lack thereof over time," Dr. Wood continued. "A lot of teachers and schools are loathe to test children. I don't see any logical justification for that. We aren't going to reach them unless we know what their strengths and weaknesses are."

Delores Scott, a teacher in the Collington Square School, a charter school in Baltimore, Maryland, says she has seen from her own experience, including most recently as a kindergarten teacher, the importance of early childhood diagnosis and intervention. "It gives them the basics and the foundation they need," explained Ms. Scott, who in 2005 was honored as Teacher of the Year by the National Right to Read Foundation.

Those children who have deficiencies — who cannot learn how to read as easily as their peers in kindergarten or first grade, perhaps because of a learning deficiency or other impediment — can receive the intensive instruction or services they need before the gap widens. "Problems have to be caught early — in kindergarten or first grade — before the children are too far behind," said Ms. Scott, who today administers testing to elementary school students at the Collington Square charter school.

Equally important, children who struggle must receive the systematic, direct instruction they need to avoid the devastating shame and humiliation that comes from reading failure. As G. Reid Lyon, PhD, former chief of the Child Development and Behavior Branch of the National Institute of Child Health and Human Development (NICHD), National Institutes of Health, noted, children who have difficulty reading in front of peers and teachers suffer on a daily basis. "It is clear from our NICHD research that this type of failure affects children negatively earlier than we thought," Dr. Lyon wrote. "By the end of first grade, children having difficulty learning to read begin to feel less positive about their abilities than when they started school. As we follow children through elementary and middle school, self-esteem and the motivation to learn to read decline even further. In the majority of cases, the students are deprived of the ability to learn about literature, science, mathematics, history, and social studies because they cannot read grade-level textbooks."[6]

Even with early childhood instruction that targets the needs of the individual learner, schools cannot assume that their work with students is done once a child reaches grade level. Very often, children who struggled to read in the early grades and who are brought up to grade level by the third grade will face challenges later on. "You can take an at-risk child and, on the basis of early screening and diagnostic testing, usually raise that child's reading performance to the average level by third grade," Dr. Wood explained. "Having only done that, however, you can expect that child to regress to near the degree of deficiency that the child was showing in kindergarten."

For example, if a child was at the 15th percentile and then was brought up to the 50th percentile, that child is likely to regress back to the 15th or 20th percentile by eighth grade. The main reason for the regression, Dr. Wood said, is the need for vocabulary enrichment. "Unless you have vocabulary enrichment and enhancement going on in kindergarten through third grade, you are failing to establish a level of skills in vocabulary that is going to be required for later reading success.

*Vocabulary does not progress as rapidly*
*as we think that reading progresses.*

— Dr. Frank Wood,
Professor of Neuropsychology,
Wake Forest University

Unfortunately, how and what to teach children remains the focus of much debate. However, that debate should now end. We know how to teach children to read — all of them. And we do know now to do accurate and complete diagnoses of learning deficiencies in children at an early age. The challenge now is to implement what we know works. Those who refuse to accept the clear findings of research in reading that has been conducted over the past half century are hurting our children. I plead with those who read my story to consider the devastation that was caused in my life and in the lives of countless others who were denied the skill of reading. Listen to the pleas of those whose stories are in this book.

Consider the solutions as illustrated by the Pueblo, Colorado, schools (which adopted Lindamood-Bell) and others who had the courage to change their instructional approach to reading and adopt what science has proven to work. Another scientifically derived new approach, the Fast ForWord series of language and reading intervention programs, has met with similar success in its translation from the scientific laboratory into classrooms nationwide. Developed by Scientific Learning Corporation and based on more than 30 years of research by Dr. Paula Tallal, a cognitive neuroscientist, and Dr. Michael Merzenich, a neurophysiologist, Fast

ForWord was initially validated in controlled laboratory studies, then in clinics nationwide, and subsequently in school trials similar to that described for Pueblo. Now comprising a dozen computerized language and reading intervention programs for pre-K through adults that individually adapt to the needs of each student, Fast ForWord has been used by more than 1 million students in 4,900 schools nationwide, as well as in 39 countries. (For detailed results of school trials, see *www.scientificlearning.com/results/.*)

Lindamood-Bell and Fast ForWord are but two examples that demonstrate definitively that scientific advances pertaining to how the brain learns, especially how we learn spoken and written language, can be effectively translated, scaled up, and scientifically validated for broad educational use to the benefit of millions of struggling readers. We have lost enough young learners to the debate over how children learn to read. Now it is time to heal the nation and to move ahead with the solution.

Canadian researcher Dr. Steve Truch confirms that teaching children to read explicitly and systematically, using phonemic awareness, phonics, vocabulary development, and oral reading for fluency and comprehension, is critical. "That's what good readers do. They develop the process of decoding until it becomes automatic," added Dr. Truch, a prominent North American learning psychologist and director of The Reading Foundation, which he started in Calgary in 1990 and in Vancouver in 1994.

## Middle School and High School

No one can refute the argument that early childhood diagnosis and intervention help to address problems and deficiencies as quickly as possible. Those who receive remediation as first graders—and who have the benefit of ongoing reading instruction and vocabulary building—have a better chance of retaining reading success in the higher grades. But what about those students in middle school or even high school who have difficulty with reading?

Yes, it is more difficult to intervene with these students, in part because they have come to see themselves as failures. As the Native Alien I once was in middle school—an angry adolescent and young teenager who acted out to vent his frustration and to hide the fact he couldn't read—I know how difficult motivating and teaching these students can be. But just because something is difficult doesn't mean there's an excuse not to do it. We need specific strategies to help close the literacy gap for these middle school and high school students so that they can go on to reach their potential and become contributing members of society.

According to research published in an Alliance for Excellent Education report to the Carnegie Corporation of New York, approximately 8 million 4th- to 12th-grade students struggle to read at grade level, and about 70 percent of older readers require some form of remediation. "Meeting the needs of struggling adolescent readers and writers is not simply an altruistic goal," wrote study authors Gina Biancarosa and Dr. Catherine Snow of the Harvard Graduate School of Education. "The emotional, social, and public health costs of academic failure have been well documented, and the consequences of the national literacy crisis are too serious and far-reaching for us to ignore. Meeting these needs will require expanding the discussion of reading instruction from Reading First—acquiring grade-level reading skills by third grade—to Reading Next—acquiring the reading skills that can serve youth for a lifetime."[7]

*America's schools need to produce literate*
*citizens who are prepared to compete in the*
*global economy and who have the skills to pursue*
*their own learning well beyond high school.*

— Reading Next, "A Vision for Action and
Research in Middle and High School Literacy"[8]

Dr. Lyon observed that by middle school, children who read well read at least 10 million words during the school year. Children with reading difficulties read fewer than 100,000 words during the same period. "Poor readers lag far behind in vocabulary development and in the acquisition of strategies for understanding what they read, and they frequently avoid reading and other assignments that require reading," Dr. Lyon wrote. "By high school, the potential of these students to enter college has decreased dramatically. Students who have stayed in school long enough to reach high school tell us that they hate to read because it is so difficult and it makes them feel 'dumb.' As a high school junior in one of our studies remarked, 'I would rather have a root canal than read.'"[9]

With middle school and high school students, the stakes are even higher. Now the issue is not just falling test scores but a greater incidence of drug and alcohol abuse, teenage pregnancy, crime and delinquency, and suicide. "Our data show that the greater the loss [in reading skills] in relative percentage terms between third grade and eighth grade, the more serious the psychiatric depression," Dr. Wood stated. "Suicidality — ranging from thoughts to actual attempts — is several times more prevalent in low-reading teenagers than in typically reading teenagers. Leaving that aside, just the depression is at least double in prevalence in low-reading eighth graders than in typically reading eighth graders — even if you control for other factors such as ADHD or socioeconomic level."

Louise's son started talking about hurting or killing himself as early as second grade, and suicide threats continued into high school. As her son struggled with reading and acted out in school, Louise was able to get him a few counseling sessions, but given the family finances, private therapy was out of the question. Finally, when her son was 14 years old, a special education teacher told Louise she could demand to have him tested through the school system. The testing revealed he had short-term memory and language-processing problems. He was reading at the fifth-grade level and writing only at the second-grade level.

"Meanwhile, the suicide talk continued to be a problem, and he was acting out so much," Louise recalled. "At one point while I was driving him to the counselor, he threatened to jump out of the car."

Finally, Louise was able to afford counseling and treatment to improve his brain function. Her son made tremendous progress, emotionally as well as academically, eventually graduating from college and getting a good job.

Reaching out to teenagers who have low reading skills or who are functionally illiterate is no easy task. Any parent knows the joys and challenges of having a teenager in the house. Now compound that with the anger, frustration, and depression that go with being a teenager who cannot read. The only way to deal with these students, I believe, is to confront the education credibility gap. The burden of proof is not on the students; it's on the schools that have to demonstrate with confidence their ability to teach these young people. I can tell you, when I was 13, if someone could have proven to me that they could teach me how to read, if they had sat me down and said, "This is what you have to do," I would have signed up. I would have been there.

"When you approach these children who weren't helped before — or they were helped but the gains they made didn't stick — you have to recognize the additional burden of depression and the tendency to want to give up," Dr. Wood observed. "Without addressing those issues in some sort of stimulating, collegial, partnership-type of experience, you're just spitting in the wind."

Once teenage learners put their trust into a program because they see it's working, they are more apt to stick to it, even though it's a long process. As students begin to make gains, they will be motivated to continue.

Based on her experience as a special education teacher who now oversees supplemental reading instruction and tutoring programs for about 400 students in six schools, including in Denver and Colorado Springs, Marianne Arling believes many secondary students lack literacy skills and need instructions in the basics. This requires systematic delivery of phonemic awareness, phonics, and vocabulary.

"Secondary students, like adults, can learn quickly. These are instructable skills," Ms. Arling said. Her advice as a practitioner is for teachers to work in small-group settings to listen to children as they read. This will allow teachers to hear, for example, whether the students are reading short *i*'s as short *e*'s. "You can't know that if you are teaching 23 kids at a time. With small-group instruction, you become aware of what the individual's problems are so that you can give the child the individualized instruction that he or she needs — provided that the tutor is well-trained in an effective method," she added.

## The High School Learner

When a student reaches high school without having the necessary literacy skills — decoding, fluency, and comprehension — it is "situation critical." These students are at high risk of becoming high school dropouts. Now a variety of factors are coming together to put a spotlight on the issue of high school reading levels, including the debate around the reauthorization of the No Child Left Behind Act and state proficiency standards and exit exams, such as those that have been implemented in California and other states.

We can't let the good news of our high expectations for high school students turn into a punishment for millions of young people across the country who lack the necessary reading and math skills to meet these standards. The risks of being a high school dropout today — given the greater technology and literacy demands of the workplace — are too great.

The U.S. Department of Education called the state of literacy among American youth "alarming and not getting better." It cited statistics revealing the following:

- One-third of students entering ninth grade have reading skills that are two or more years below grade level.

- Twenty-eight percent of 12th-grade public school students (or about 800,000 young people) scored below the Basic level on the National Assessment of Education Progress (NAEP) 2002 reading assessment.

- Thirty-five percent of undergraduates participate in remedial education during their first two years of postsecondary enrollment.[10]

Teaching reading to high school students is a particular challenge for many reasons. First, there is the expectation on the part of most teachers that by the time students reach ninth grade, they have learned to decode and have adequate reading comprehension. Thus, teachers who specialize in a particular subject (e.g., history, science, math, etc.) are focused on imparting knowledge related to a particular curriculum, not on detecting reading deficiencies or teaching reading. Some high schools do have reading programs, but given the statistics that one-third of ninth graders are reading below grade level, most schools are woefully understaffed to meet the literacy needs of their students.

Many well-intentioned teachers try multimedia approaches to impart knowledge to students who have difficulty reading. For example, a language arts teacher shows a movie based on a book in class so students who can't read the book independently still learn the story. However, these teachers need to see that they are only accommodating, not addressing, a reading or learning deficiency. This is not the teacher's fault. Teachers are required to teach curriculum — whether it's science or literature or another subject area. Most teachers do not have the specialized training to recognize and understand a reading deficiency, let alone address it. Even in special education, students may be accommodated instead of diagnosed and instructed.

This type of accommodation will not help teenagers and young adults who will very soon enter society; instead, it hurts them deeply. Giving these students only the bare minimum of skills, instead of assessing their strengths and weaknesses and teaching them accordingly, is only another form of social promotion (see Chapter 3). The result is a wider gap between the haves and have-nots, which damages society.

"Reading (decoding, fluency, and comprehension) is a gateway skill that allows students to access the knowledge and skills they need to acquire through their high school education. We cannot allow today's group of high school students to leave high school with inadequate reading skills, and hope that the next generation of students will arrive at high school with higher levels of proficiency in reading," the U.S. Department of Education stated. "Nor should we focus exclusively on students who enter high school with lower reading and writing skills. To prepare young people for the many challenges that await them as adults, high schools must enhance and strengthen the reading and writing skills of all students through their high school careers."[11]

School districts need to implement screening and diagnostics for older students who are behind in their literacy skills and then provide intensive remediation to bring them up to grade level. This may involve time dedicated every day to reading, as well as intensive tutoring.

For higher-grade students especially, computer-based exercises and reading drills can be particularly effective, as long as the students have been assessed and are monitored by a trained teacher or tutor. As Marianne Arling noted, the computer is especially useful for high school students who may need repetition to develop a particular set of skills, whether for two weeks or two months. "They can do this repetition with a computer program, which is always patient and always affirming," she added.

The needs of the high school students offer a unique opportunity for school districts to foster closer ties with adult literacy programs. This may involve studying adult learning models or joining forces with an adult learning center to teach these older students.

Mary was a high school senior who struggled in reading. Born prematurely at 24 weeks and weighing only 1 pound, 6 ounces, Mary had already beaten the odds of survival. As an infant, she had been given only a 5 percent chance of living. Even though she had developmental delays, including those related to walking and talking and later in the classroom, Mary was destined to beat the odds again. She was particularly blessed with parents who believed in her, a special education teacher who wanted the most for her, and a district that was willing to try something new.

Mary and her classmates were among the high school students to take part in a cooperative literacy effort, begun in 1998, between the Carlsbad Library's adult learning program and Carlsbad High School. Students were bused to the adult learning program, where 9th through 12th graders were tutored one-on-one in basic reading and writing skills by their special education teacher and aide and by staff and volunteers at the adult learning program.

"It was a plus for the students just to get off the school campus, where they didn't have to worry about other kids seeing them in [special education], and then to have uninterrupted time in an adult environment," observed Lynda Jones, retired director of the adult literacy program. "The one-on-one tutoring was making a difference."

By the next semester, the high school program at the library's adult literacy program doubled to 12 students, then increased to 40, which Lynda says is capacity for now because of school scheduling and transportation issues. "Working with the teens has added a wonderful dimension to our program," Lynda added. "The tutors love the teens and are devoted to them."

For the high school students, enrolling in the adult literacy program is voluntary; the course is considered an elective. Thus, the young people have chosen this for themselves, recognizing it as an opportunity to get the reading and writing skills they need for life. "It's helped a lot. Ever since I got to the program, I've been more confident in my other high school classes," Mary said. "When I read now, if there is a big word, I try to pronounce it, or I would ask the teacher to help me. I still struggle with spelling every once in a while."

Mary is literate and is able to write emails and send instant messages to friends. Asked to reflect on her experience in the program, Mary credits the adult environment and the one-on-one attention she received. "I had one tutor who, when she sat down with me, I felt comfortable. She told me, 'The best thing you can do is try. You never know until you try.'"

Mary's tutor was not making an empty promise. The program had a proven track record of teaching adults with learning and reading deficiencies how to decode and build their fluency, vocabulary, and comprehension. For students like Mary to commit the time and effort, teachers and administrators must be willing to back the efficacy of their programs and have the ability to deliver to them to learners.

## Dropouts and Adult Literacy

Mary's story illustrates what happens when two literacy programs that serve separate populations — one for high school special education students and the other for adult learners in a community-based program — agree to interact and collaborate. This kind of interaction among programs is essential for the literacy movement to embrace the bigger vision that will open doors to the resources they need.

This interaction is already happening on some levels because of a change in student populations in the adult literacy programs. The typical adult learner is older, someone who already has a job and very often a family. The need to get a better job creates the impetus to enroll in a program to improve literacy skills. Increasingly, however, adult literacy programs are seeing an influx of younger students — sometimes as young as 16 or 17 — who have dropped out of high school and now want to improve their literacy.

"There is some controversy surrounding these younger students who have left school and now want the education, and so they end up going to adult literacy programs," commented Dr. Dominique Chlup, assistant professor and director of the Texas Center for the Advancement of Literacy & Learning (TCALL), the state's literacy resource center.

These younger students can be a challenge to the typical adult learning program, which is used to an older, more mature learner. Getting 16-year-olds to commit to a schedule, to come in when they are supposed to, and to understand that literacy is not achieved overnight can be difficult.

> *One adult unable to read is one too many in America. We must take a comprehensive and preventive approach, beginning with elementary schools and with special emphasis in our high schools. We must focus resources toward proven, research-based methods to ensure that all adults have the necessary literacy skills to be successful.*
>
> — U.S. Secretary of Education Margaret Spellings [12]

## Adult Literacy

Based on my experience, high school students and adult learners share one significant commonality: they know from bitter experience not to get their hopes up. They are guarded with others and with their expectations. They've tried, other teachers have tried, other schools have tried, and nothing has worked. And yet, the desire to read — to have a skill that the rest of the world has but they do not — is bigger than their fear and cynicism. Why should the learner trust or believe someone now? What is different this time?

Every adult program must be aware of these questions and be capable of answering them truthfully and completely. This involves using data and assessment and being willing to re-examine teaching practices and programs based on what has proven to work best. For adult literacy programs to take on these challenges, they must have better funding and support on the federal and state level and from private sources.

Sadly, adult literacy lacks a champion on the national level. There are, however, some efforts to include an adult education component in No Child Left Behind as it is considered for reauthorization. There is also a federal-level adult literacy program, known as the U.S. Adult Education and Literacy System (AELS), a name coined by international literacy expert Dr. Thomas Sticht. AELS received a significant boost with the passage of the Economic Opportunity Act of 1964, which provided federal laws and funding for adult basic education. AELS is funded in part by federal monies and in larger part by states and local communities. However, many community-based programs have pulled out of AELS, Dr. Sticht said, because of an accountability requirement that imposed a burden on volunteer organizations with very few paid staff members.

While adult literacy programs face more demands to show their results, they must be given the resources to do so. As Dr. Sticht points out, it is ridiculous to expect a program that is run largely by volunteers with little professional staff to undertake the kind of data gathering and analysis that's now being required. What's needed is professional staff to run and evaluate the programs — and professional staff takes money.

As he noted, AELS has seen more than 100 million adults enrolled, yet we spend very little on adult programs — some $800 per enrolled student. By comparison, about $8,500 per enrolled student is spent in kindergarten through grade 12, and in Head Start, the investment per enrollee is about $7,000. Given the importance of adult literacy — not only for the adult learner but also to prepare their children for school — we must provide additional resources and support for adult programs to continue to operate and to collect and analyze data that measures effectiveness.

"We have to remember why we're all in this field, to help the learners and meet their needs," Dr. Chlup observed. "If we can use the data to help the learners, then instead of program administrators thinking, 'I'm held accountable by the data,' they realize that the ones to whom they are the most accountable are their learners — helping them with their immediate goals, their long-ranging goals, and the goals they haven't thought to have as of yet."

Adult literacy is hard work on both sides. Adult learners are usually juggling jobs and family responsibilities along with the long-term commitment to a literacy program. Often these students need more flexibility and access. Programs often accommodate this by allowing students to "stop out" — whether because of job concerns, a temporary lack of transportation, child care or family care demands, or other issues — instead of "dropping out." In the interim before they return, they need to have access to the resources that will help them continue to practice and build their literacy skills. On the other side, adult literacy programs take well-trained and dedicated volunteer tutors, who give up so much of their lives for students whom they've never met before. When a student and a tutor really click, the synergy feels like magic.

Celeste Nowak, a teacher by profession, became an adult literacy tutor as a way to give back to her community in northern California. Her students have included adults who needed basic reading skills and learners for whom English is a second language. "It takes a lot of fortitude to continue on," she observed. "But as the community has become more and more involved, our budget has increased. We've gotten grants from community sources because they see the value of the program."

Too often, these real-life experiences, which occur in literacy programs across the country, stay in the realm of stories and anecdotal evidence. These situations and, more importantly, the solutions that are implemented need to be quantified, analyzed, and shared. In fact, that is exactly what was done in a project spearheaded by the National Center for the Study of Adult Learning and Literacy (NCSALL). The study looked at the real-world challenges of adult learners in literacy programs who "must make an active decision to participate in each class session and often must overcome significant barriers to attend classes."[13]

Based on the findings of the NCSALL study, Dr. Chlup believes one of the important ways to build persistence among adult learners is to discuss the learner's goals and set realistic expectations around them. She used the example of a student who states her goal is to earn a GED. After her literacy skills are tested, it is determined that this person has relatively low reading and writing skills, which will affect how long it will take to achieve a GED. Now the literacy instructor can explain that, based on these pretest scores, the adult learner will likely take between 18 months and two years to get a GED. That may be a sobering reality for the learner, who expected to get a GED in two months, but persistence is built on realistic expectations.

"Now the conversation can be, 'We're really committed to helping you get your GED. For you to achieve this goal, you'll have some other issues to think about. Have you thought about child care or transportation? What happens when or if you need to "stop out" temporarily? Let's think about some self-study strategies we'll be able to use for you.' The goal is to help them persist in the program, and for that to happen, there needs to be an open, honest, and upfront conversation," Dr. Chlup added.

Staffed by volunteers and managed by administrators who are usually extremely passionate and very overworked, community-based literacy programs do what they have to do to satisfy a local, state, or federal funding source. Too often, however, these programs have not utilized the data to their own best interest. Instead of just collecting the data on the number of learners to register each year, the average number of sessions attended, months in the program, and so forth, programs could really study their own data and see what these experiences are telling them.

Adult learning programs also need to tap into a resource that they have at the ready but may underutilize: the learners themselves. Often, programs ask learners to share their success stories to attract other learners and to put a human face on the work that is being funded.

Marty Finsterbusch, a former adult learner who is now executive director of VALUE Inc., believes adult learners can do so much more. VALUE's mission is to strengthen adult literacy in the United States through learner involvement and leadership, a goal that he is passionate about. "We bring the unique perspective that other national organizations do not have. They may have one or two students on the board, or they have a committee of learners, but they have no real say in what goes on. VALUE, on the other hand, is made up of adult learners from across the country and from multiple organizations," he commented. "What we bring is the truth. We prove that adult education does work."

Rather than have adult learners "tell their story and leave," Mr. Finsterbusch firmly believes these individuals have valuable skills and expertise to offer a literacy program. Granted, it may take training, but adult learners can and want to help. Literacy programs, he said, have not fully done their jobs unless adult learners are helped to become more involved, whether in fundraising, teaching, or administration. "Adult learners can do that work. Once the organization understands that student involvement is not just one more thing to get done, but it's part of their job, then they buy into it.

They say, 'Why couldn't I train one of my alums to be my secretary, or train one of my learners to be one of the tutors?' We have jobs and we have our own businesses. Our family members may include the mayor in town! We can't improve adult education in the U.S. until we have changed the image in the minds of the people of who the adult learners are."

For adult literacy programs to reach the next level of effectiveness, they must see themselves as a key part in the continuum. Yes, they serve a specific population: local adults who want to gain or improve their literacy skills. But as we've seen, the population of learners is diversifying, including ESL adults and younger students who have recently dropped out of high school. As we have seen in Carlsbad, there will be opportunities for adult programs to work with school districts to teach older students.

In Carlsbad, an important and symbolic step is being taken to recognize the importance of the adult learning program as part of the literacy continuum. The new Carlsbad City Library Learning Center will house the library and all its programs for adults and children who are already literate, who know the joy and power of the written word. The learning center will also encompass the Adult Learning Center, as well as the library's Centro de Información, which offers programs in English and Spanish with an emphasis on family participation.

As I see it, including the Adult Learning Center in the new library campus brings the problem of adult illiteracy out of the shadows to address a problem that many people in the community do not know exists. More importantly, the new location not only showcases the Adult Learning Center and the work that is done there, but it also celebrates this mission in a highly visible way: bringing literacy in English to adults who lack adequate skills, as well as to the community's large ESL population. The Carlsbad City Library Learning Center is not just a building campus but also an acknowledgment that everyone has a place at the library. This includes those who take their literacy for granted, as well as those who struggle to claim their right to read and write.

## Family Literacy

With family literacy programs — working with parents and pre-school or school-aged children — the literacy cycle is completed. Both ends of the spectrum are engaged, the emerging reader and the adult learner. Literacy skills are imparted, and family ties are strengthened. Parenting skills are reinforced. All components come together here to help an adult learn how to read to get a job or a better job and to give a young student a stronger start.

> *Research shows that children with educated mothers*
> *are most likely to learn how to read at a young age*
> *and to thrive in the classroom. A mother who reads*
> *can introduce her child to the joy of words*
> *and learning at a young age.*
> — U.S. Secretary of Education Margaret Spellings[14]

To be effective, family literacy programs should have four essential components, according to Benita Somerfield, executive director of the Barbara Bush Foundation for Family Literacy. The first is to provide literacy instruction to the parent or primary caregiver. The second is preliteracy instruction for preschool children (since most children attend family literacy programs before school starts). The third component is to enable parents and children to learn together, showing parents how to share books with their children and engage in literacy activities with them.

"Our perspective is that when you're funding a family literacy program, you are getting double-duty for your dollars because you are working toward preventing delays in children and working with the adults to improve their literacy," Ms. Somerfield said.

Most adults in a family literacy program range from those having no reading skills at all to adults having a fifth- or sixth-grade reading level. In addition, an increasing number of ESL parents and families are participating in these programs. Through family literacy outreach, adults who lack literacy in English can still become their children's first teachers, bolstering their parenting skills. This is where the fourth element of the family literacy program comes in: parenting skills are imparted and reinforced.

As with adult literacy programs, family literacy initiatives must embrace data collection, measurement, and assessment. It's not enough to "just tell the stories," Ms. Somerfield commented. "There must be real evaluation of the program, based on measurable objectives. That way the family literacy or other literacy program can go to a policy maker or private foundation and say, 'See, this works.' It's not about telling the passionate stories; that's been done to death. The story is still essential, but to prove that you're doing the work, you must have the data showing that adults are getting more jobs and their children are starting school and they are ready to learn."

The challenge for teachers in adult literacy programs is to see all participants as learners — the adults as well as the children. "We try to move the schools from parent involvement to parent engagement, to really seeing parents as learners," explained Sharon Darling of NCFL. "I keep telling teachers, you do so well identifying the individual needs of learners — why can't you see parents the same way? These parents probably had a bad experience with school when they were students, and now we have to reach out to them in another way. Plus, you may have a parent in the program who is working two jobs."

Family literacy programs not only provide a chance for parents to learn how to interact with their children around literacy activities, but they also give the parents a venue to talk about issues from child development to alcohol abuse and spouse abuse. "The goal is to help parents get the skills they need, the children the skills they need, and help to change things at home," Ms. Darling added.

Family literacy programs have been put in place in every conceivable location: in Appalachia, on Native American reservations, in Spanish-speaking communities, in inner cities, in rural areas, and in Title I schools across the country, where parents work alongside the children in kindergarten through third grade. NCFL also is working closely with specific communities, such as through its Hispanic Family Learning Institute, which it launched four years ago. "Haven't we learned from what happened to the African-American and the Native American community? This is happening now in the Hispanic community. We are fragmenting the family by teaching the children and not the parents," Ms. Darling said. "We must preserve the strength of the family."

Asked about the reaction to the family literacy programs from the various communities, she explained, "As soon as we open a program, there is a waiting list."

## Success Along the Continuum

To gauge our success in delivering literacy along the continuum — from preschool to adulthood — we must look at the data. We need to see hard evidence that things are changing: that children are gaining proficiency based on standardized test scores, that the high school dropout rate is declining, that more high school students have achieved literacy, that adults are able to get jobs and better jobs, and that parents who read can help their children become better prepared for school.

This will require change in the systems with which we teach and assess the effectiveness of our programs. All programs must commit to better teacher training and use of proven, research-based tools and methodologies to teach learners to read. At every juncture, we must hold ourselves accountable in ways that we have not before. We must use the gains we've already made along the literacy cycle to attract more support and funding from policy makers and private sources. Success must build upon success.

The bridge is built. Now we must get more people across.

# CHAPTER 7

# The Failing System

When children have difficulty learning how to read, when students do not perform up to expectations on standardized tests, the first question that's usually asked is, "What are they being taught in school?" Parents, students, community members, even other teachers wonder what's happening—or not happening—in the classroom that produces such a poor result. Teachers often feel the brunt of this questioning, which at times feels like an accusation that they're not doing their jobs. The reality, however, is that teachers are being let down, too. Teachers see their students struggle, and they feel underprepared and ill-equipped for the job of teaching all learners. There are even some teachers whose own children have learning deficiencies, particularly in reading, and they feel powerless to help them.

Years ago when I was a teacher, I was acquainted with a man whom I'll call Donald. He was a real advocate for teachers: active in the union and a supporter of the teaching profession and his colleagues. Years later, after reading a newspaper interview with me about my first book, Donald called me to discuss his son who, at the time, was in special education. As a math teacher, Donald was able to work one-on-one with his son to teach him math, but when it came to reading, he didn't know what to do. Yet Donald believed that his son could be taught to read and wanted to hear more about my experience at the Lindamood-Bell Clinic.

Throughout our conversations — as Donald tried to get services for his son at the local high school and later took him to Lindamood-Bell for testing — I was struck by how frustrated this master teacher was by the system. The system that he had participated in and advocated for throughout his career had let him and his son down. As a concerned parent, he came face-to-face with the inadequacies of his district's services for students like his son, who have learning and/or reading deficiencies.

Donald's battle was a personal one as he fought, and later prevailed, to have his local district pay for the services to which his son was entitled. Although other teachers may lack the personal connection, they still feel anger toward a system that gets in the way of doing their job they want to do — namely, teach students. In conversations with teachers coast to coast, I've heard numerous dedicated professionals admit that they were not adequately trained in college or university to teach reading. They may have learned a lot about education theory, but nothing prepared them for what they would later face in the classroom: a diverse population of learners, some who seemed to learn how to read naturally, some who required a little extra attention, and about a third who needed specific intervention, whether in small groups or one-on-one.

"The fact that teachers need better training to carry out deliberate instruction in reading, spelling, and writing should prompt action rather than criticism," the American Federation of Teachers (AFT) stated in a report. "It should highlight the existing gap between what teachers need and what they have been given. It should underscore the obligation of teacher preparation programs to provide candidates with a rigorous, research-based curriculum and opportunities to practice a range of predefined skills and knowledge, as well as the need for licensing authorities to assess that knowledge."[1]

Sometimes publicly, but more often reluctantly and in private, teachers admit the bitter truth: the system is failing. The disappointment is felt most bitterly by those for whom teaching is more than a profession but instead a real vocation. These are the people who have wanted to be teachers all their lives, since they were youngsters in schools. Some were the bright students who took to learning naturally, with eager minds. Others, including many who ended up in special education and struggled with learning, especially reading, have real empathy for students who face similar challenges. Frustrated by the system's failure to teach all students and angry at such things as the high school dropout rate and the lack of adequate services for special education students, these teachers often wonder why they persist. Surely there's a better way to make a living.

Teachers' frustration, I believe, stems from their fundamental desire to make a difference in the lives of their students and the feeling of their failure to do so. Teachers want to do the right thing and must be given the information and tools they need to carry out their mission. More than ever, schools need teachers who are willing to admit the system's failure and to become accountable for their own part in making it better.

Dr. Elaine Cheesman was running an adult literacy clinic in Connecticut when she began encountering younger students for whom "unnecessary reading failure" was something she just couldn't accept. "When I got 18-year-old students, I started getting really angry," she explained. "We know what it takes to teach people to read. There is no question about that."

For Dr. Cheesman, who is now on the faculty at the University of Colorado–Colorado Springs in the Special Education Department, her motivation stemmed from a personal encounter with the failure of the system to educate all students because teachers are not properly trained. "At the age of 48, I entered a doctorate program expressly because I wanted to get into teaching teachers at the preservice level," she added.

> *If teaching children to read was as simple*
> *as providing the attention of an enthusiastic*
> *but untrained tutor, we would have discovered*
> *that and been doing it. Learning how to read is*
> *difficult for many people, and science … is helping*
> *us understand why and what can be done about it.*
>
> —Louisa C. Moats, EdD, in testimony before the
> House Committee on Education and the Workforce[2]

Teachers do not bear all the blame for students' poor performance, nor should they become scapegoats in the failing system. At the same time, they are most definitely a key part of the solution. As we examine the failing system, teachers must commit to changing their attitudes toward such things as inservice training. They need to embrace the fact that every educator, regardless of subject area, specialty, or grade level, plays a role in promoting student literacy. And as difficult as this subject is to broach, teachers must be willing to look at their own deficiencies, particularly with the written word, to become more proficient with literacy and, therefore, more effective as educators.

For teachers to be most effective, it is imperative that they be properly educated and better trained by colleges and universities in the latest, scientifically proven methods of teaching reading. New tools and better training are the only ways to counter the problem of teachers who are unprepared to teach children how to read. This is even more important for special education teachers, who are in classrooms where half of the students have serious reading deficiencies that might have been alleviated or prevented with earlier and more effective treatments or instruction.

Ten years ago, national education expert Louisa C. Moats, EdD, testified before the House Committee on Education and the Workforce that "things are bad all over when it comes to the preparation of teachers of reading."

Dr. Moats told the committee then, and remains firm in her belief today, that "Teacher preparation in reading will require a systemic overhaul to reach every part of the problem: preservice and in-service training, teacher textbooks and state credentialing standards, instructional materials, the design and operation of departments of education, and the ways in which information is disseminated into the field. Only systemic rebuilding is likely to establish a profession that is informed by science, a profession that will meet every child's need for reading success."[3]

Today, Dr. Moats believes there is inconsistency between what teachers are taught in college and university and what works in the classroom. "That gap is still enormous. It has not changed very much," she added. "The schools of education are the last to get on board and are the most resistant to the findings of the research consensus."

## The Failing System

Despite some stellar examples to the contrary, overall our education system is failing. The problem is systemic and must be addressed as such. Without action to overhaul the system — to fix what is broken by engaging all parties in an honest dialogue and an earnest partnership — it will continue to flounder.

One of the big pushes to improve our educational system has been the No Child Left Behind Act of 2001, the sweeping federal education reform legislation that has forced school districts to take a realistic look at their results. Importantly, No Child Left Behind was approved with strong bipartisan support. In 2008, this ground-breaking education reform—which remains highly controversial and openly opposed by many teacher groups—is expected go before Congress for reauthorization. Rather than become discouraged or abandon the education reforms, I believe that school districts, teachers, policy makers, parents, and, importantly, institutions of higher education that train teachers must redouble their efforts to commit to the goals of No Child Left Behind. No matter what becomes of this federal education reform law through reauthorization hearings and beyond, we cannot go backwards. We must continue to strive to close the gap between the haves and have-nots in literacy. As Senator Edward Kennedy (D-MA) said of the education reform act, "The Act's accountability and focus on every child has been instrumental in turning our national attention toward the worthy goals of closing achievement gaps and securing educational opportunity for all students."[4]

My view is that No Child Left Behind has made an important and much-needed impact on education in this country by boldly pointing out what students should be achieving and what they are not achieving and forcing teachers and administrators to look for the best methods to be used in the classroom. I wholeheartedly concur with the *New York Times* editorial that stated, "The core part of the law, which requires the states to close the achievement gap between white and minority students, must remain sacrosanct, and the Bush administration must stand firm against the districts that simply don't want to make the effort."[5]

The literacy gap must be meaningfully addressed by policy makers and educators for the sake of all students, especially minority and underprivileged students who are not receiving the education they need and that their families desire for them. As Professor Alfred Tatum of Northern Illinois University, author of *Teaching Reading to Black Adolescent Males: Closing the Achievement Gap*, stated, "It's a point of urgency. We cannot continue to stay the course we have been on for African-American adolescent males. We need to rally people around the complexity of addressing the literacy needs, not only of African-American adolescent males, but of all students in the face of national legislation."[6]

For all the criticism of the federal education reform act, there is far more right with it than wrong with it — including the required testing. Unless we collect data through standardized testing, how can school districts know how well they are performing? Without diagnostics to show what's really broken, how will we know what to fix?

Similarly, we must take an analytical, data-driven approach to identify school districts that are failing and to take bold action to correct the problems. As the AFT noted, "Many schools are not educating students at the high levels needed to prepare them to lead successful and productive lives. It is also no secret that many students in these schools have been placed at an educational disadvantage as a result of social and economic factors beyond the purview of the educational system. In far too many cases, these conditions have been exacerbated by education policy decisions that deny schools the resources they need, allow poor management to continue unabated, and deprive school staff of quality professional development."[7]

AFT has published a list of indicators of a failing school district, which should be followed up with a more comprehensive investigation:

• Lack of academic standards

- Low student performance

- Lack of improvement over time

- High levels of disruption and violence

- High rates of student absenteeism

- High rates of staff absenteeism

- High dropout rates

- High rates of staff turnover

- A negative school atmosphere

There is an obvious, but terribly unfortunate, correlation between poorer school districts that cannot afford to pay a competitive wage and the quality and experience of the teachers they attract. An idealistic, young, but inexperienced teacher may go to an inner-city school to teach but often, after a year or two, seeks a position in a district with better pay and fewer challenges. This leads to high turnover (one of the AFT's symptoms of a failing district) and a staff that is disproportionately inexperienced.

Poor and minority children don't underachieve in school just because they often enter behind but also because the schools that are supposed to serve them actually shortchange them in the one resource they most need to reach their potential — high-quality teachers. "Research has shown that when it comes to the distribution of the best teachers, poor and minority students do not get their fair share," stated the Education Trust, which was established in 1990 by the American Association for Higher Education to encourage colleges and universities to support K–12 reforms.[8]

The Education Trust noted that students in high-poverty and high-minority schools are "disproportionately assigned" to new teachers — almost twice as often as children in low-poverty and/ or low-minority schools. The Trust also observed that students in high-poverty and high-minority schools are further "shortchanged when it comes to getting teachers with a strong background in the subjects that they are teaching." It added that classes in these schools "are more likely to be taught by 'out-of-field teachers' — those without a major or minor in the subject they teach."[9]

The problems may be most dramatic in failing school districts that have serious problems with teacher inexperience, high staff turnover, a lack of training and resources, and a student population that is performing poorly academically. However, school districts face challenges at every socioeconomic level. A wealthier school district that offers lucrative teacher salaries may attract more talented and experienced staff. Nonetheless, certain problems exist in virtually every district to some degree:

- *A lack of targeted, proven, preservice training for teachers — experienced and inexperienced alike — particularly to prepare them to teach reading.* Many teachers, including reading specialists, admit that they did not learn in college or university the skills, strategies, and techniques they need in the classroom to teach children how to read. They need to be given scientifically based knowledge about the process of learning to read and how directly and systematically to teach phonemic awareness, phonics, vocabulary development, oral reading fluency, and reading comprehension.

- *The "flavor of the month" initiative that is launched with great fanfare and then fades away, rather than meaningful inservice training and professional development.* Teachers who have been around for a while are understandably cynical when their districts announce new programs that will be the magical solution to the problem of illiteracy and reversing the dropout rate. Who wants to commit to something that may be abandoned in a year or two? However, when districts offer inservice training on teaching methods that are research based and have generated proven results in other districts, teachers need to keep an open mind and give the new approaches their best efforts.

- *School administrators' lack of accountability for the test data from their schools and lack of authority to work to improve that data.* Standardized testing is needed to determine where students are in their achievement of certain skills and subject matter. Taken together, student achievement provides a snapshot of a school's performance. As the saying in business goes, "Results don't lie." If standardized test scores are low, the school administration must be accountable for the problem and exercise the authority to address it head-on — even if it means staff changes, a new curriculum, or additional teacher training.

- *An unwillingness to analyze and address teachers' own problems with language mastery.* If approximately one-third of the general population experiences some degree of difficulty learning how to read, it only follows that at least some portion of the teaching population also has problems with the written word. Granted, this is a highly controversial topic, but unless we are willing to ask the tough yet necessary questions, we will only have excuses and rationalizations.

- *A lack of accountability on the part of colleges and universities for training teachers who will be able to educate our children, particularly those who have difficulties with reading.* These institutions of higher learning must commit to being an active part of the solution for addressing student illiteracy. It is a simple, indisputable fact that to have properly trained teachers in the classroom, colleges and universities must re-evaluate their curricula. Although many teachers gain important skills and needed training through inservice professional development, these resources could be much better applied if teachers began their careers with stronger foundations in reading instruction already in place.

## Boston University/Chelsea Partnership

In all ways, Chelsea, Massachusetts, was a district in crisis. The community, itself, was in distress, with an average annual income that was 44 percent below the state average. In 1988–89, more than half of the students who entered high school did not graduate; only a fifth of high school graduates planned to attend a four-year college; a quarter of teenage girls were pregnant or already mothers; and only a quarter of students took the Scholastic Achievement Tests (SATs), and those did not distinguish themselves. A detailed study of Chelsea schools revealed that the changes needed were so extensive, and local politics so intrusive, that a ten-year period of management by an outside agent would be required.

In March 1989, the Chelsea School Committee committed to a bold and innovative plan: a partnership with Boston University. A long-term program of educational reform was put in place to prepare children to learn, equip teachers to teach, restructure the curriculum, and promote community involvement. All parties had a strong commitment for the long haul. Even when the city of Chelsea went into financial receivership in September 1991, Boston University remained in the partnership, although the city could not afford to fund the school system as it had in the past. The university established A Different September Foundation to help make up for the deficit and fund other initiatives. The partnership between Chelsea schools and Boston University was so successful that it was extended until 2003 and again until 2008.

Looking back on his five years as superintendent of Chelsea, from 1995 through 2000, Dr. Douglas Sears acknowledged that it was "the most compelling experience of my life." Now associate provost and assistant to the president at Boston University, Dr. Sears has a wealth of experience to share with other school districts based on his involvement in the Chelsea partnership.

Among the lessons he learned was to identify and prioritize what needs to be done — even though at the beginning, everything appears to be critical. This means engaging in some form of triage to do what absolutely must be done first among all the pressing needs that demand attention. By not giving into the temptation to try to do everything at once, school districts will be less likely to feel overwhelmed and underprepared.

"We tried to do too much too early. We didn't get as clear with each other and the community about what we wanted to accomplish in curriculum and other goals," added Dr. Sears, who was the second person from the university to serve as superintendent in Chelsea and who held the post the longest.

The Chelsea district's needs were deep and serious, including a curriculum overhaul and better standards and compensation for teachers. At the same time, it needed to replace all of its school buildings soon for the sake of student and teacher safety, comfort, and effectiveness. With changes in school configuration came shifts in student populations, staffing changes for teachers and principals, new bus routes — all of which had to be explained to parents, many of whom did not speak English or for whom English was a second language.

A long-term plan needed to be driven top-down, which meant that administrators — and in this case, superintendents appointed by the partnership — would need to exercise authority and be accountable. This balance between accountability and authority is essential, Dr. Sears explained, as school districts implement long-term solutions to entrenched problems. "One of my rules is that authority and accountability have to align. Superintendents and principals are responsible if something goes wrong, if something does not meet the standards. If they are not given legitimate authority to actually get the work done and to make the personnel changes, then they end up being the scapegoats," he added.

> *Expenditures for education are investments*
> *in educational capital... the moral and*
> *intellectual capital of the nation.*
>
> — Dr. John Silber, former President
> of Boston University[10]

As the Chelsea partnership committed to a turnaround of the district schools, 17 goals were identified. These goals responded directly to major problems that were identified at Chelsea. Moreover, these same goals were the standards by which progress was measured over time.

Three of the goals were to revitalize the curriculum; establish programs for professional development of school personnel and expand learning opportunities for parents; and improve student test scores. Clearly, these three objectives were interrelated. Improving the curriculum would require professional development for staff and parental support and understanding. With new curriculum and better teaching methods, the expectation was that student scores would improve.

"Inservice training is very important, but it needs to be good. We had a good early orientation, summer retreats, and a palette of inservice offerings or professional development," Dr. Sears explained. "We tried not to do it during the day to protect the instructional time."

Other goals were straightforward: to decrease the dropout rate, increase average daily student attendance, increase the number of high school graduates, increase the number of high school graduates who went on to attend four-year colleges, and increase the number of job placements for high school graduates. Another goal was to develop a community school program that offered before-school, after school, and summer programs to students, and also offered adult education classes.

Other goals of the partnership were to identify and encourage the utilization of community resources; establish programs that link home and school; decrease teacher absenteeism; improve financial management and expand the range of operating funds; increase salaries and benefits for all staff and raise the average teacher salary to be competitive; construct effective recruiting, hiring, and retention procedures for all staff; establish student assessment designs and procedures to assist in monitoring programs and to act as incentives for staff; and expand and modernize physical facilities.

Reviewing the list of the goals set forth by the Boston University/Chelsea Partnership, what is most notable is how concrete they are. A school district's mission, after all, is fairly straightforward and does not change much from year to year. It is to teach all learners, from kindergarten through grade 12, providing them with the instruction they deserve and the resources they need to graduate and for a majority to pursue postsecondary education.

"You can get diverted by ideas. We have been at our best in Chelsea when we concentrated on the basics — making sure that students are showing up, hiring good teachers and making sure they show up, and making sure conditions for teachers are better," Dr. Sears said.

Today, the partnership has reported that, even as enrollments in Chelsea increased, average systemwide daily attendance has reached 94 percent. Scores on the SAT, the Iowa Literacy Test, the

Massachusetts Comprehensive Assessment System (MCAS), and Advanced Placement exams all showed "steady improvement."[11]

Chelsea continues to face challenges, including budgetary. For example, federal Title I funds have been cut back, although the district has received additional monies from the Massachusetts state legislature. Still, the partnership has remained firm in moving forward in Chelsea, where its population of "urban, at-risk, limited English, and minority students" now has the benefit of a well-run and efficient system.

## Better Training for Better Teachers

As we look at turnaround districts like Chelsea — and even others that have been operating fairly well over the years — we see an important, common strategy: better training makes for better teachers. With better teaching, improved student achievement follows. In particular, inservice training helps to put teachers on the proverbial same page when it comes to such things as curriculum and teaching practices. The sad reality about inservice, however, is that it often means "unteaching" what teachers learned at colleges and universities about reading instruction and introducing them to methods and strategies that, according to the experts, they should have been taught in the first place.

For reading curricula, inservice is essential for rolling out a specific approach districtwide, instead of having teachers apply what they know or what they've gleaned on their own. Many experienced teachers, including reading specialists, admit that inservice allowed them to hone their skills and to master new techniques related to instruction — for example, moving from whole language to a scientifically based approach that stresses direct and systematic instruction in the essential components of reading instruction.

Understandably, many longtime teachers are skeptical when it comes to new curricula, approaches, and teaching methods. They have seen so many programs come and go. Therefore, when districts decide to launch new programs — whether in reading or another academic area — administrators had better be prepared to counter teacher resistance with solid information and thorough explanations.

"You need to show teachers something that will work and explain the benefits in a common-sense way. If you do, they'll implement it because teachers are there to work hard and to teach children," Dr. Sears advised. "Just show them what the new program will do and why they should teach it to the children. A lot of what has been done in the name of education reform has been junk. Most of what works in education now is not new. It's not about a new idea, but getting clarity about what needs to be done, and then getting down to do it and assessing the results."

The National Reading Panel determined that inservice professional development for teachers results in "significantly higher achievement for their students," adding that these findings were true for both established and new teachers. "More research is needed, however, to determine the best combinations of inservice and preservice training, the appropriate length of each, and how teachers should be supported over the long term to improve student performance."[12]

Reading begins in early childhood. Kindergarten has the foundation protocol of teaching the 26 letters of the alphabet that make up 44 sounds and 6 types of syllables. Although some teachers fear drilling young children, the needed repetition can be made fun. Teachers can engage students with stories and conversations to build their oral vocabularies.

Using assessments, teachers can group children with similar skills, including those who need remedial instruction. One size doesn't fit all. Skill assessments can direct the type of instruction that a student needs to strengthen identified weak areas. An experienced teacher can sometimes do this without a curriculum; however, not every student has an experienced teacher. Furthermore, every student should have equal access to a structured, evidenced-based reading program.

*Learning how to read is not natural or easy for most children. Reading is an acquired skill.*

— American Federation of Teachers,
June 1999 report, *Teaching Reading Is Rocket Science*[13]

With the range of students in our classrooms today, primary teachers, especially, must have a clear understanding of how to teach reading to children. They need to have knowledge of the literature of reading research and an understanding of the concepts and methodology of teaching a student to read that is consistent with the latest findings of research in reading instruction. They need to know how the brain is affected by various kinds of instruction and know which reading programs work and which don't. Teachers have always been "diagnosticians" and thus are able to analyze a learner's skills and know how to improve them. The result of the analysis is the development of a logical course to build the foundational skills for the struggling reader. This provides a sense of peace and hope—for the teacher, the student, and the parents. Students who have language-processing deficiencies need additional help, and that should be provided early on in their schooling. Teachers must have access to scientifically developed tools to teach such children how to decode the written word, to understand the sounds represented by letters and groups of letters, and, ultimately, to read.

## Testing Teachers

When I was a teacher, I did not belong in a classroom. As painful as that statement is for me, it's the truth. I did not have the adequate literacy skills to teach students — especially those who needed help that I could not give them. Therefore, as I approach the controversial topic of testing teacher skills, I know the lay of this land. I know what it's like to be a teacher who struggled with the written word, in my case because of a severe language-processing disorder. And, at least anecdotally, I know I am not alone. There are teachers for whom the written word is a challenge, whether because of dyslexia or another language-processing deficiency.

Dr. Cheesman related from her experience at a Connecticut adult literacy clinic that one of the adult learners was a certified teacher who was very ashamed of her low level of literacy. To hide her lack of proficiency, the teacher worked only with very young students. After two years at the clinic, the woman was able to read college-level material. As an adult learner, I applaud this teacher for recognizing her deficiency and committing the time and effort to overcome it.

Teachers' fear of being tested reminds me of something that happened several years ago when one of California's largest school districts adopted Open Court, a phonics-based curriculum for reading, which was good news. A teacher trainer, who had more than 25 years' experience teaching Open Court and training teachers, was doing the inservice training for this large school district. When I met him at a conference and asked how the training was going and, specifically, what the teachers' pre- and post-tests were showing, he said the district wouldn't allow him to do any pre- and post-testing of the teachers. Shocked, I asked him why. He told me, "They don't really want to deal with the truth." The school district didn't want to face how unprepared their teachers might be, many of the teachers didn't want to acknowledge their own deficiencies, and their union protected and supported them.

Although I do not have statistics on the number of credentialed teachers who have struggled with learning deficiencies, including reading problems, I can cite an article from the *Annals of Dyslexia* that noted, "Students with LD (learning disabilities) are no longer a rare phenomenon in higher education. One of the major factors leading to the increase in enrollment of students with LD is the enactment of Section 504 of the Rehabilitation Act of 1973," which mandates that institutions of higher education that receive federal funds cannot discriminate on the basis of a disability. "To date, no large-scale, systematic research has investigated the major areas of study among students with LD in higher education," the article continued. "However [one study] reported that 24 percent of the students with LD who were receiving support services at a small, private, competitive Midwestern college had chosen a major in education. Moreover, approximately half of these students chose to certify in special education. Similar data were found in a large, doctoral degree granting university; there, 25 percent of the undergraduate and graduate students with documented learning disabilities were in teacher preparation programs."[14]

I do not doubt the motivation of these individuals with learning disabilities who decided to become special education teachers. Having experienced the frustration of special ed when they were students, many are highly empathic and passionate about helping young students. At the risk of offending those who have these high ideals and motivations, I must state that unless teachers have specifically addressed their own learning deficiencies, they cannot adequately help these students.

When I was an adult student of the Lindamood-Bell Clinic, one of my best teachers was a young man named Steve. A clinician, Steve came from a family of doctors and for a long time had his sights on medical school, although decoding and comprehension problems held him back. Instead, he enrolled in Lindamood-Bell for two years of intensive remediation and eventually became a teacher — most importantly, a teacher who had been diagnosed and received specific instruction to overcome his deficiencies. In fact, Steve was one of the best clinicians I had the privilege to work with, even though his difficulties had been as severe as mine. What this shows is, just because a person has a learning deficiency doesn't mean that she can't teach. However, that learning deficiency must be addressed first. It is unacceptable, I believe, for an elementary school teacher to have the "accommodation" of someone else reading to the children in the classroom. This is not fair to the children or to the teacher, who deserves help to overcome the deficiency.

> *Researchers consistently have found that*
> *a teacher's level of literacy, as measured*
> *by vocabulary skill and other standardized*
> *assessments, is related to student achievement.*
>
> — The Education Trust[15]

Teachers typically are opposed to such measures as assessments of their skills, tests of their knowledge and abilities, and other means to certify their qualifications. Such scrutiny makes people uncomfortable, and those of us who have struggled with a learning deficiency of some type have learned to hide to protect ourselves. However, teachers need to address their own deficiencies to elevate the profession as a whole and command the respect, recognition, and compensation that they deserve.

A teacher in a California state prison, who was well liked and well respected by his colleagues and students alike, taught automotive repair and was highly knowledgeable about the subject matter, which had few reading requirements. He was also an adult student working to mastery literacy. When he finally learned how to read, he was so overjoyed by this accomplishment that he told his supervisor. He was fired. Like so many people, including myself for many years, he was trapped in an education system that did not allow him to admit his weakness. Luckily for this teacher, he was able to appeal his supervisor's decision and prevail. He kept teaching—and he kept learning as an adult student to advance his literacy skills.

Now it's time for us to come clean about what we all know: the better equipped the teacher, the more likely students are to succeed. As the Education Trust stated, "Two reviews of the research on teacher quality concluded that teachers' levels of literacy accounted for more of the variance in student achievement than any other measured characteristic of teachers… The findings are so robust and so consistent that there is broad agreement that teachers' academic skills have a considerable impact on student achievement."[16]

## Where the Blame Rests

But what about the teacher who is highly literate, knows the subject matter, and is passionate about teaching? Indeed, these individuals are the ones the system needs the most. They have the knowledge to share and the commitment to the students, which makes their profession more than just a job. And yet, they, too, are being shortchanged by the system—in this case, the system of higher education.

Consider this story told by Dr. Carol Tolman, a national literacy expert and a national trainer for the Language Essentials for Teachers of Reading and Spelling (LETRS) program. While doing Christmas shopping in December 2005, she met a young woman who, between customers in a busy store, was trying to study from a book on reading and literacy. When it was Dr. Tolman's turn to be waited on, she asked about the book. The young woman explained that she had just graduated from a well-known school with an education degree and wanted to become a reading teacher. As she prepared for the certification examination, she was dismayed by the amount of material she would be tested on that she had never even heard about in college.

"She told me, 'I just went through four years of school and now I have to take this certification test, and I don't know any of this stuff in the test preparation book,'" Dr. Tolman explained. "She gave me the example of phonology, saying she had only heard it mentioned once — and that was by a substitute instructor when her regular professor was out sick."

Dr. Tolman agreed to meet with the young woman on her break and gave her a crash course in phonology and phonemic awareness to help her study. Beyond this remarkable chance encounter between the young graduate and the national reading expert is the sad fact that this young woman had gone to college expecting to be adequately trained and educated to become a teacher — yet when she faced her certification examination, she was not prepared. "The higher education system, in many instances, fails our future teachers. We truly have to open our eyes and our minds to address this crisis in America," Dr. Tolman added.

Colleges of education have failed to adequately train teachers in how to teach reading. Early-education researchers point out that each year, thousands of graduates from these colleges of education flood into first-grade classrooms all across America, and for the most part, they have been taught that direct and systematic instruction in the essential components of reading instruction is not only wrong but harmful to students. Unless and until there is a revolution in the content of preservice teacher education in reading instruction, we are fighting a losing battle.

"The buck stops in the schools of education," observed Robert Sweet, president and cofounder of the National Right to Read Foundation and recently retired professional staff member of the U.S. House of Representatives. "Colleges of education have been specifically tasked with providing teachers with knowledge of how to teach a child how to read. Most have dropped the ball. Not only are they not doing their job, they are making things worse."

The scientific findings both shine a light on the failure of and provide direction for our system. On the hopeful side of things, there have been decades of research into how to teach children to read. On the other side, however, the education field, by and large, continues to ignore these findings. In a study, the National Council on Teacher Quality noted that the "science of reading has led to a number of breakthroughs that can dramatically reduce the number of children destined to become functionally illiterate or barely literate adults. By routinely applying the lessons learned from the scientific findings to the classroom, most reading failure could be avoided." In fact, the study noted, the current failure rate of about 20 percent to 30 percent could be reduced to as little as 2 percent to 10 percent, in the primary grades at least.

However, a study of 72 institutions of higher learning that educate and train teachers found a shocking gap between what the science of reading has proven and what future teachers are being taught. "Almost all of the 72 institutions in our sample earned a 'failing' grade, even though a passing grade was possible if a professor devoted less than 20 percent of the lectures to the science of reading," the study authors noted. Furthermore, the study found that much of current reading instruction for teachers is "incompatible with science."

"Many reading teachers and textbooks describe the process of becoming a reader as a natural, organic process, though there is no scientific basis supporting such a view for any child, even for children who seem to find it easy to learn how to read," the study added. "Many courses indicate that exposing children to literature that speaks to their own experience will spark a natural development of reading skill; the right motivation is sufficient to build skill. However, these assertions are also unsupported by scientific evidence."[17]

Asked how such a gap between reading science and reading instruction could exist, Dr. Moats explained that a college or university's department of education may be staffed by a professor with a doctorate in education theory — but with little or no training in content. "There is a total division in the academic enterprise between people who are trained to think about reading as a kind of social, emotional, and humanistic activity — in which the student voice is valued and teachers have to discover their own philosophy, and there is no truth that resides outside — and the group of people who do the research," she added.

Dr. Tolman observed that, in higher education, reading instruction can become "wedded to an approach that may not be as research-based as they'd like it to be." Authorship of a particular reading program or curriculum can lead to a great deal of reticence to change. She added, however, that not all reading curricula have to be abandoned but instead should be expanded to include other elements based on reading research, such as the importance of phonemic awareness to establish a foundation in reading. Through phonemic awareness, young children (like all emerging readers, including adult learners) are able to build a foundation with speech sounds that will later support their decoding of an alphabetic system for both reading and writing.

Another possible approach would be to require that all teachers — regardless of subject area — be taught at least the fundamentals of reading instruction. Dr. John Strucker of the Harvard University Graduate School of Education observed that "regular teachers are getting fewer courses in reading or about reading than my parents got in teachers' college in the 1940s... It would be a good idea if all teachers, including those in physical education and art, as well as the content areas, were required to take courses in reading development," he added. "If all teachers had a basic understanding of how children learn to read and how to recognize reading difficulties, they would be better prepared to meet children's classroom instructional needs, and they would be better prepared to engage and contribute to discussions about reading difficulties with reading specialists, special education teachers, and parents."

The AFT has also called for "higher standards and substantive courses" for teacher preparation, noting that as these policies are adopted by colleges and universities, "the two million new teachers projected over the next decade may be equipped to minimize reading failure in all but a small percentage of students." AFT added, "Only recently has basic research allowed the community of reading scientists and educators to agree on what needs to be done. This new information about language, reading, and writing is just beginning to shape teacher preparation and instructional programs. This knowledge must also form the basis of in-service professional development for practicing teachers."[18]

## Call to Accountability

The reality of the failing system is a wakeup call to accountability. Each of us — whether parent, student, administrator, teacher, or policy maker — must do whatever it takes to effect change within the system, including holding others accountable. The failing system requires that teachers look honestly at their own strengths and weaknesses and get the help, training, and support they need — whether professional development or improvement of their own literacy. District-wide, teachers and administrators must commit to inservice training that works, based on scientifically proven tools and methodologies that make sense. Parents must play their part, too, taking an active interest in their children's education and modeling good, literate behaviors to the best of their abilities.

Ultimately, responsibility for the quality of education in our schools comes to rest on the doorstep of our institutions of higher learning. Colleges and universities must be held accountable for preparing teachers. It is time for policy makers in particular to put teacher-training programs to the test, holding them not only accountable but also responsible for how well our children are learning how to read.

## CHAPTER 8

# Teaching Our Teachers

Throughout this book, I have advocated for learners, both adults and children, to support the cause of their getting the literacy skills that they desire and deserve. As I've stated before, teaching children and adults to read requires properly trained teachers who have access to the latest research-based tools and techniques. Now I'm turning the tables. In this chapter, I am advocating for teachers — for these professionals to get the training they need do their jobs.

Putting teachers in classrooms without the research-based methodologies proven to work is grossly unfair. Without proper preparation and instruction, teachers face unfavorable odds of ever being successful. Add to that the very real struggles of this profession, from tightening school budgets to adversarial relationships with administrations, and it's no wonder that teachers so often feel burdened, frustrated, and unappreciated.

The greatest tribute we can give to teachers in particular and the teaching profession as a whole is to acknowledge their essential role in the delivery of literacy skills to every learner. In every venue in which literacy skills are taught, from the preschool through the adult learning center, the teacher is the essential element. For these teachers to succeed in their jobs and, more importantly, to feel successful in their chosen profession, they must be properly trained and equipped with proven, scientific research-based tools and methodologies.

Before going further, it is important to define what is meant by "scientifically based reading research." For that, we turn to the U.S. Department of Education's definition included in the No Child Left Behind Act. Scientifically based reading research must do the following:

- "Employ systematic, empirical methods that draw on observation or experiment

- Involve rigorous data analyses that are adequate to test the stated hypotheses and justify the general conclusions

- Rely on measurements or observational methods that provide valid data across evaluators and observers, and across multiple measurements and observations

- Be accepted by a peer-reviewed journal or approved by a panel of independent experts through a comparatively rigorous, objective, and scientific review."[1]

Let me also say at the outset of this chapter discussion that I come from a family of teachers. My father was a teacher, and I have teachers among my siblings and in my wife's family as well. I have nephews and nieces who are teachers. Thus, in my normal, day-to-day life, I'm well aware of the issues that teachers face. And I've heard from teachers over the years all the so-called reasons why students don't learn how to read. Students don't care or they won't try. They don't come in for extra help after school. Parents aren't aware, or they can't or won't help with homework.

These are not reasons; they are excuses. Finding a scapegoat in the blame game is a defeatist circle. We cannot point fingers at each other—teachers to parents to children to teachers and back again—and expect to get anywhere. The reason that children don't learn how to read in school is because teachers don't know how to teach them. I do not say this to condemn or blame anyone but to state the facts as I see them. When children—no matter what their socioeconomic background or how literate their parents—come into a classroom, teachers have a professional and a moral obligation to teach them. In some situations, parents are able to partner in the education process; in other cases, they cannot. Simply stated, parents who are not literate are not able to teach their children. For these children to learn how to read, schools must make even more of an effort for the sake of these youngsters and for all of society.

Teachers do face some formidable challenges in the classroom because of the natural learning demographics of their students. For example, we know that approximately one-third of learners will have some degree of difficulty learning how to read. Given this fact, it only makes sense that teachers be given the tools, resources, training, and proven methodologies to help them be successful in their mission to teach children. To approach it any differently is to set up for failure.

Over the years, I've said these same things to thousands of teachers. Often, I'm brought in as the motivational speaker who puts a human face on the problem of illiteracy and to enlighten them with real-life stories of what it's like when you can't read. The audience hears from Johnny the Innocent, the little boy who wanted so much to learn how to read like the other children, and from the Native Alien, who acted out his anger and frustration of not being able to read. Then Mr. Corcoran paints a vision of a world in which all learners are taught to read, write, and spell. Sometimes I inspire; sometimes I irritate.

I remember one of the most difficult audiences of teachers I ever addressed. It was October 1995, and the Sacramento City Unified School District had invited me to be the keynote speaker at a two-day inservice session on the topic of renewing and revitalizing a commitment to literacy. My audience was 3,000 teachers and other staff—the first time in more than a decade that the school district had brought all of its employees together for a meeting. The event was held at the Sacramento Convention Center, but to me it felt more like the coliseum of ancient Rome and I was about to be fed to the lions.

## An Unwelcome, but Necessary, Message

My speech in Sacramento came only a year after my memoir about being "the teacher who couldn't read" was released, and I was still fairly new on the speaking circuit. My emotions on the topic were still raw, and although I probably wouldn't have admitted it at the time, there was still much growth and healing ahead for me. My audience was also raw: teachers who were in the midst of contentious contract talks with the district and who had not received a pay raise in four years. District officials, too, were under very real pressure from the city government to improve schools. The mayor's commission on the city's schools in Sacramento had presented "strong recommendations" to the school district and also issued a "warning that it would not stand for inaction."[2]

These were strong words from city government to school district officials. (They also serve as an example of how, on the local, state, or federal level, lawmakers can put pressure on school districts to improve performance.) The commission's recommendations included demands "to produce educational results, to put aside internal differences, to identify resources to get children books and supplies, to clean up schools and to reach out to parents, especially those with limited English ability."[3]

Against this contentious backdrop, I was sent in to be a motivational speaker. Is it any wonder that my mission — to remind teachers that it is their job to teach children to read — wasn't exactly a welcome topic? A flyer that was handed out to all attendees brought that point home. I still have a copy of that flyer in my files. Across the top is the bold headline "Nobody Asked Us." The message was that for years, inservice days were planned with teacher input, but not this event. Referencing my message about literacy and the need to teach all learners, the flyer went on to say, "You are professionals who are working hard. You can and do teach reading. You have a lot to contribute. You are doing all this despite the fact that you have not had a raise in four years." I was handed a copy of the flyer as I entered the convention center. Then, once I got inside, I saw that virtually every person there was wearing a bright pink badge that said, "Read This: How About a Raise?"

Thanks goodness I'd had the foresight to ask Pat Lindamood, my teacher, my mentor, and my friend, to come with me. I wanted her beside me for moral support as much as for her expertise. I spoke for 45 minutes, and afterwards my reception from the elementary school teachers was very positive. I received good feedback and compliments from them after I spoke. They were the ones who stood in line later on to buy a copy of my book. One reason that the elementary teachers warmed to me was that I had told the secondary teachers that they had to stop blaming their colleagues for the failure of students to read. It was every teacher's job to teach children. Mind you, this was a dozen years ago when people weren't saying this as often as they are now.

Looking back, I should note that the responsibility for teaching children how to read rests squarely on the shoulders of elementary teachers. I'm not suggesting that a high school history teacher also teach reading. However, we are in crisis situation in our schools across America. Therefore, it is the responsibility of every teacher, regardless of subject area or specialty, to be knowledgeable enough about reading and how to detect deficiencies among students to be part of the solution. That history teacher in my example, therefore, should be on alert for students who are struggling with reading and be able to have an intelligent conversation with the school's reading resource team to advocate for that learner.

By and large, that day in Sacramento, the secondary teachers reacted coolly, apparently put off by my message. One of the questions I'm often asked in these presentations is how I hid my illiteracy from my teachers. At Sacramento, as I have in many other presentations, I told the truth, "Do you really think I hid the fact that I couldn't read from my teachers? Don't you think they knew?" I asked them. "Aren't there students in your classes today who can't read the textbook? Don't you know kids who are failing your classes because they can't read the materials and they have been passed along anyway thanks to social promotion?"

I knew this kind of talk was not going to help me win any popularity contests that day, but it needed to be said. These teachers were ignoring the fundamental issues of student achievement and lower literacy levels, while trying to steer attention toward their issue of pay.

This experience was a real eye-opener for me. It was the first time that I'd faced such a large and hostile audience, but it wasn't about me. The teachers were genuinely upset by the friction with administration over contract talks and the issue of pay. They weren't angry about literacy, nor were they rebelling about having to teach children. Granted, my message about literacy and a commitment to teach all learners rubbed some of these teachers the wrong way. But the bigger issue was that they felt underpaid and overburdened.

Across the country, school districts face the same contentious setups, with administrators on the one side talking about budget cuts and tight resources and, on the other side, teachers who feel unsupported and unappreciated. This doesn't mean we should back off on our demands that schools teach all learners. Rather, we need to help our teachers by giving them the information, training, and research-based tools that they need to do their jobs. Teachers should be trained in research-based techniques and approaches to teach all students, from those who take to reading naturally to those who will need specific help, from an entire class to small instructional groups to one-on-one. This information can be—and is—imparted through inservice training paid for by school districts, but a far better approach would be to give teachers this knowledge preservice—that is, before they begin teaching. Then inservice training can become the professional development that it is meant to be, to further enhance the skills and techniques of properly trained, empowered teachers.

> *True understandings require some*
> *measure of science and the willingness*
> *to seek information when making decisions.*
>
> —National Institute for Literacy,
> *What Is Scientifically Based Research?*
> *A Guide for Teachers*[4]

## Focusing on Teacher Education

Giving our teachers what they need will require change in the curricula taught at colleges and universities and in the licensure and certification requirements put in place by state authorities. In no way is this change meant to punish or penalize teachers. Rather, it is to make sure that they are being taught what works, that they are being given what they need, and that they are prepared in the best possible way for the difficult yet rewarding job that awaits them in the classroom.

This raises the question: What and how are our teachers being taught? As stated in Chapter 7 and as will be explored in several examples in this chapter, institutions of higher learning that train teachers must re-examine their curricula. Although professors at universities and colleges may resist this change — feeling, no doubt, that it is an imposition for them to be told what to teach — we must all be on the same page. Egos must be put aside for meaningful dialogue to take place. Educators at all levels, from the K–12 system through the universities, need to communicate openly about what scientifically conducted research has shown, what is needed in the classroom, and how teachers can reach out to all learners — especially the approximately 30 percent of the population who will have some difficulty learning how to read.

The National Council on Teacher Quality report, as discussed in Chapter 7, examined a representative sample of universities and colleges that train teachers, looking at curricula on the basis of the five components of effective reading instruction as identified by the National Reading Panel: phonemic awareness, phonics, fluency, vocabulary, and comprehension. "Given the strength of the scientific research in reading instruction, there is genuine cause for concern that only one in seven education schools appears to be teaching elementary teacher candidates the science of reading," the report stated. "Perhaps in twenty years, with some perspective, we will not be surprised to find that it took several decades for the science of reading to be absorbed into mainstream thinking and practice. But that kind of long-term perspective will mean that yet another generation of children will have been deprived of the benefits of the science."[5]

It is no longer acceptable for there to be such a wide gap between what teachers are taught and what they need to teach in the classroom. Steps must be taken now to align university curricula with classroom practices. Thankfully, such efforts are already underway. The solution, no doubt, will take time to implement. It is unreasonable to expect teacher candidates who have not been taught the required knowledge to be suddenly tested on it for state licensure. Yet until state licensure requires knowledge of research-based reading instruction (such as the five components identified by the National Reading Panel), there will be no way to pressure universities and colleges to change their curricula. Indeed, it is a chicken-and-egg dilemma with no clear clue of which should come first. The status quo, however, is no longer acceptable, and action must be taken.

## Maryland: Training for Professors

Over the past several years, the Maryland State Department of Education has taken bold steps to create greater alignment between the methodologies of reading instruction that are taught at colleges and universities and the knowledge that teacher candidates must demonstrate to be licensed in the state, as well as to maintain that licensure. Starting in 1999, universities and colleges in the state were required to submit their courses for approval, based on mandates from the state. Any reading program that did not meet the state criteria put the accreditation of the entire teacher-preparation program in jeopardy.

Although that was a tough stance to take, anything less would have perpetuated the problem in Maryland that is also plaguing other states. "We had teachers matriculating through teacher-preparation programs coming into our schools and requiring so much professional development to be effective as teachers of reading," explained Dr. Nancy S. Grasmick, state superintendent in Maryland. "Then we began looking at the results of our reading scores on standardized tests, and we saw that we were not accelerating the performance of our students."

Moreover, the state found that many teachers were not able to differentiate their approach based on the abilities and diagnostic profiles of students in their classrooms. "When we observed teachers in the classroom, few were able to do differentiated instruction in the classroom," Dr. Grasmick added. "I'm not talking about special-needs students, but random groups of students with whom the teacher ought to be able to do that type of differentiated instruction."

Maryland's response was to begin mandating a series of courses as part of the curricula in institutions of higher education. The courses had to be grounded in research-based reading methodologies, focusing on areas such as the processes and acquisition of reading, instruction of reading, materials for reading, and assessment for reading instruction.

Not only did Maryland target preparation programs to ensure that new teachers were better prepared, the state also required teachers who were already in the classroom to demonstrate they had the necessary knowledge to teach reading. These teachers have been given the option of either taking additional reading courses or — in lieu of courses — of passing an examination developed for the state by Educational Testing Services.

Admittedly, the state's actions and mandates met with resentment and resistance, particularly initially. However, the state's tough line on program approval meant that colleges and universities had to get on board or risk losing their state approval and accreditation. The state also has had the backing of key stakeholders from pre-K through college, as well as the secretary of higher education and the chancellor of the university system.

Over time, what began as an adversarial relationship at times has become more of a partnership between Maryland's school systems and higher education. For example, when the state revised its elementary course guidelines, it brought together reading professionals from higher education and school systems. "They worked together diligently. What we saw was that, as a group, they took a big step toward working with our state education department to lead this change," commented Dr. Virginia Pilato, director of certification and accreditation in Maryland. "That settled a lot of the antipathy we saw early on. It was professionally gratifying for them to work with their peers. It was a very powerful experience."

Maryland also used a grant from the federally funded Reading First program to bring in top-notch people, including Dr. Louisa Moats and Dr. Carol Tolman (see Chapter 7), to review Maryland course guidelines and provide training to school district and higher education faculty. "We have more to do, but we're on the right track," Dr. Grasmick commented. "We're not going to be satisfied until every teacher matriculating through these institutions and coming into the classroom is really being prepared."

The success of the program thus far can be seen in student achievement. Each of Maryland's 24 school systems has shown improvement in reading, and every subgroup has also shown improvement. State officials are convinced that improved teacher preparation is largely the reason. Dr. Grasmick shared the story of visiting a school where Reading First curriculum was put in place. Although 65 percent to 70 percent of the student population at the school is entitled to receive free meals or meals at a reduced cost (an indication of low-income level), student achievement has surpassed expectations. "If you see a school is doing well, you would expect a large group of students to be proficient, a smaller group being advanced, and a very small group being basic," she added. "In this school, which started at a very low level, the largest group was in advanced. It was just amazing."

## Colorado: Setting Standards and Examining Curricula

The State of Colorado has embarked on an initiative to examine the education and training that teachers are receiving to improve student performance. The foundation of this drive is the Colorado Basic Literacy Act, which was enacted by the Colorado General Assembly in 1997 with the goal of ensuring "that by third grade all students have the literacy skills essential for success in school and life." The act calls on local school districts to identify students who are reading below grade level and to provide them with "necessary reading interventions."[6]

Colorado recognized that to improve student performance, it had to look at the knowledge and training of its teachers at colleges and universities in the state. In 2006, the Colorado Reading Directorate (CRD) was formed and given the responsibility to review and evaluate applications for teacher-preparation program approval "in all areas touching on literacy." To accomplish this, literacy courses are reviewed by CRD to "ensure that teacher preparation programs address the most current scientific research on literacy standards, assessment and instruction."[7]

Dr. Debora L. Scheffel was appointed chair of the CRD and is also director of the state's Reading First program. Now, through the CRD, Dr. Scheffel is part of a team of educators who are working to close the achievement gap in the state by focusing on teacher preparation. Specifically, the CRD is evaluating all teacher-preparation programs offered by Colorado institutions of higher education, as well as designated agencies that have been approved by the Colorado State Board of Education to offer alternative licensure programs. These programs are reviewed to determine the inclusion of research-based tools and methodologies for teaching reading.

*Recent advances in scientific research in reading*
*have necessitated a sense of urgency to move knowledge*
*acquired from the convergence of research findings*
*into daily practice in the classrooms of Colorado.*

— Colorado Teacher Preparation Program,
*Approval Rubric and Review Checklist*
*for Literacy Courses* [8]

Authority for the curriculum review comes from the state's statutory responsibility to evaluate teacher-training programs. To carry out its mission to improve teacher preparation and student achievement, the CRD first had to develop a rubric by which to evaluate reading education programs. Using the initial rubric, the first programs were evaluated by the CRD starting in August and September 2006. As of early 2007, about 20 programs had been reviewed, with some variability in curricula. At some universities, programs are being enhanced to include more research-based reading methodologies, while at others, there has been a more significant overhaul of programs.

A college professor who has taught literacy in the schools of education at three universities in the state — most recently at the University of Northern Colorado — Dr. Scheffel said she believes the curriculum review by the CRD is a benefit to the colleges and universities by strengthening their teacher-preparation programs. Further, as teacher-preparation programs are aligned with research in reading instruction, the state can use its licensure requirements to determine if new teachers entering the field have the requisite knowledge and skills to teach all learners. "We want to ensure that teachers in these programs in the state or who are licensed from another state are able to show a threshold level of knowledge in the area of teaching reading," she explained.

As teacher preparation and licensure are put into place, Dr. Scheffel believes the state can move forward with another "leverage point" to enhance teacher effectiveness and close the achievement gap among students: namely, inservice training for teachers who are already in the field. "We know that professional development for teachers has been weak or inconsistently strong. The question now becomes, how can we make it better so that when teachers are asked to renew their licenses, we make sure that the hours they have put in [for continuing education requirements] really do help make students successful," she added.

Admittedly the concept of the CRD and the curriculum review has met with some resistance and outright criticism. One can see how some professors might feel as if Big Brother is watching what they're doing a little too closely and dictating what must be taught. Such resistance is understandable given our human nature, but it cannot be a permanent roadblock to such necessary steps.

Dr. Scheffel also acknowledged that universities and colleges in the state have been underfunded in the past, which has made it more difficult for them to do their job. The purpose of the CRD review is not to be heavy-handed, she said, but to help the institutions of higher education to utilize their resources more effectively with assistance and partnership from the state.

Dr. Elaine Cheesman, who is on the faculty at the University of Colorado–Colorado Springs in the special education department and also serves on the CRD, explains that she has exposure to "three sides" of the CRD. First, she served on the directorate committee that developed the rubric. Second, she now is part of the committee that evaluates college and university syllabi. Third, as a professor, she has to create her own syllabus. Yet she's committed to these necessary changes to prepare teachers for the task and responsibilities of teaching children to read. Ultimately, she says, the authority — and the responsibility — rests with the states. "It's the duty of colleges of education to prepare teachers, but they don't license the teachers — the state does," she added.

Dr. Scheffel believes that by engaging the colleges and universities in productive dialogue, the process will be seen as positive — not punitive. "Without that positive attitude and buy-in from the teaching preparation programs, it won't be successful. Yes, you can handle something legislatively and people will comply by the letter of the law. But we want to get people to buy into it, who want to participate in it. Otherwise, this will just be a compliance issue," she added.

For example, she noted, the CRD is hosting research forums several times a year to engage constituents in a legitimate discussion of the implications of scientific research. Nationally known researchers are invited to present their work, and members of institutions of higher education and school districts are invited to attend.

## A National Approach to Teacher Training?

More states must be willing to take the bold moves that Maryland and Colorado have undertaken to close the gap between what teacher candidates are taught at colleges and universities and what they need to teach in the classroom. Unless our teachers are properly trained in the latest, proven, and scientific-based research, the achievement gap between haves and have-nots in our schools will persist. Learners will continue to struggle, and school districts will lose ground.

The only approach is systemic change, both at the university level where tomorrow's teachers are taught and in the K–12 classrooms where today's teachers are working. Preservice training in proven, research-based methods is essential for the future. But more must be done now. We cannot wait until the next cycle of teachers graduate and begin teaching—honing their skills that may take a few years to develop more fully with experience — to bring research-based methodologies into schools today.

> *Even if by some miracle a scientifically proven*
> *reading curriculum was adopted by the schools,*
> *teachers would need extensive retraining.*
> *This would entail workshops and ultimately*
> *a complete overhaul of elementary education*
> *departments in nearly every university.*
>
> —Diane McGuinness, PhD,
> *Why Our Children Can't Read*
> *and What We Can Do About It*[9]

Maryland officials are interested in leading a drive to push for greater standardization on a national level in reading education. The model is the reform that took place nearly a century ago in medical schools, thanks to the efforts of an educator named Abraham Flexner. His report, *Medical Education in the United States and Canada,* more commonly called the Flexner Report, triggered reform in the standards and curricula of medical schools in North America. Some medical schools closed down, and those that remained conformed their curricula to Flexner standards.

Dr. Grasmick would like to take a "Flexner approach" to reading curricula across the country with Maryland as the testing ground. Although this concept did generate some initial interest, she noted, it has not advanced. She is hoping, however, that increased focus on Reading First curriculum development in other states might spark the drive to apply the Flexner approach to all accredited colleges and universities where teachers are trained.

## The Whole Language Debate

The discussion of reading curricula at universities and colleges brings to the foreground the debate around the whole language approach to teaching children to read. As a child who did not learn how to read in the classroom and an adult who learned how to read through a systematic, research-based approach grounded in phonics, I have strong views. I am living proof of the National Reading Panel's findings that the foundation of reading instruction comprises phonemic awareness, phonics instruction, fluency, vocabulary, and comprehension.

As Dr. Diane McGuinness, a cognitive developmental psychologist and researcher in reading instruction, observed in her book *Why Our Children Can't Read and What We Can Do About It*, children must be trained to hear the individual sounds, or phonemes, of their language. "They must be able to disconnect or 'unglue' sounds in words in order to use an alphabetic writing system."[10]

Dr. McGuinness further states that, based on research in the classroom and the clinic, "when the sequence of reading and spelling instruction is compatible with the logic of the alphabet code and with the child's linguistic and logical development, learning how to read and spell proceeds rapidly and smoothly for all children and is equally effective for poor readers of all ages."

Her findings, she says, are outside of the debate between whole language and phonics. While I respect Dr. McGuinness and her work, I would like to place the emphasis on systematic phonics-based instruction and other research-based methodologies as a contrast to whole language. Whole language is based on a belief that exposing children to reading will help teach them to read. The biggest drawback to whole language is that it is not scientifically based and, in fact, runs completely contrary to the findings of research. Reading is a skill to be learned. We are not born with the ability to read; otherwise, there would be no need to be taught. In fact, there is evidence that the scientific approach can teach all but 3 to 5 percent of the population in the first few grades of school.[11]

In her book *Overcoming Dyslexia: A New and Complete Science-Based Program for Reading Problems at Any Level*, Dr. Sally Shaywitz, professor of pediatrics at Yale University School of Medicine, makes the point that effective reading programs teach children about phonics systematically and explicitly. "There is no subtle or subliminal teaching here; children are not left to their own devices," Dr. Shaywitz wrote. "In general, systematic phonics programs also directly teach letter-sound relationships… Children are taught to transform letters into sounds and then blend (synthesize) the sounds together to form a pronounceable word."[12]

She contrasts this systematic approach to whole language, which does not focus on the sound of the words but on meaning and context. "It is assumed that reading is acquired naturally, just as speech is (which is, as we know, an incorrect assumption). In this view, letter-sound relationships will be learned naturally, seemingly by osmosis, as children are surrounded by literature and exposed to printed materials," Dr. Shaywitz explained.

With a systematic phonics instruction, children are taught that the clues to a word lie within it, so that a word can be analyzed and sounded out. In whole language, the clues are external to the word, meaning children are supposed to guess or somehow derive the meaning of a word from the context or even the illustrations in the story. Again, sound science stands on the side of phonics for all learners and especially those for whom reading is a struggle.

"The National Reading Panel found that children who are taught phonics systematically and explicitly make greater progress in reading than those taught with any other type of instruction," Dr. Shaywitz wrote. "The panel found that beginning the teaching of phonics in kindergarten or first grade produces the best results. Once a child demonstrates that she has some understanding of how spoken language works, it is time to learn how letters link to these sounds. In general, phonics instruction extends over two school years. All children benefit from it."[13]

Ample evidence shows that research-based reading curricula work best for all learners.[14] I sought out the advice and perspective of experts in research-based reading curricula for their perspective on the whole language debate.

Dr. Scheffel of the CRD explained that the major drawback to whole language is that it is a philosophy-based practice grounded in the belief that reading is a natural skill. Unlike speaking, however, using the written language is not a natural skill. Rather, students need to be taught explicitly how to read. "Reading is not going to happen by osmosis," she added.

Whole language poses a major problem for many students, including the approximately one-third of all learners who will have some difficulty with the written word. For these learners, deciphering the 26 letters of the alphabet and the 44 phonemes made up of those letters must be taught directly.

"Some students do deduce those structures of language, but those students are few and far between, and they are not the ones who struggle in reading," Dr. Scheffel added. "All students can benefit from systematic, explicit, and intensive instruction to master these skills, but those students who struggle with reading will likely not be successful without this type of instruction to acquire proficiency in reading."

Robert Sweet, Jr., president and cofounder of the National Right to Read Foundation (NRRF), retired professional staff member of the U.S. House of Representatives, and former acting director for the National Institute of Education, spoke strongly against the use of whole language to teach children how to read. "Brain imaging studies have confirmed that whole language instruction affects the right hemisphere of the brain, where memory and picture images are stored," he said. "Intensive instruction in systematic phonics, on the other hand, programs the left hemisphere of the brain where sound/symbol relationships are learned and stored. That is why it is so important for little children beginning in kindergarten and first grade be taught correctly."

A *Time* magazine article discussed the areas of the left side of the brain that are key to reading. They can be described in layperson's terms as the "phoneme producer," the "word analyzer," and the "automatic detector." Using MRI, the article stated, scientists learned that beginning readers rely most on the phoneme producer and the word analyzer parts of the left hemisphere. Then, as readers become more skilled, the automatic detector becomes more active, allowing readers to recognize familiar words on sight. "As readers progress, the balance of the symphony shifts and the automatic detector begins to dominate," the article explained. "If all goes well, reading eventually becomes effortless."[15]

Once children understand the "code" to the point of decoding being an automatic process, they can unlock any word in the English language, Sweet explained. Whole language, however, does not provide that to students, and it is actually damaging to those who struggle with learning how to read.

As we continue our battle to prevent and eradicate illiteracy, we must fearlessly take on the whole language debate. It still boggles my mind that, in the face of such indisputable scientific evidence, this debates continues at all. Could it be that those who have the power to change things really haven't read the research, or are they so arrogant that they stick to their ways in spite of it?

We need to support and demand the inclusion of systematic phonics instruction in our schools consistent with the findings of the National Reading Panel and in line with the philosophy of the Reading First program for K–3 students. Otherwise, far too many children will be at risk for low literacy, becoming adults who lack the skills they need to succeed in life.

"Yes, we need to help the current population of adults who have been damaged by whole language, but if we are to ever stop the uninterrupted flow of new children into the system ... we must shut off the spigot of illiteracy at the source," Mr. Sweet noted. "That is what Reading First is all about: shut off illiteracy at the source so that we no longer damage children and send them into adulthood handicapped for life."

In the midst of the debate around reading programs in school districts and curricula at colleges and universities, we cannot lose sight of the purpose — that is, to ensure our children learn how to read. We can talk all we want about academic freedom on the university campus or the need for teachers to be creative in the classroom, but the bottom line is the performance of the students. If a significant percentage of our children fail to acquire the necessary reading and writing skills they need to advance in school and in life, then the system has failed. A failed system must be overhauled. The number one focus in any education reform must be to teach all learners how to read.

Advocates, researchers, educators, professors, parents, and community leaders at every level must keep the spotlight of attention on this drive to improve our students' performance. That requires more effective and empowered teachers who are given the tools they need. Professionals in the classroom should demand nothing less. Those who have spent four years and thousands of dollars receiving an education from an accredited college or university have the right to be properly prepared for the challenge that awaits them.

The ball is now in the states' courts, to use their authority through state approval and licensure to examine what and how teachers are being trained. The lives of the children in those states demand it. As Dr. Grasmick poignantly observed, "If a child cannot read in today's world, that child has no window for opportunity."

CHAPTER 9

# A Vision for the Future

Throughout this book, I have painted a vision of what is possible, of collaborative efforts to close the literacy gap for children and adults. The experts interviewed have offered their wisdom and advice on what needs to be done at every level, from the preschool to the university. Now, in this chapter, I will share some scenes from what is already being done. However small or large, these endeavors chip away at the obstacles of illiteracy and open the pathway to the bridge to literacy.

Some are global and others are local, but in every instance, they show what is needed: commitment on the part of literate people to share what they have and what they know with those who cannot read and write. Yes, we need the power of Capitol Hill and the mandate from state legislatures to back literacy efforts. The grassroots, however, is more powerful than it realizes. This is where the tutor meets the adult learner and where the properly trained teacher opens the eyes and ears of the struggling child to the beauty, joy, and power of the written word.

One of the most poignant examples of literacy in action on the community level is Highlands, North Carolina. I did not know anyone in Highlands before I was contacted by telephone nearly two years ago, but now I consider it a privilege to be acquainted with many fine people in this community. Highlands is a community blessed with natural beauty, a place that offers "a mountain respite" to visitors and residents. It is a retirement community with residents who are both well educated and from professional backgrounds.

As I also discovered about Highlands, it is a community with heart. I first received a call from Breta Stroud, director of the Literacy Council of Highlands, in 1995. Newly hired in her position, she made up for what she acknowledged was a lack of experience in the literacy field with great enthusiasm, commitment, and an orientation of serving others, which had come from working in the service industry, including restaurants, over the years. From the first moment we spoke, I knew this was a very bright woman who knew how to connect things. She had read my book and wanted to brainstorm how to get me to Highlands to raise awareness of literacy issues in the local community. Although Highlands has a highly educated and literate population, many people in the outlying rural areas shoulder the double burdens of high poverty and low literacy.

Ms. Stroud had an idea: Highlands had a new Community Read program, which is like a townwide book club. One book is chosen each month, which is read by everyone who wants to participate. Discussion groups are then held throughout the community. She wanted to make my first book a Community Read project. I didn't hear from her again for nearly a year, but when she called back, it didn't surprise me at all that she had managed to bring her idea to fruition. Pitching the idea to various groups in the community, such as the local library, schools, and churches, Stroud had found the way. The local Rotary Club offered tremendous support.

(As will be discussed later in the chapter, Rotary International is providing exceptional support worldwide for literacy.)

In September 2006, I traveled to Highlands, a place I had never visited before. From the moment I arrived, it felt like a second home to me. Many of the people in town had read my book and were eager to discuss it with me. I made four or five presentations to groups throughout the community, at schools and churches. I have spoken many times in the past to local Rotary Clubs, especially in California. Because this service organization holds its meetings at lunch during the workweek, programs are short but well attended. I knew from this experience that I would have about 20 minutes to speak and then everyone would return to their jobs and businesses. Not so in Highland. Many Rotarians stayed long after my program was over to talk with me.

Everywhere I turned in Highland, people were eager to engage in a dialogue about the problem of illiteracy and what could be done about it. What also impressed me was that, at many of the presentations, I saw some of the same faces. This was a community committed to action. Also striking was the fact that most of the people were not advocating for their children, their families, or themselves. Instead, they were called to action because they were alarmed at the high levels of illiteracy in the surrounding community, as reflected in the Literacy Council's statistics. When the council was founded in 1992, a literacy survey of the local area found that one-third of the adult population in Macon County did not have a high school diploma and almost 15 percent of those adults had less than a ninth-grade education.

Today, the Literacy Council is small but thriving with a full-time executive director. It stretches its modest budget dollars with reduced rent and continued support from the Rotary Club, which offered $2,500 in seed money to found the Stroud council, as well as support from local churches, merchants, businesses, and residents. When asked about the work of the council, Breta Stroud is eager to credit others in the community for taking up this cause so enthusiastically. "The council would not be able to conduct its daily business without the tireless efforts of its volunteer tutors, who give of their time and energy with big hearts and intelligent minds — and without financial compensation," she said.

To me, Highlands provided a snapshot of what can — and is — being done on the local level to make real inroads in the fight against illiteracy. We need many more communities like Highlands, where there is a real awareness of the problem and the commitment to find and implement a solution. The good people of Highlands whom I met did not think it was just the job of the school district or the local library or some other party to teach adults and children to read. They looked at themselves and asked the question: What can we do to help?

The Literacy Council offers several programs: afterschool tutoring, GED, English as a second language (ESL), and adult literacy. The biggest program is the afterschool tutoring with more than 70 students enrolled. The council also partners with a local community college to offer GED and ESL classes. It uses tutorial and language-learning software in its new computer lab. Interestingly, the adult literacy program at Highlands is its smallest. When I visited Highlands, it had only one adult student, and a few months later, it signed up a second learner. Reading that, one might feel discouraged, or even a bit cynical, and believe that a program so small doesn't deserve all the accolades that I'm heaping on it. But read on. In grassroots efforts such as in Highlands, everyone agreed that learning to read was the most important skill. And in Highlands, the community rallied around the one man who was the program's first adult learner.

When this man first came to the Literacy Council in 2004, he had virtually no reading skills whatsoever. He could not recognize letters or even read his own street sign. After enrolling in the adult literacy program, he began attending tutoring sessions five days a week — after working a full day. Three years later, he is still committed to daily tutoring sessions through the program. With the help of three volunteer tutors, he logged more than 600 hours of tutoring time — and counting. He has completed all 12 levels of the Wilson Reading Program and is learning how to type using the software in the computer lab. In 2006, he passed a major milestone when, for the first time, he was able to vote in an election.

When I heard about this adult learner's success story, I knew that I, too, had to reach out to this fellow traveler on the bridge. Through my foundation, I was able to link this learner with Marianne Arling, who heads the foundation's instruction program. Among her many talents as a teacher (and I'll be writing more about her in the Epilogue) is her skill as a trained evaluator and tutor. She has worked with both school-aged and adult learners via distance learning, using a special online software program. This program enabled Ms. Arling, who is in Colorado, to work with the Highlands student in North Carolina. She tested the adult learner and devised a program to continue his literacy education. In addition, she trained eight of the Highlands tutors in the online program, giving them coaching that will help them as they reach out to more students in their local community. As a result of my visit to Highlands, Breta Stroud later traveled to Colorado to observe Marianne Arling's tutoring program firsthand to see how Highlands's efforts could be expanded.

As I observed in Highlands, the whole community rejoiced with the accomplishment of this one learner as another person crossed the bridge to literacy. Rather than feeling smug satisfaction over the success of this "poster child," the opposite occurred. Highlands and its Literacy Council wanted to do more — and more must be done. According to Ms. Stroud, recent census data has shown that 51 percent of the adult population in Macon Council has only basic or below-basic literacy skills. "We are not satisfied with our outreach and the success of the adult literacy program as a whole," she added. "We want to, and feel it is our duty to, find a way to reach out to more adults in our area who need help with basic reading skills and who might benefit from the adult program in any way."

That was the real purpose of the Community Read project in 2006. I was brought in to be a catalyst to spark a community poised to expand its commitment to adult and child literacy. Everywhere I spoke — at the school, at the Literacy Council, at local churches, and in many impromptu and casual conversations — I was struck by the heartfelt desire of these residents. There is so much more to be done in Highlands, but they have all the necessary elements for success on the grassroots level. They have dedicated adult literacy volunteers who say yes to advanced training; they have teachers and school administrators who engage in open and constructive dialogues; they have support from local civic, religious, and other community groups; and they have citizens who have stepped up personally to the challenge, including by becoming tutors. Most importantly, they have awareness throughout the community.

Literacy programs cannot thrive in an environment of closed minds and barricaded hearts. If people think that a lack of literacy skills is a problem that affects someone else's children or some other adult, or they think that it is someone else's job to teach them, then the status quo of the haves and have-nots is reinforced. The literate take their gift of the written word and jealously guard it, while so many others are left empty-handed in the dark.

At the grassroots level, community awareness is the first little spark that ignites a fire. It begins with one person or a handful of people, and it gradually spreads its heat and light. In Highlands and everywhere, the literate people must be the flag bearers and sol-diers in the fight against illiteracy. It is not too late to close the gap between the haves and the have-nots. Yes, it will take years, maybe decades, but if we don't start now, the problem will only get bigger and more entrenched. However, unless our efforts ensure that reading instruction for adults is based on the same foundational principles as those needed for young learners, the situation will only get worse. That is simply not acceptable when we do know what to do.

Make no mistake, as evidenced by the NAAL statistics in Chapter 1—showing 43 percent of the adult population in the United States as being at basic or below-basic literacy levels—we are entrenched in a national illiteracy epidemic. It is so easy in the face of those numbers to throw up one's hands in despair and say, "What can I do? I'm only one person." On the local level, however, one person can make a tremendous difference. One person joining with others can turn the tide of any problem. One person can turn despair to hope, move from powerlessness to empowerment. As we have seen in politics—from state referenda to national agenda—when the grassroots gets big enough, change on a large scale is possible.

## Chicago Public School Turnaround

Big, urban school districts are burdened with low-performing schools, especially in neighborhoods that have high poverty and/or high minority populations. That's a given, right? Not so in Chicago, which has become a model for urban districts everywhere. Reform in Chicago has reflected the belief that "strong parent, teacher, and principal involvement with authority decentralized to the schools" produces results, according to John Simmons, president and founder of Strategic Learning Initiatives, a nonprofit organization that works with urban school districts.

As Mr. Simmons wrote in his book *Breaking Through: Transforming Urban School Districts,* "Success in reform efforts has come primarily from activity at the local level and through the implementation of practices developed in the past fifty years by high-performing organizations."[1] Although improvements have been dramatic, Mr. Simmons indicated that change has taken hold thus far in about half of the low-scoring elementary schools. But the experience of those 181 schools deserves both notice and careful study for the lessons it yields for other districts.

According to Mr. Simmons, 82 percent of the total number of Chicago public elementary schools had very low results on the 1990 Iowa Test of Basic Skills (ITBS). Only 20 percent of the students in these schools scored at or above the national average. By 2005, half of these schools, 181 of them, saw significant improvements in performance, with 49 percent of the students at or above the national average, an increase of 150 percent. The ITBS is "norm-referenced," meaning that half of students must fall below the national average.

> *What we are calling for . . . is really*
> *no less than a cultural revolution of sorts*
> *in urban school districts across the nation.*
>
> —John Simmons, *Breaking Through:*
> *Transforming Urban School Districts*[2]

In an interview, Mr. Simmons attributed the successes realized in Chicago to three principles that are grounded in the experience of high-performance companies and that can be adopted by school districts as well. Key to the Chicago turnaround has been decentralization of authority and responsibility, moving it from the central district office to the local, neighborhood schools, including the formation of local school councils. "We've known forever in the private sector that pushing responsibility to the people closest to the problem and closest to the customers gets the best results," Mr. Simmons explained. "They need to be empowered to identify and solve their problems, they need training to do their jobs well, and they need support, not mandates, from senior management to solve the problems that they have no control over."

In education, the concept plays out with autonomous schools that do not have any responsibility to the central office other than what is required by federal and state laws. The schools in Chicago that perform the best, Mr. Simmons went on, are those in which principals have developed high levels of trust among key stakeholders in the building, including parents, teachers, and other administrators. "We have a high correlation between buildings that have high trust and high rates of improvement on standardized tests," he explained.

The experience and results realized in the Chicago Public Schools since 1990 highlight the importance of three principles:

1. *Consistency:* One vision in the classroom and the central office

2. *Simultaneity:* Working everywhere at once

3. *Quality:* Learning from the best

Consistency, Mr. Simmons said, means having all teachers using similar strategies and tools so that when students move from classroom to classroom and from neighborhood to neighborhood — which is common in an urban area — they are taught in a similar way. He stressed that these strategies and tools can be based only on the "strongest research." Skills and techniques are enhanced by meaningful and effective professional development, which results in "growing great professionals," he added.

"Teachers are the most disrespected professionals I've ever seen," Mr. Simmons commented. "They also get the lowest-quality and less frequent development of any profession I've ever seen. If the principal respects teachers and trains them, schools get impressive results. This philosophy of support unlocks the creativity and energy of principals and teachers. When they are motivated and supported, they can transform the results in their classrooms, and that's what we've been seeing."

Simultaneity means restructuring and decentralizing the school district office while rolling out new leadership and training programs in local schools at the same time. The goal is to empower building principals and teacher-leaders in each school. "Most people in business will recognize immediately what we're talking about — that is, combining a restructuring strategy to transform school decision making with training and support and empowerment at the school level to create a high-performance system," Mr. Simmons said.

Quality speaks not only to results but also to the means to get there. Specifically, in Chicago, that meant highly effective professional development for teachers as a means to empower and elevate professionals. Using networks of neighborhood schools, the staff shares in the training and expense. "This also speeds up the diffusion of best practices," Mr. Simmons added. "We found that at every school building in the city, regardless of how low the school scores were, there are always a couple of teachers whose students were getting impressive results. By bringing those teachers together with the others regularly, they can begin to share what they are doing."

Similarly, among a group of five school principals, there are usually one or two who are "head and shoulders above the others — and when they talk, the others take notes and listen," Mr. Simmons said.

"At the grassroots level, it is very important to create the environment where stakeholders can work together to first design what they want to do, and then transform the results," he noted, adding there are four components to making this happen. First is providing high-quality professional development to teachers over a four-year period. Second is helping parents to assist their children with learning at home. The third is working with principals in the school buildings so that they understand how to support professional development and parents helping their children to learn. The fourth is accelerating trust across all stakeholders.

School districts from Washington to Sacramento have studied the success that's been realized in Chicago, Mr. Simmons said. The first consideration is whether the districts are willing to change the way they operate. "Is the leadership in the central office in these school districts ready to study other districts that have transformed themselves? Are they ready to learn and to develop demonstration areas in their own districts for five years to try these ideas out?" Mr. Simmons asked. "These aren't pilot programs, but demonstrations, because we know this works. We are demonstrating how to scale up best practice across the city."

## The Charter School Option

As school districts undertake meaningful reform, I believe one of the forces for change will be charter schools. Charter schools are typically the undertaking of a group of parents, teachers, or other involved and concerned citizens who get together to form a school "option," which must be sanctioned by the state to be part of a local district. Charter schools are not private; they are public, and they are free. What's interesting about charter schools is that by bringing together people with a passion, a commitment, and a desire to change, all schools benefit. Not only does the charter school establish itself with a commitment to high education standards and academic goals, but its very existence tends to elevate other schools around it.

"What charter schools are doing is going to have a lasting impact," commented Jeanne Allen, president of the Center for

Education Reform. "Charter schools have an effect on the traditional system — especially when they have to think about closing failing schools."

According to the Center for Education Reform, there were nearly 4,000 charter schools operating in the 2006–07 school year in 40 states and the District of Columbia, an 11 percent increase from the 3,600 schools open in 2005–06. Ms. Allen believes the trend will continue, thanks to more former teachers and parents who are piloting charter schools, as well as the growth in technology that can bring new and innovative instructional programs to these schools.[3] (The John Corcoran Foundation is providing the literacy portion of an online home charter school in Colorado through a computer-based program.)

Ms. Allen believes that charter schools play an important role in closing the achievement gap, particularly when it comes to literacy, by overhauling or eliminating programs that don't work and bringing in new teaching approaches that are proven to be effective. She added that charter schools, which are more decentralized, put the decisions about program selection — such as reading curriculum — into the hands of those who will be implementing and using it.

"Most literacy issues are directly attributable to a lack of effective education," Ms. Allen said. "That's not to say that every charter school is successful or more accountable, but … charter schools, I believe, have a better chance of hitting the nail on the head, because they are set up to be schools, and not for bureaucracy."

*No school, teacher, administrator, parent, or*
*student should be required to tolerate a failing school*
*when thousands exist that succeed despite all odds.*

—Jeanne Allen, President of
The Center for Education Reform[4]

Founding a charter school requires tremendous commitment and involvement of parents, teachers, and others in the community. This speaks to me of true grassroots leadership and passion to make a difference in the way that students are taught and education is delivered to meet specific needs of learners. Pamela Grubbs, who lives in Oceanside, California, is an example of a parent who became involved in a charter school in an effort to find the best education for her son and daughter.

It began when her daughter was in first grade and a lack of classroom space resulted in 40 students in a class with 2 teachers. Unhappy with her daughter's education, Pamela made the decision to homeschool her daughter. A college graduate, Pamela said she used her common sense, focused on the fundamentals, and tried to make learning fun. Her daughter progressed quickly. She also homeschooled her son for kindergarten, at the end of which he was able to read chapter books.

From homeschooling, Pamela began to investigate charter schools that would allow her children to continue learning at home, while providing an enriching classroom and group atmosphere. She learned about The Classical Academy, a homeschool public charter, in Escondido, and even though it meant an hour drive, she enrolled her children. (Pamela later became involved with the establishment of The Classical Academy in Oceanside, even though her children did not attend there, to bring the experience to more learners in her area.)

Pamela's children, like the other students, went to school in Escondido two days a week and were homeschooled on the other days, following a curriculum that met or exceeded state education standards. "It was the best of both worlds. My kids could go to school, learn to speak publicly as they shared reports in front of peers, do experiments, and engage in activities that work better as a group," she observed. "By homeschooling them, we were able to eliminate so much of the downtime. We could cover in three hours what it would take a whole day in school, so my children had time for art and piano lessons and still had ample time for playing, family, and travel, and all the things we value."

Today, Pamela's daughter is in high school, following an independent study course at Escondido Charter High School. Her son, who was advanced enough to skip eighth grade and go directly into ninth, is at The Classical Academy High School in Escondido, which Pamela also helped to found.

Her advice for other parents who are interested in charter schools is to start talking to others and asking questions. "I was looking for such a thing that I didn't know already existed, but the reason I found it was I kept looking," she said. "I kept hanging in there and brainstorming. If you hear about a charter school, even if it is hours away from you, go and visit. Find out how they started, and maybe they'll help you." Above all, Pamela advised, and this rings true for every parent with a child of any ability in any school, "Don't settle. Just don't settle when it comes to your children's education. And even if it doesn't happen for your child, you can open the door for someone else."

## Rotary Lends Its Muscle to Literacy

As these examples show — in Highlands, North Carolina; Chicago public schools; and in charter schools that are founded locally — grassroots involvement can create learning miracles in local communities. As powerful and important as the grassroots is, we also need change on the global scale. Here, Rotary International has demonstrated the power of its commitment. From local groups, such as the one in Highlands that provided seed money for the Literacy Council to its work worldwide, Rotary International has adopted literacy as one of its causes.

Rotary is also using the latest technology to extend the reach of its helping hand through the new Computer-Assisted Literacy Solution (CALS), which the organization is making available to virtually any child or adult who has access to a high-speed Internet connection. The technological link enables CALS to deliver its self-paced, interactive instruction in English-language literacy and math not only throughout North America but also in developing countries, where broadband Internet service is becoming increasingly widespread.

Rotary International's commitment is an exciting development for the cause of literacy. First, consider the sheer magnitude of the size of this organization. There are approximately 1.2 million Rotarians in more than 32,000 clubs in more than 200 countries and geographical areas. Rotarians are known for their commitment to humanitarian goals and their drive to achieve them.

Now think of what Rotary International has accomplished since adopting the goal of a polio-free world (which it has virtually accomplished, except for four areas). To tackle this mission, Rotary International has become the leading member of the Global Polio Eradication Initiative and the largest private sector donor. It has contributed more than $600 million to polio eradication in 122 countries. Plus, as Rotary International noted, "Tens of thousands of Rotarians have partnered with their national ministries of health, UNICEF, the World Health Organization, and the U.S. Centers for Disease Control and Prevention, and with health providers at the grassroots level in thousands of communities."[5]

To think that the muscle behind the effort to eradicate polio worldwide is now behind other humanitarian causes such as literacy gives me great hope. This is truly cause for celebration. As Rotary International states, "Literacy empowers people. It is the foundation for virtually all forms of education and an essential component in poverty reduction, social inclusion, and economic development.

Despite the importance of literacy, there are over 800 million people unable to read or write in the world today, and 64 percent of
these people are women and girls."[6]

Rotary International (RI) Past President Bill Boyd observed
that for the past four or five years, Rotary has focused on international needs of literacy, water, health, and hunger, encouraging
local clubs to become involved with these projects as they fit within
their regional and local framework. "There is a large amount of
interconnection among these four needs. If you can't read or write,
you are seriously handicapped to keep your family healthy. If you
don't understand written instructions, you can't produce crops
effectively. Hunger follows. Without literacy, understanding clean
water safety becomes a significant issue. You can see how all four of
these emphases do connect," Mr. Boyd said.

Literacy is also a personal mission for many of its top leaders.
Bill Boyd explained that, after leaving school at the age of 15, he
became self-taught and a voracious reader, thanks in part to the fact
that his father owned a bookshop. "I am what I am because of what
I have been able to read," he explained. "It was a very logical connection for me to get involved in literacy."

Rotary International President Wilfrid J. Wilkinson, in a foreword to this book, said that in his year of leadership (2007–08), he
was "personally committed to helping build the bridge to literacy."
He further called on others to "listen to the clarion call…and join
us in solving this crisis by meeting the challenge, using the opportunities available to bring all people — one at a time — into the literate world."

Rotary International's commitment to service locally and glob-
ally deserves to be lauded. From grassroots involvement to the new
CALS program that is being made available in numerous countries,
Rotary is making meaningful efforts in the global battle against

illiteracy. The use of technology makes CALS particularly exciting, because it can reach learners virtually everywhere.

Before Rotary launched CALS, the program was subject to efficacy tests in Canada and Australia, which yielded strong and convincing results. Positive testimonials from parents, teachers, and students continue to attest to the value of this technological literacy tool. Rotary is making CALS available through AutoSkill International Inc., which creates research-based programs for at-risk students to build reading and math skills. (For more information on the Rotary-AutoSkill collaboration, see *www.autoskill. com/rotary/.*)

"Recently available to Rotary, [CALS] enables users of any age to improve quickly their English language and math skills in a measurable way," RI President Wilkinson said in a statement.[7] "Where broadband connected computers are available, I would recommend that clubs and districts consider using CALS as an opportunity to help others, one person at a time, in the true spirit of Rotary Shares."

Also thanks to Rotary, CALS is available to any learner — adult, child, ESL student — at a subsidized cost. The only caveat is the person must come through a local Rotary Club or district. Every Rotary Club is autonomous, undertaking projects that best meet the needs of its community. In addition to offering access to CALS, other local efforts to reduce illiteracy range from building schools and paying teachers to serve as tutors to collecting and distributing books. One of Mr. Boyd's personal favorites has been a project within Rotary to distribute dictionaries to third graders. For some of these children, it is the first book they have ever been given. "I love the letter we received from one child that said, 'This is the first book I ever owned. I'm up to page 138 now.' Another said, 'Thank you for the book. I will value it for my whole life, and I will give it to my children when I die,'" he recalled.

Rotary's efforts are also global, such as building a school in South Africa; putting in benches and desks in schools in India; teaching reading and writing in Lagos, Nigeria; and teaching reading to some 100,000 people — nearly all of them women and Kurdish refugees — in Turkey, where Rotary has also opened elementary schools and a high school. Across the globe, in Cedar Rapids, Iowa, Rotarians have become mentors working with very small groups of children and going into school libraries to help impart the value of books and the joy of reading.

> *The ability to read, write, and do simple math is*
> *not only critical to progress and prosperity, it is necessary*
> *for the very survival of individuals in a modern society.*
> *Literacy and numeracy projects allow Rotarians to make*
> *a creative contribution to building nations, reducing poverty,*
> *and opening up opportunities for those who need them.*[8]
>
> — Rotary International

When Rotary declares its global polio campaign a success, another cause will be elevated to the same status as eradicating polio. Literacy is certainly on that list of causes to be considered. Although it will be up to Rotary leadership at that time to decide which cause is the successor to polio, Mr. Boyd noted that if the organization chooses literacy after his tenure as international president is over, "then there will be one former Rotary International president with a smile on his face."

Through local clubs that build schools and give away books to the rollout of CALS, Rotary has shown the strength of its commitment to literacy. Just as we have seen with its campaign to eradicate polio, Rotary takes on causes with conviction and knowledge. Literacy advocates everywhere should watch this organization closely, as I believe they will accomplish great things in the future.

## Media and Technology Link

For any campaign to succeed, the grassroots is critical. In the drive to prevent and eradicate illiteracy, resources must be deployed on the local level to meet the needs of individuals, both children and adults. One of the most effective ways to link the grassroots with a national or even global vision is through the media. From traditional television programming to emerging venues, such as the Internet and other new modes of electronic communication, the literacy movement needs to harness the power of media to increase awareness, inspire volunteers, and reach out to learners and potential learners who need help.

As we look at how to accomplish that mission of enlightening and empowering the grassroots, we can draw upon the experience of Project Literacy U.S. (PLUS). From the mid-1980s through the mid-1990s, PLUS spearheaded a national public awareness campaign through its two sponsors, the American Broadcasting Company (ABC) and the Public Broadcasting Service (PBS). Led by these two media powerhouses — competitors that worked together in support of a cause that was bigger than any business rivalry — PLUS took on the mission to raise awareness about illiteracy and to attract the critical support and resources needed to combat the problem. The tools that PLUS used included community outreach, increased visibility through on-air programming and national and local public service announcements, and partnerships with affiliated member TV stations and national and local literacy and education organizations. Importantly, PLUS was committed to continue sending this message over a long period of time.

The PLUS formula appeared simple: combine national and local television and radio messages with grassroots efforts by service providers and literacy organizations. That simplicity of a two-pronged approach was also its brilliance. On the national level, ABC and PBS put their strengths into raising awareness through documentaries, news programs, public service announcements, and even story lines in popular television programs and movies. On the local level, volunteerism was encouraged, and resources were made available in communities so that when learners stepped forward for help, someone was there to meet them.

As ABC president and national literacy advocate Jim Duffy, who led his network's efforts in PLUS, explained at the time, "Everything we learned about the illiteracy problem so far tells us that it is absolutely essential that community resources be mobilized, organized, and in place before awareness raising with on-air programming begins in earnest. This is so that people who respond to that programming—those who need and want help and those who are able to help—will have somewhere to turn to in every sizeable community in the United States."[9]

The PLUS vision was to rally the troops in the battle against illiteracy from every corner, including other broadcasters, print media, business, labor, farm groups, religious leaders, church groups, and service organizations. "If we can blend all of those resources, if we can work together, then we will really make a difference," Mr. Duffy wrote in his memoir.[10]

PLUS was an unprecedented effort that worked. To back that claim, Mr. Duffy cited several statistics from the lifespan of the PLUS initiative:

- An impressive 800,000 calls made to the National Literacy Hotline and a like number made to regional and local hotlines

- Volunteer programs: Literacy Volunteers of America and Laubach services (which have since merged to become Pro-Literacy Worldwide) saw doubled and even tripled student enlistment

- Service program organizations more than doubled the number of volunteer tutors.

- The Adult Basic Education (ABE) programs, administered by the U.S. Department of Education, went from 2.8 million students in 1985 to approximately 4 million by 1991.

- Federal funding for literacy programs increased from about $98 million in 1985 to more than $200 million in 1991.

- State funding for literacy programs increased from $240 million in 1985 to $750 million in 1991.

- Further, PLUS helped the National Literacy Act of 1991 to pass, which established the National Institute for Literacy (NIFL).[11]

PLUS received more acclaim than any other broadcasting public service campaign, including President Reagan's Volunteer Action Award in 1987 and the American Legion Distinguished Service Award in 1988, among many other honors. The initiative leaves us a powerful legacy, showing what can be done when various factions commit to work collaboratively for the common good. Further, it demonstrates what we must do now, employing the power of the media once again through television, radio, and new channels of communication. We must educate people in America that the illiteracy epidemic is still a major societal and economic issue that affects all of us, while deploying resources on the grassroots level to offer help to individuals wherever it is needed.

Another important component of today's awareness campaign must be the tremendous advances in scientific research conducted over the past several decades. Through this research, we know much about how to teach children and adults to read using science-based methodologies. However, there is no quick fix to overcoming illiteracy. It requires a long-term commitment to do what is necessary: assessment, intervention, remediation, testing, data analysis, and follow-up throughout the life cycle of the learner.

The message we have to deliver today is a powerful one. Twenty years and hundreds of millions of dollars in research later, we know that reading is not a natural process; however, reading failure can be overcome with screening, intervention, and proper instruction. We have the knowledge that will enable us to prevent and eradicate illiteracy.

This is also a sobering message that we must have the courage to deliver: there is a tremendous gap between what we know and what we do with regard to teaching reading, writing, and spelling, particularly in our schools. Some may not want to hear this message, and others will not want it to be broadcast. For the sake of the children and adults who remain on the other side of the bridge without the written word, however, we must declare our message to all who will hear to rally support and resources for what must be done — once and for all — to close the literacy gap.

## Reaching Learners Wherever They Are

Donald Colhour, a 20-year veteran of ABC who was a unit production manager and producer of special projects for ABC Entertainment between 1969 and 1989, became involved in literacy while working in PLUS. Reverend Colhour, whose credits include everything from *General Hospital* to the Academy Awards, is now a clergyman with an ecumenical and global vision. As senior minister at the Wilshire Christian Church in Los Angeles, he saw the link between faith and literacy.

"In our market research at ABC, a very interesting find was that a primary motivator for adults to learn to read was to read their faith-based texts," Reverend Colhour said. "So it seemed natural that faith-based institutions could possibly be the untapped providers of a safe place for nonreaders to learn to read. By providing sanctuary for these nonreaders, they could tell their friends they were going to church, or temple, or the mosque and still be telling the truth. What they didn't have to reveal was that they were going there to learn to read."

With this vision, he founded Project Literacy Los Angeles, a broad-based organization that provided free instruction in basic skills to nonreaders using the volunteers and facilities of local churches coupled with those of schools, libraries, literacy organizations, corporations, and service organizations. Since becoming a pastor, Reverend Colhour has expanded the project's vision beyond Los Angeles into Project Literacy America.

Now with Project Literacy America, the model is that faith-based institutions across America (whether Christian, Jewish, Muslim, or another faith) can partner with multidisciplinary educational, corporate, and service clubs in every city of America to declare the eradication of illiteracy as a mission of their organization. Combining these community partners creates the bridge across communities and the nation whereby every conceivable partnership of public, private, and nonprofit organizations can contribute to eradicating illiteracy in America.

Literacy and ESL classes are held at Wilshire Christian Church and in the senior housing next door. Expanding this project beyond Wilshire Christian Church and Wilshire Center is imperative, said Reverend Colhour, because in the Los Angeles metropolitan area, 53 percent of the adult population cannot read above a third-grade level.

"The economic, political and cultural consequences of such a statistic are dire when one contemplates the capability of America's workforce and the ability of its people to go to the polls to vote and to discern what is truth," he added. "We can never fulfill the goals and dreams of the framers of our Constitution if we fail to resolve this crisis."

## Shining Light in Darkness

To reach learners wherever they are, we cannot limit our efforts to schools, libraries, and churches. We have to go into the trenches to reach those for whom illiteracy has become a life sentence. There is a direct link between illiteracy, juvenile delinquency, and adult crime. According to expert estimates, illiteracy rates may be 75 percent or higher among the prison population.

Whenever I speak in prisons and juvenile detention facilities, I come face-to-face with a population that, in addition to "correction," also needs to receive literacy education. Growing up, my problems were with school, not with the law. And yet, when I address an audience of juvenile offenders, I see in their faces the same pain, anger, and rejection that I experienced as the Native Alien.

In February 2007, just as this chapter was being written, I was invited by the Knox County Library Program in Vincennes, Indiana, to be a guest speaker as part of a literacy awareness campaign focusing on adult literacy. I made five presentations in one day in the midst of a spell of bitterly cold weather in the Midwest. Coming from southern California, it was a long trip, indeed.

I spoke to two groups at the Southwestern Indiana Regional Youth Village Incarceration Facility for Teenagers: a group of about 75 or 80 boys and another group of approximately 25 girls. When the boys came in for their presentation, about a third wore camouflage attire as part of a voluntary boot camp program that many of them liked for the structure and discipline. They looked to me like cadets — their postures rigid and their eyes straight ahead. The rest of the boys had the same guarded expression that I have seen often in settings like this. They are wary of others: the guards, the teachers, their peers, and certainly outsiders. This was not a warm audience. But I know from experience how to melt an icy crowd like this one — that is to help them see me differently: not as a man in a suit and a tie but as Johnny the Innocent and the Native Alien. I began to tell the story of these two characters, or subpersonalities, that I carry within me. There weren't any smiles or dialogue with my audience at this point, but their nonverbal language showed the thaw was beginning.

Toward the end of my presentation, several boys started to ask questions. One asked if I thought I could have gotten away with the same things today that I did when I was in school — the incidents and events that I shared in the introduction of this book, which culminated in my graduating from high school and then college — even though I could not read or write. I paused and told him, "I'm not sure. I think I might have been able to do something to get by because a lot of people still do: they graduate from high school without having the reading and writing skills they need to function in life. There are still ways to be 'pushed through' the system."

The point I wanted to make with these boys, however, was not about getting by or getting around the system but about getting the education I wanted and deserved. It's the same education that these teenagers need if they are to have any hope of turning their lives around and breaking a vicious cycle that has already put them in a detention facility.

"What I really do know from my past experience is that I learned how to read and write when I was 48 years old and I could have learned when I was 8 years old. If I had the choice, I would not have gone through what I went through," I told them. "But I cannot do anything about my past — and neither can you. We can do something about our futures; it's not too late. It wasn't too late for me to learn to read, and it's not too late for you."

I told them that I had come to speak that day to bring a message of hope and possibility and to accomplish another important mission. I came to speak to the teachers and administrators at the facility about the importance of properly trained teachers who are able to meet the needs of all learners. "They have an obligation to you to come to the table with the right skills," I told my young audience — as teachers, administrators, and others also listened. "You have to come to the table with the right attitude. You cannot give up."

Afterwards, several teachers came up to me and said they were so pleased with how the youth interacted with me. They were not just listening; they were engaged. I was happy to know that, even in a small way, I had helped bring a positive message to youth who need to know there are people who truly care about them and want them to succeed.

Perhaps the most gratifying moment, however, came when a boy approached me after my presentation to speak with me privately. He looked at me, his expression showing how much thought he had given to what he had to say. "You know," he told me, "before today, I never thought about why I acted so crazy and angry in school. It's because I can't read."

Fortunately, within the system, advocates and champions are working to improve the literacy skills of juvenile offenders and incarcerated adults. One of the notable ones is Judge James Milliken, whose career includes sitting on the bench in superior court as well as in juvenile court in San Diego. In 1996–97, he recalled, 4,900 felonies were committed by juveniles in the county of San Diego alone — 80 percent of which were serious crimes committed by recidivist juveniles who were on probation for committing some other crime.

Judge Milliken saw the same pattern over and over again: juvenile offenders were released from incarceration, sent home, and placed on probation with the instructions to go to school, stay sober, be in by eight o'clock at night, and to stop hanging around with the peers who had gotten them in trouble in the first place. "We didn't have any probation officers supervising them; consequently, the kids would go right back to the street, get in trouble again, and then be sent to the youth authorities," he recalled.

The response was intensive supervision of youth on probation, requiring inpatient or outpatient drug and alcohol treatment for those who were addicted, follow-up drug and sobriety tests, and an emphasis on education. When he learned that two-thirds of the juveniles who came before him were reading at the fourth-grade level or below, Judge Milliken knew something had to be done.

It began with a young man named Andrew.

Connie Messina was a literacy champion who was instrumental in Andrew's transformation. She was a former school counselor who was working at the time as a counselor for the San Diego Urban League, a social service agency for African Americans. Asked to form an anger-management counseling group for three teenaged youth who were having problems with truancy, Ms. Messina agreed — and Andrew was among the three boys who came to the program.

After testing the boy for learning skills and discovering that Andrew performed well, she went to his school — a storefront charter school — to find out why he was truant so often. No one knew what Andrew's reading ability was, except that he was below grade level and he had been in special education since elementary school. He was labeled defiant, unmotivated, and uncooperative.

Suspecting that Andrew had a phonemic awareness problem that no one had detected, Messina told his probation officer that she was going to ask the judge to send Andrew to a literacy clinic for assessment and treatment. The probation officer thought the request was inappropriate, but Ms. Messina proceeded anyway. She managed to convince the court to share the cost of the reading clinic with probation and the special education department of the San Diego School District. At the clinic, Andrew was assessed and began reading instruction for four hours per day, five days per week.

"When the director of the reading clinic presented Andrew's reading scores, there was silence in the courtroom," she recalled. "Judge Milliken was ecstatic. As Andrew stepped forward and handed him a paper he had written on the Civil War, you could have heard a pin drop."

Judge Milliken called Andrew "the one who opened my eyes." In a few weeks, Andrew went from reading at third-grade level to testing in the 75th percentile of high school juniors with the word-attack skills of a graduate student. "He wrote for me a five-page paper on the origins of the Civil War as a condition of getting off probation," the judge added. "It was amazing! After that experience, I got on the reading campaign, and we started widely requiring all kids who were going to work camps for felonies to be tested and put into our reading programs."

Leaving the courtroom, Ms. Messina asked Andrew what he had written on the note to the judge. Andrew told her, "Thank you for helping me to turn my life around, and now that I can read, I'd like to go to college."

## Champions and Unsung Heroes

Everywhere I go, I meet champions of literacy. They are the students and teachers, the volunteers and the parents, the school administrators and community leaders, researchers and advocates, and other people who are committed to change. Some of them earn a moment in the spotlight, justifiably, for the work they do and to inspire others to pick up the torch and carry it their share of the distance. Some of those voices have been heard in these pages; there are many others out there as well.

# The Bridge Builder

Throughout the writing of this book, the visual image of a bridge to literacy has helped me. The bridge recalled my own journey from being illiterate, to a developing literate, and then to literate. The bridge also speaks to the journey that must be undertaken by all parties involved in this issue. The literate must span the gap from those who are literate to those who are illiterate. Those who lack the necessary reading and writing skills need to step forward to begin this crossing.

I have been on both sides of the bridge, and this experience has given me an unobstructed view. Writing this book has helped me to increase my awareness of each side, to experience a deeper understanding of the transformation I have undergone, and to help me bridge the gap so that others might make the journey that I have.

When I was illiterate, I thought in pictures. People say a picture is worth a thousand words, and I know many painters, photographers, and other visual artists use images to convey thoughts, knowledge, and emotions. Now that I am literate, I have searched for the right words to express my thoughts and feelings about America's illiteracy epidemic and what must be done to fight it. Since then, I have found that the written word can paint pictures, too. (A writer friend of mine now assures me that thinking in pictures and looking for the words to express what I "see" makes me a poet; I would love to believe that is so.) Intuitively, the image of a bridge helps to crystallize my thinking around what needs to be done. We need an infrastructure — as real and tangible as a bridge — to span the achievement gap and link those who have the precious literacy skills with those who are lacking them.

I trusted my intuition long before I knew what the word meant. I depended on it, acted on it, and have observed intuitiveness in others. From my observations, admittedly not pure science, I have concluded that some people are more intuitive than others, or at least it seems that way. Perhaps some people just trust their intuition more than others. We are all smart in different ways; we have special talents, and we all have deficiencies. *Book smart* and *street smart* or just plain *common sense* are all vernacular terms used to define intelligence. The book-smart kids do better in the classroom than the street-smart kids as a rule, and as adults, they seem to have better jobs. It didn't take much observation for me to conclude at an early age that I needed and wanted some book smarts.

Most of my life, I could not consider myself book smart, because I really did not know how to read, write, or spell. However, I have known for a very long time that people learn differently through my own acquisition of knowledge and skills without the support of the printed word. As an illiterate, I called upon an elaborate repertoire of resources. Today, as a literate person writing this book, I have examined illiteracy in America in a scholarly and scientific fashion — something I certainly could not have done as a college student. So now, at long last, I have finished my assigned essays and term papers; I have done the needed research. I know I am almost 50 years late in completing my written assignments, and

I don't even know to whom or where to submit them. Finally, I can truly say that I have done the work to graduate into literate society and into the circle of higher learning.

Writing this book would be difficult for most people. For me, writing presented the challenge of sifting through and forming my thoughts and opinions. I had to define what I really think. Writing, as I have found, is not the same as speaking. Writing requires the right combination of words to say what you mean and to mean what you say. Writing also requires several skills, from research and interviews to the use of grammar, including syntax, and proper spelling—all of which I am still learning with the help of my writing and research assistant Patricia Crisafulli. Tricia helped me with the writing, but I know (and she reminds me) that I own every word in this book.

By putting my ideas on the printed page, I have taken another step and made another commitment to remind literate society that those of us with learning deficiencies—including those of us who are dyslexic—can learn. It is never too late to learn how to read and write.

I am deeply grateful that I had the opportunity to learn how to read and write, and I am beholden to those who helped me learn. Although I did not know it at the time, these people enabled me to write about my life in my first book, *The Teacher Who Couldn't Read*. I have coined terms that I use in this book; for instance, America's "dominant literate culture," a culture that holds power because of its literacy skills, and the "subculture of illiteracy," whose members are second-class citizens. No other literacy advocate, perhaps, could use these terms. They would appear too harsh, too politically incorrect. But as someone who spent four decades in the subculture of illiteracy and another two decades among the literate, I have earned the right to use these words. My brethren in the subculture understand; they don't mind straight talk — in fact, they champion it.

In the past 20 years, many people have told me how inspiring my story is — the struggles of one person to overcome what seemed like insurmountable obstacles and, finally, by the grace of God, to learn how to read. I'm proud and humbled that I have been able to inspire others. And I would be remiss if I did not acknowledge all those who have inspired me. At the top of my list is my teacher and my friend, the late Pat Lindamood, who unlocked the mystery of an auditory-discrimination problem that was the reason I had not learned how to read in the classroom.

There are so many others whom I have met along the way, some of whom I have written about in this book or in my previous one. Former First Lady Barbara Bush has been an inspiration for championing programs for adults and families and to me will always be the first lady of literacy. I am ever grateful for her support. There are also unsung heroes in literacy, advocates who are motivated by passion. Many have a personal connection with literacy, often a child or other family member who has struggled to learn how to read. Others feel a call that compels them into action. One such person is Marianne Arling.

In the interest of full disclosure, let me tell you that Marianne is now the programs director of the John Corcoran Foundation, and in that capacity she oversees tutoring programs that in the 2006–07 school year served more than 700 students in Colorado. Marianne is also a skilled online instructor who can assess and teach students who have already worked with a qualified tutor. Her vision and technology savvy will extend the reach of literacy tools beyond physical locations into virtual classrooms. Marianne is a quiet woman who does not draw attention to herself. She is, however, a strong force to be reckoned with and a champion of great courage and vision. Her story is worth telling.

After graduating with a master's degree in special education in 1991, Marianne had hoped to be able to help students with learning deficiencies. "Unfortunately, I discovered after completion of the program that I really hadn't learned any skills that would really empower students to overcome those problems," she recalled. "I learned how to go into classrooms and help children by reading to them, or writing for them, or discussing with teachers how to modify lesson plans to make them easier for my students. However, I didn't know how to help students read for themselves, so that they could do the same work that other students were doing. This was a great frustration for me as well as for the students."

Marianne, whom I consider to be a role model for teachers everywhere, did not surrender to her frustration. She reached out to learn more, to find out what she could do to help her students. While attending a special education conference, she heard Pat Lindamood speak, which prompted Marianne to pursue additional training in Lindamood-Bell and, later, in other reading methodologies as well. About this time, Marianne read a magazine article about me and the publication of my first book. She contacted me, and I was happy to be a resource person for her.

Marianne's professional journey included a special teacher-training program offered by the Colorado Department of Special Education, which she found to be very valuable when working with her students. She met resistance, however, for thinking and acting outside the box in special education. Marianne's desire was to pull students out of the classes where they could not function and to teach them to read. The special education model at the time, however, was inclusion instruction, in which she was expected to go into the classroom and help students with their work.

Although frustrated and discouraged, Marianne was not defeated. When she couldn't work inside the system, she decided to work outside of it. "Parents always encouraged me to use my methods, because they could see them helping their children. They asked me to start an afterschool program," she recalled. "I prayed hard and started to look for some kind of funding. My good husband agreed that I could try to just work with an afterschool program instead of trying to continue teaching in a system that wasn't working for me, even though it meant a drop in income."

From there, Marianne's work in education has taken many twists and turns, from work with school districts to a community college, where she trained tutors for students needing remedial instruction. Now, through the John Corcoran Foundation, she continues to work with afterschool reading programs in several schools for students needing intensive instruction and remediation. In a fashion that is typical of her, Marianne takes none of the credit for her accomplishments, instead seeing herself as part of a much bigger picture of the good work that is done in the name of literacy. "I consider myself greatly blessed to have been given the gift of understanding how to teach children to read," she said.

Working with Marianne has been like collaborating with an angel. She is among the many good people who have helped me professionally and also personally as I have taken up the cause of literacy while unburdening myself from the shackles of illiteracy.

Through my writing, over the past 20 years or so, I personally have unloaded most of the negatives that impacted my life related to my illiteracy, the feelings of shame, frustration, humiliation, fear, anger, lost opportunities, guilt, and sometimes rage that affected my well-being emotionally, physiologically, and spiritually. Yet in the course of writing this book, some old negative feelings were rekindled.

In April 2006, I received a letter from the superior court of California informing me that the San Diego County Sheriff's Department had provided information to the court and a determination was made based on that information not to nominate me to serve on the 2006–07 San Diego County Grand Jury. The letter further stated, "If you have reason to believe the background information is incorrect, please contact the Sheriff's Department." Of course I had reason to believe it was incorrect; I knew my record was clean as a whistle. When I was appointed to the board of the National Institute for Literacy by President George H. W. Bush and confirmed by the U.S. Senate, and later served under President Bill Clinton, I was subject to an FBI investigation. I don't think I've even had a traffic ticket on my record for years. I ordered a copy of my police records from the sheriff's department, paid the $15 fee, and got the results of their search. It was clean. There was nothing negative on the report.

Anyone who has ever had incorrect information reported about them understands the urgency of my efforts and my diligence in correcting any errors. Rejection is one thing I have learned to live with over the years, but please get the facts straight. Eight phone calls, three letters (one certified), and three weeks later, I received from the court the letter shown in Figure E.1 on the next page.

After reading this letter a few times and reflecting on it for a day and a restless night, some of the "boys" showed up to offer their opinions. You remember Johnny the Innocent, one of my subpersonalities that I wrote about in the introduction. Johnny the Innocent recalls the little boy I once was, who was banished to the dumb row in second grade and never knew why. Johnny the Innocent always trusted adults to do the right thing. His advice was always, "Tell them again and again; if you share a good idea long enough, eventually the good people will hear it."

Johnny the Innocent didn't say much about that letter, though. It just looked like he had been crying. The Native Alien, the angry teenager I once was, had plenty to say about that letter: "I warned you to keep your big mouth shut. You know we can't trust the literate world. They just don't get it." The Native Alien told me he saluted the impressive effort I was continuing to make, devoting myself to the problem of illiteracy. "But believe me, trust me, I have a lot of experience with this type of thing. I have been misunderstood and felt isolated most of my life. And once you are labeled and typecast as an outsider, it is very difficult to change that image and their attitudes. In their eyes, once you are an outlaw, you will always be an outlaw. Bottom line, what the judge means is that he does not think you are trustworthy. And that is an insult, and that's not cool."

𝕿𝖍𝖊 𝕾𝖚𝖕𝖊𝖗𝖎𝖔𝖗 𝕮𝖔𝖚𝖗𝖙
OF THE
𝕾𝖙𝖆𝖙𝖊 𝖔𝖋 𝕮𝖆𝖑𝖎𝖋𝖔𝖗𝖓𝖎𝖆

CHAMBERS OF            May 3, 2006         MAILING ADDRESS

JUDGE OF THE SUPERIOR COURT        SAN DIEGO, CALIFORNIA 92112-2724

Mr. John Corcoran

Oceanside, CA 92054

Dear Mr. Corcoran:

       Thank you for your Prospective Grand Jury Nominee Questionnaire for the 2006-2007 County Grand Jury, and your follow-up letters of April 18 and 19, 2006.

       The San Diego Superior Court appreciates your concern about the letter you received from Neal Methvin, Jury Services Manager. The standard wording referred to could have been modified to deal more directly with the decision concerning your application. As you learned from the Sheriff's department, your "record is as clean as a whistle".

       Please be assured that the decision not to nominate you as a grand juror was in no way based on your dyslexia. Your dyslexia was not known to the San Diego Superior Court Jury Manager, to the San Diego Superior Court Jury Commissioner, to the Presiding Judge, or to me, let alone considered, in reaching the decision not to nominate you. The San Diego Superior Court makes it a priority to comply with all non-discrimination laws, including the Americans with Disabilities Act. Jurors with any physical conditions or limitations requiring special arrangements are asked to contact the Jury Commissioner's Office, so that appropriate arrangements for accommodation can be made.

       Instead, the Superior Court's concerns with your application centered on the longtime deception throughout your formal education, and into your early adult life, as revealed in your biographical materials and on your John Corcoran Literacy Foundation website. There, you admit to "living a masquerade" and "a serious charade."

       While we salute the impressive effort you are continuing to devote to the problem of literacy, and to helping others cope with the challenges you faced, the Superior Court must ensure the utmost integrity in the administration of justice. Accordingly, you were not nominated for consideration for the 2006-2007 Grand Jury.

*Figure E.1*   Letter from the Superior Court

I could see the Native Alien clearly in my mind: arms crossed defiantly across his chest and a smile on his face that was more of a sneer. He had some advice for "Mr. Corcoran," the man I am today, the one who vowed never to silence these voices inside. "You know I am right on this one, Mr. Corcoran. Why don't you just blow up your silly bridge in protest?"

The Desperado — the college student who couldn't read and resorted to desperate measures to get a degree by hook or by crook — reminded me that it had been more than 45 years since college graduation and 30 years since I left teaching. Since then, Mr. Corcoran has been a respected national literacy advocate, telling his story for 20 years. "Is there anything you can do to restore the various rights lost as a result of telling your story, our story? In the Presidential Appointment, you are called the 'Honorable John Corcoran.' Doesn't that stand for something if the president says so? Could you ask for a presidential pardon? What about the governor? Maybe amnesty?"

The Desperado's face reflected his hurt and anger but also his shame for what he had done such a long, long time ago — sins and trespasses that have been confessed and recounted numerous times. "Isn't there a statute of limitations on our crimes and indiscretions? We've taken responsibility for them and expressed our remorse — especially for having been the 'teacher who couldn't read.'"

The Desperado wanted to know the specific charges and demanded a trial by jury — a jury of our peers. "We can't expect a fair trail from a literate judge, can we?" he said passionately. "Today our peers are our illiterate fellow travelers and the literacy advocates who have proven themselves trustworthy, who understand and take their share of the responsibility. Those are the people who can see the bridge. We are the new citizens of the dominant literate society, and we are called on to do our civic duties. Teaching people to read is our civic duty. It cannot wait. Don't wait. Go, go to the bridge now."

Mr. Corcoran responded to the judge's letter within 24 hours. I did not consult with anybody, although I did consider the verbal and nonverbal comments from the "boys." When I was done, I asked my wife, Kathleen, to read my letter to the judge. It was an unprecedented first: no editing suggestions, not even a raised eyebrow. The boys approved of it also, even the Native Alien, who said, "This letter is better than blowing up the bridge. Writing can be more powerful than any explosive — dynamite and maybe even nuclear warheads. Maybe you're right about this reading and writing stuff. It is cool! Now I understand what is meant by the expression 'the power of the pen.' And we got some of that power, too." His smile was genuine; his sneer was gone. "Do you really think we can get more of us across the bridge?"

When I told Kathy that I was going to include the judge's letter and my response in this book, she asked me why. Then the inquisition started. She put on her devil's advocate hat. I had been through the routine before during 42 years of marriage to this literate lady. I am a conceptual thinker, and Kathy needed to hear my explanation word for word. If I did not value and respect her opinion, I would not have told her what I was thinking about doing.

"It's your book and I support your decisions," Kathy began, and then gave me several considerations to think about. She also asked what was wrong with the judge's letter. Wasn't he just doing his job?

I told her that yes he was but that I have a job to do, too. I explained that I needed to show the "boys" that I am true to my word. I had promised that I would never abandon or betray them when speaking publicly. This is our struggle as we have crossed over the bridge together. I have preached the power of literacy for years to these boys, who represent so many fellow travelers I have met over the years. I needed to show them that we can hold our heads up; we can stand on our own. We can ask questions and make requests on our behalf in the language of the literate world. We are not frightened of the printed word any more. We don't have to feel like outsiders; we are not outlaws, and we do belong. We are not the victims; we are the victors. And we have the power of our own pens and keyboards.

The letter in Figure E.2 is my response to the letter from the court.

May 9, 2006

Chambers of
████████████
Judge of the Superior Court
P.O. Box 122724
San Diego, California

The Honorable, ████████

Thank you for your letter, thank you for dealing directly with the decision concerning my application. Your honesty is refreshing, it rivals my own honesty.

Do you think if I had continued "living a masquerade" I may have had a better chance of being nominated for the Grand Jury?

My love for the truth, seeking the truth and fair play was and is the driving force that motivates me to tell and write my "story".

I do understand the courts need to ensure the utmost integrity in administration of justice, which includes perception. The court does not need any controversies.

You stated in your letter "in no way" was your decision based on my dyslexia. You got the information off my web-site, there would not have been a website if it were not for my dyslexia. So, in that "way" you did base your decision some what on my dyslexia, without intent or malaise.

I respectfully accept your decision and accept the fact that there is a price to pay for telling the truth.

Enclosed is a copy of my book, I would be pleased if you read it.

Respectfully yours,

John Corcoran
████████████
Oceanside, California

*Figure E.2* Response to Superior Court

Being able to respond to the judge's letter and to write these words caused the boys and me to feel a new freedom (even though I later discovered I had written "malaise" instead of "malice"), pleasure and a satisfaction that shows we are ready to face the literate world. We are more than able to confront and encourage the literate and illiterate alike to understand the problems, conflicts, and clashes that the two groups experience every day. We live in a multidimensional, multicultural world, and cultural blindness is all around us.

I was an illiterate student in classrooms for 18 years. I was an illiterate teacher in classrooms for 17 years and a fly on the wall in the teachers' workroom and lunchroom. I have lived on both sides of the bridge and have seen and experienced the cultural bias, attitudes, and behaviors toward illiteracy. A change in one's perception can affect the problem and help implement a solution. The problem may not be as much about learning disabilities as it is about teaching disabilities.

Maybe the judge will read my books someday. Maybe he might even take a walk on the bridge. What really matters is that I have the ability to respond in the language of the dominant literate world: the written word.

I am literate. I am a literate student, committed to lifelong learning. I am no longer the teacher who couldn't read. Now my experience as an illiterate is behind me. I have crossed over the bridge many times. Now I am a builder of bridges. I am a teacher who can read. My classroom is not in the schoolhouse; it is on the bridge.

I have hope for America and high hopes and high expectations for our public school educators and educational system. I believe that teachers want to do the right things and will do the right things if they are given the correct information. I also know they must be properly taught in teacher-preparation courses; sadly, many are not. The teacher-training and education departments in our colleges and universities need to be held accountable for their part in perpetuating the problem of illiteracy in the classroom.

The challenge facing America is telling the truth, that we have failed to teach our people basic language skills. We have failed to train our teachers properly how to teach their students properly how to read and write. That must change. No more abuses. No more excuses. The real challenge is to have the political will and leadership to implement the plan based on the proven, scientific research that we already have.

Real reforms must be initiated from inside and outside our institutions. We must push the formal process and work outside the formal process. Since society and business are prime beneficiaries of quality education and literacy is the cornerstone to quality education, all facets of American society — business, policy makers, places of worship, local communities, service organizations, and others — must vigorously support and take a leadership role in reaching our noble goal of equal opportunity for all. All people must become literate if we are going to close the gap between rich and poor. This cannot be left entirely to the educators. We cannot wait for someone else to take care of our illiteracy epidemic; it is up to us — all of us.

I hope to see you on the bridge.

# *Endnotes*

## Chapter 1

[1] National Center for Education Statistics, "2003 National Assessment of Adult Literacy (NAAL)," March 2003, http://nces.ed.gov/naal/.

[2] Ben Feller, "Study: H.S. Dropouts Face Steeper Costs," Associated Press, September 12, 2006.

[3] Brent Staples, "How Schools Pay a (Very High) Price for Failing to Teach Reading Properly," Editorial Observer, *New York Times,* June 19, 2006.

[4] U.S. Department of Education, "Building on Results: A Blueprint for Strengthening the No Child Left Behind Act," January 2006, www.ed.gov/policy/elsec/leg/nclb/buildingonresults.html.

[5] James E. Duffy, *The Wind in the Trees: From the Farm to the Front Line of Television's Influence* (Waterford, VA: Endymion Publishing Company, 1997).

[6] Polly Curtis, "Lack of Education 'A Greater Threat Than Terrorism': Sen," *Guardian,* October 28, 2003.

[7] NAAL.

[8] NAAL.

[9] NAAL.

[10] NAAL.

[11] U.S. Department of Education, "Building on Results."

[12] John Kenneth Galbraith, *The Affluent Society,* 40th anniversary ed. (New York: Houghton Mifflin, 1998).

13 Donna Archer, "First Person: The Secret They Shared," *Golf for Women,* March/April 2006.

14 Ibid.

15 Mitch Albom, "The Painful Secret That Millions Hide: 'I Cannot Read,'" *Parade,* February 12, 2006.

16 Laura Bush, "Remarks by Mrs. Laura Bush, House Education and Workforce Committee: Preparing Tomorrow's Teachers," *News from the Commission on Education and the Workforce,* March 14, 2002, http://republicans. edlabor.house.gov/archive/issues/107th/education/nclb/flotus31402.htm.

## Chapter 2

1 G. Reid Lyon, testimony before Subcommittee on Education Reform, Committee on Education and the Workforce, U.S. House of Representatives, "Measuring Success: Using Assessments and Accountability to Raise Student Achievement," March 8, 2001, http://republicans.edlabor.house.gov/ archive/hearings/107th/edr/account3801/lyon.htm.

2 U.S. Department of Education, "Reading First: Student Achievement, Teacher Empowerment, National Success," April 2007, www.ed.gov/nclb/methods/reading/readingfirst.html.

3 Patrick Werquin, "Literacy: Words Count," *OECD Observer,* January 2006, www.oecdobserver.org/news/printpage.php/aid/1725/Literacy:_Words_ count.html.

4 National Institute for Literacy, press release, "Focusing on Adult Literacy Is Key to U.S. Success in the Information Age," December 6, 1995.

5 U.S. Department of Education, President's Commission on Excellence in Special Education, "A New Era: Revitalizing Special Education for Children and Their Families," July 2002, www.ed.gov/inits/commissionsboards/ whspecialeducation/reports.html.

6 Lois Romano, "Literacy of College Graduates Is on Decline," *Washington Post,* December 25, 2005.

7 Lyon testimony.

8 National Reading Panel, press release, "Northrup Hails Final Report of National Reading Panel as Much-Needed Resource in America's Classrooms," April 13, 2000, www.nationalreadingpanel.org/Press/press_rel_ northup.htm.

[9] George W. Bush, "No Child Left Behind," the White House archived information. www.whitehouse.gov.

## Chapter 3

[1] U.S. Department of Education, archived information, "Taking Responsibility for Ending Social Promotion: A Guide for Educators and State and Local Leaders," May 1999, www.ed.gov/pubs/socialpromotion/execsum.html.

[2] National Association of School Psychologists, "Position Statement on Student Grade Retention and Social Promotion," April 12, 2003, www.nasponline. org/about_nasp/pospaper_graderetent.aspx.

[3] Department of Education, "Taking Responsibility for Ending Social Promotion."

[4] New York City Department of Education, press release PR-276-05, "Mayor Bloomberg Announces End of Social Promotion in the 7th Grade," July 18, 2005, www.nyc.gov/html/om/html/2005b/pr276-05.html.

[5] Department of Education, "Taking Responsibility for Ending Social Promotion."

[6] Teresa Garcia, "No Diplomas After Failing Exit Exam," abc7news.com, June 1, 2006.

[7] Ibid.

[8] Rubin.

[9] Jay P. Greene, Manhattan Institute for Public Research, "Civic Report: High School Graduation Rates in the United States," November 2001, revised April 2002, www.manhattan-institute.org/html/cr_baeo.htm.

[10] Nathan Thornburgh, "Dropout Nation," *Time,* April 17, 2006.

[11] Greene.

[12] U.S. Department of Education, press release, "Remarks by Secretary Spellings at No Child Left Behind Summit," April 27, 2006, www.ed.gov/print/ news/pressreleases/2006/04/04272006.html.

[13] Ibid.

## Chapter 4

[1] Rebecca Pollard Pierik, "Literacy Redefined: Changing Adult Education in the Information Age," *HGSE News,* November 1, 2003, www.gse.harvard.edu/news/features/comings11012003.html.

[2] Ibid.

[3] Mary Beth Bingman, Olga Ebert, and Michael Smith, National Center for the Study of Adult Learning and Literacy, NCSALL Report #11, "Changes in Learners' Lives One Year After Enrollment in Literacy Programs: An Analysis from the Longitudinal Study of Adult Literacy Participants in Tennessee," December 1999, www.ncsall.net/?id=662.

[4] Mel Levine and Oprah Winfrey, "Dr. Mel Levine on Learning," *The Oprah Winfrey Show,* March 27, 2002.

[5] Forrest P. Chisman, Council for Advancement of Adult Literacy (CAAL), "Adult Literacy and The American Dream: An Essay by Forrest P. Chisman," February 22, 2002, www.caalusa.org/caaloccasionalpaper1.pdf.

## Chapter 5

[1] Mark Sadowski and Victor L. Willson, "Effects of a Theoretically Based Large-Scale Reading Intervention in a Multicultural Urban School District," *American Educational Research Journal* 43, no. 1 (Spring 2006): 137–154.

[2] Ibid.

[3] Ibid.

[4] *School District 60, Pueblo, Colorado, Closing the Achievement Gap*, DVD.

[5] Sadowski and Willson.

## Chapter 6

[1] PR Newswire, "National Center for Family Literacy and Toyota Join Forces in Hispanic Literacy Initiative," March 16, 2003, www.hispanicbusiness.com/news/newsbyid.asp?id=9613.

[2] Sheldon H. Horowitz, Laura Kaloi, and Susan Petroff, National Center for Learning Disabilities, "Transition to Kindergarten: Policy Implications for Struggling Learners and Those Who May Be at Risk for Learning Disabilities," March 2007, www.ncld.org/images/stories/downloads/school_transition_policy_paper.pdf.

[3] Janet Steffenhagen, "Test Early for Literacy, MLAs Urge," *Vancouver Sun,* December 5, 2006.

[4] U.S. Department of Education, "Building on Results."

[5] U.S. Department of Education, "Reading First Support," www.readingfirst-support.us/default.asp?article_id=8. (Accessed July 17, 2007.)

[6] G. Reid Lyon, "Reading Disabilities: Why Do Some Children Have Difficulty Learning to Read? What Can Be Done About It?" *Education News,* March 28, 2003, www.ednews.org; reprinted from *Perspectives* 29, no. 2 (Spring 2003).

[7] Gina Biancarosa and Catherine Snow, *Reading Next: A Vision for Action and Research in Middle and High School Literacy,* 2nd ed., a report to Carnegie Corporation of New York (Washington, DC: Alliance for Excellent Education, 2006), www.all4ed.org/files/archive/publications/ReadingNext/ReadingNext.pdf

[8] Ibid.

[9] Lyon, "Reading Disabilities."

[10] U.S. Department of Education, "Every Young American a Strong Reader," Issue Papers, The High School Leadership Summit, 2003, www.ed.gov/about/offices/list/ovae/pi/hsinit/papers/reader.pdf.

[11] Ibid.

[12] Greg Toppo, "Survey Finds 1 in 20 Lack Basic English Skills," *USA Today,* December 15, 2005, www.usatoday.com/news/nation/2005-12-15-literacy_x.htm?POE=NEWISVA.

[13] John Comings, Andrea Parrella, and Lisa Soricone, "Persistence Among Adult Basic Education Students in Pre-GED Classes," NCSALL Report #12, December 1999, www.ncsall.net/?id=663.

[14] U.S. Department of Education, press release, "Secretary Spellings Delivered Remarks at the White House Conference on Global Literacy," September 18, 2006, www.ed.gov/print/news/pressreleases/2006/09/09182006.html.

**Chapter 7**

[1] American Federation of Teachers, "Teaching Reading Is Rocket Science: What Expert Teachers of Reading Should Know and Be Able To Do," June 1999, www.aft.org/pubs-reports/downloads/teachers/rocketsci.pdf.

[2] Louisa C. Moats, testimony before Committee on Education and the Workforce, U.S. House of Representatives, September 3, 1997, www.arthurhu.com/97/07/moats.txt.

[3] Ibid.

[4] Senator Edward M. Kennedy, press release, "kennedy.senate.gov/newsroom/press_release.cfm?id=7FDF423A-8BE5-48C0-AAD7-3AF9625086E8, "Kennedy on No Child Left Behind Policy Announcement," March 18, 2008.

[5] Editorial, "Fixing 'No Child Left Behind,'" *New York Times,* April 5, 2005.

[6] Mark McGowan, "NIU Literacy Professor Works to Close Reading Achievement Gap for African-American Adolescent Males," *Northern Today,* August 2005, www.niu.edu/northerntoday/2005/aug29/tatum.shtml.

[7] American Federation of Teachers, "Indicators of Low-Performing Schools," www.aft.org/topics/school-improvement/downloads/indicators.pdf.

[8] Heather Peske and Kati Haycock, "Teaching Inequality: How Poor and Minority Students Are Shortchanged on Teacher Quality," A Report and Recommendations by the Education Trust, June 2006, http://hub.mspnet.org/index.cfm/13140.

[9] Ibid.

[10] Boston University/Chelsea Partnership, "Need for Reform," www.bu.edu/chelsea/needfor.htm.

[11] Boston University/Chelsea Partnership, "Performance Indices," 2003, www.bu.edu/chelsea/performa.htm.

[12] National Reading Panel, "Teaching Children to Read: An Evidence-Based Assessment of the Scientific Research Literature on Reading and Its Implications for Reading Instruction," 1999, www.nichd.nih.gov/publications/nrp/upload/smallbook_pdf.pdf.

[13] American Federation of Teachers, "Teaching Reading Is Rocket Science."

[14] Cheruta Wertheim, "Students With Learning Disabilities in Teacher Education Programs," *Annuals of Dyslexia* 68 (1998): 293–309.

[15] Peske and Haycock.

[16] Peske and Haycock.

[17] Kate Walsh, Deborah Glasser, and Danielle Dunne Wilcox, "What Education Schools Aren't Teaching About Reading and What Elementary Teachers Aren't Learning," *National Council on Teacher Quality* (May 2006, rev. June 2006).

[18] American Federation of Teachers, "Teaching Reading Is Rocket Science."

## Chapter 8

[1] National Institute for Literacy, "Using Research and Reason in Education: What Is Scientifically Based Research? A Guide for Teachers," 2005, www.nifl.gov/nifl/partnershipforreading/publications/html/science/stanovich.html.

[2] Carlos Alcala, "Mayor's Panel Issues 'Demands' for Improving Schools," *Sacramento Bee,* October 26, 1995.

[3] Ibid.

[4] National Institute for Literacy.

[5] Walsh, Glasser and Wilcox.

[6] Colorado Department of Education, "Colorado Basic Literacy Act (CBLA)," last updated January 26, 2006, www.cde.state.co.us/action/CBLA/index.htm.

[7] Ibid.

[8] Colorado Reading Directorate, Colorado Department of Education, "Colorado Teacher Preparation Program Approval Rubric and Review Checklist for Literacy Courses: Introduction," July 2006, www.cde.state.co.us/edprepprogram/downloads/Rubric.doc.

[9] Diane McGuinness, *Why Our Children Can't Read and What We Can Do About It* (New York: Touchstone, 1997).

[10] Ibid.

[11] Peggy McCardle and Vinita Chhabra, *The Voice of Evidence in Reading Research* (Baltimore, MD: Brookes, 2004).

[12] Sally Shaywitz, *Overcoming Dyslexia: A New and Complete Science-Based Program for Reading Problems at Any Level* (New York: Alfred A. Knopf, 2003).

[13] Ibid.

[14] National Reading Panel, "Teaching Children to Read: An Evidence-Based Assessment of the Scientific Research Literature on Reading and Its Implications for Reading Instruction; Reports of the Subgroups," February 2000, www.nationalreadingpanel.org/Publications/subgroups.htm.

[15] Christine Gorman, "The New Science of Dyslexia," *Time,* July 20, 2003, www.time.com/time/magazine/printout/0,8816,465794,00.html.

## Chapter 9

[1] John Simmons, *Breaking Through: Transforming Urban School Districts* (New York: Teachers College Press, 2006).

[2] Ibid.

[3] Center for Education Reform, press release, "Charter Schools Number Nearly 4,000 Nationwide," September 19, 2006, www.edreform.com.

[4] Center for Education Reform, press release, "A Sense of Urgency for Education Reform," January 23, 2007, www.edreform.com.

[5] Rotary International, "Polio," www.rotary.org/foundation/polioplus/index.html. Accessed July 13, 2007.

[6] Rotary International, "Literacy," www.rotary.org/aboutrotary/president/boyd/literacy.html. Accessed July 13, 2007.

[7] "New Literacy Program Earns High Praise From Rotarians," *Rotary News,* July 2007.

[8] Rotary International, "Literacy and Numeracy." www.rotary.org/programs/service_opportunities/participate/literacy.html.\ Accessed July 13, 2007.

[9] Duffy.

[10] Duffy.

[11] Duffy.